INTEGRATIVE SPIRITUALITY

D1258359

In *Integrative Spirituality*, Patrick J. Mahaffey elucidates spirituality as a developmental process that is enhanced by integrating the teachings and practices of multiple religious traditions, Jungian depth psychology, and contemplative yoga. In the postmodern world of religious pluralism, Mahaffey compellingly argues that each of us must fashion a unique path to wholeness that integrates aspects of life and of the self that have become disconnected and disowned.

Integrative Spirituality uniquely conjoins four components: exemplary religious pluralists from three traditions, individuation, the forms of contemplative Hindu yoga that have been successfully transmitted to the West, and a presentation of two models for integrating psychological growth and spiritual awakening. The book presents pioneering practitioners in each field who exemplify how we may fashion our own approach to integrating both spiritual awakening and psychological development and delineates an array of practices that integrate the somatic, psychological, interpersonal, and spiritual aspects of life. Ultimately, Mahaffey contends that integrative spirituality is a mode of being that fully embraces the divinity inherent in each of us and in the world.

Integrative Spirituality will be essential reading for academics and students of Jungian and post-Jungian studies, transpersonal and Jungian psychology, and religious studies and contemplative education. It will also be of interest to analytical and depth psychologists in practice and in training, and to anyone seeking a greater understanding of spirituality, psychological growth, religious traditions, individuation, and contemplative yoga.

Patrick J. Mahaffey is Professor and Associate Chair of the Mythological Studies Program at Pacifica Graduate Institute, California, USA, where he teaches Hinduism, Buddhism, and depth psychology and the sacred. He is the editor of *Evolving God-Images: Essays on Religion, Individuation, and Postmodern Spirituality* and the author of essays on Hindu yoga traditions, Buddhism, and Jung's depth psychology.

"Patrick Mahaffey's *Integrative Spirituality* is a beautiful testimony to the challenges and rewards of deep engagement with inner work, soul work. He easily persuades us of the importance of both centering on the perspectives that speak most powerfully to us and of honoring those of others. His own journey has led him to balance the complementary perspectives of Jungian depth psychology and contemplative yoga, to attend to both a quest for psychological wholeness and for spiritual awakening. His book culminates in a moving account of his own integration of these traditions and the daily practice that issues from it, an account that beautifully serves to encourage us in our own attempts to cultivate soul."

—**Dr Christine Downing**, author of *The Goddess: Mythological Images of the Feminine* and *Gods in Our Midst: Mythological Images of the Masculine*. Downing is a distinguished scholar of religious studies and depth psychology. She is Professor of Mythology and Depth Psychology at Pacifica Graduate Institute, the author of several other books and many scholarly essays, and a past president of the American Academy of Religion.

"Dr Mahaffey's book is a veritable tour de force that guides the reader unerringly through the intricacies of several religious and psychological traditions. With deeply moving openness about his own life path, he shows how these may be integrated. The reader will be rewarded with both a deepened inner life and a profound appreciation for the complementary nature of our spiritual traditions. This book will expand the reader's spiritual and psychological horizons."

—**Dr Lionel Corbett**, author of *Psyche and the Sacred* and *The Sacred Cauldron: Psychotherapy as a Spiritual Practice*. Corbett is a distinguished Jungian analyst and scholar of depth psychology. He is Professor of Depth Psychology at Pacifica Graduate Institute.

INTEGRATIVE SPIRITUALITY

Religious Pluralism, Individuation, and Awakening

Patrick J. Mahaffey

Routledge
Taylor & Francis Group

LONDON AND NEW YORK

First published 2019
by Routledge
2 Park Square, Milton Park, Abingdon, Oxon OX14 4RN

and by Routledge
711 Third Avenue, New York, NY 10017

Routledge is an imprint of the Taylor & Francis Group, an informa business

© 2019 Patrick J. Mahaffey

British Library Cataloguing-in-Publication Data
A catalogue record for this book is available from the British Library

Library of Congress Cataloging-in-Publication Data
Names: Mahaffey, Patrick J., 1952– author. Title: Integrative spirituality :
religious pluralism, individuation, and awakening / Patrick J. Mahaffey.
Description: Abingdon, Oxon ; New York, NY : Routledge, 2018. |
Includes bibliographical references and index.
Identifiers: LCCN 2018025951 | ISBN 9781138610385 (hardback) |
ISBN 9781138610392 (pbk.) | ISBN 9781138610408 (master ebook) |
ISBN 9780429879746 (mobipocket) | ISBN 9780429879760 (Abode Reader) |
ISBN 9780429879753 (ePub)
Subjects: LCSH: Religious pluralism. | Spirituality. | Individuation
(Psychology)—Religious aspects. Classification: LCC BL624 .M2948 2018 |
DDC 204—dc23
LC record available at https://lccn.loc.gov/2018025951

ISBN: 978-1-138-61038-5 (hbk)
ISBN: 978-1-138-61039-2 (pbk)
ISBN: 978-1-138-61040-8 (ebk)

Typeset in Bembo and Stone Sans
by Florence Production Ltd, Stoodleigh, Devon, UK

For Nina

CONTENTS

ACKNOWLEDGMENTS

Writing this book has evoked deep gratitude for so many people who have been important in my life. I was fortunate as a doctoral student to have many extraordinary teachers in the field of religious studies: Arabinda Basu, Walter Capps, John B. Cobb, Jr., W. Richard Comstock, Nancy Falk, Gerald Larson, Ninian Smart, and Raimundo Panikkar.

I am grateful to my Pacifica Graduate Institute colleagues for their collaboration in developing a unique doctoral program dedicated to the study of religious traditions, myth, literature, and depth psychology: Charles Asher, Lionel Corbett, Christine Downing, David Miller, Daniel Noel, Walter Odajnyk, Ginette Paris, Safron Rossi, Glen Slater, Dennis Slattery, and Evans Lansing Smith. The hundreds of passionate students I have been privileged to teach for nearly twenty-five years have also inspired me. Most of them came to Pacifica not only to pursue graduate study but also to deepen their commitment to psychological and spiritual growth.

In this book, I argue that psychological growth and spiritual awakening are different, yet interrelated, processes of human development. With gratitude I acknowledge the many spiritual teachers who have guided me and informed my spiritual practice: A. H. Almaas, Gurumayi Chidvilasananda, Mark Griffin, Sally Kempton, Sri Raushan Nath, Paul Muller-Ortega, Swami Shankarananda, Pandit Rajmani Tigunait, B. Alan Wallace, Christopher Wallis, and Ken Wilber. My psychological development has been supported by Jungian analyst Kurt Goerwitz, and psychotherapists Janice Hamilton, Cynthia Haskell, Pamela McLean, and Jack Zimmerman.

Writing a book is a daunting process, and it depends upon the generosity and assistance of others. Throughout the final stages of the publication process I received skillful support from Susannah Frearson and Elliott Morsia at Routledge. Janet Bubar Rich provided editorial assistance with an early version of the manuscript. I am grateful for permission to reprint two figures from *Integral Spirituality*, by Ken Wilber, Copyright (2006) by Ken Wilber, by arrangement from The Permissions Company, Inc., on behalf of Shambhala Publications Inc., Boulder, Colorado, www.shambhala.com.

Throughout this creative endeavor, a beautiful portrait of Sarasvati, goddess of learning and wisdom, hung above my desk—I acknowledge the presence of the divine feminine. I am mindful of the many splendid women who have graced my life, including my grandmother, my mother, and my former wife, Susan. Dr. Carol Geer, a former colleague at the University of California, Santa Barbara, has been a loving mentor since my graduate school days and a benefactor who has supported the publication of this book; Christine Downing, my dear Pacifica colleague, offered thoughtful, extensive suggestions for the final version and encouraged me to take the time to let the book become all it wanted to be; and Sally Kempton graciously agreed to write the Foreword. Most especially, I thank my wife, Nina Mahaffey, whose painstaking rounds of copy-editing greatly enhanced the quality of the writing. Within the sacred container of marriage, she and I have been blessed to individuate, together and alone, toward wholeness and awakening.

FOREWORD

If only this book had been around when I was studying comparative religion in college! It might have helped me integrate my religious instincts with my gut-level suspicion of religious orthodoxy. Patrick Mahaffey's study of religious pluralism and individuation speaks to the heart of the dilemma I felt then, asking some of the great questions that contemporary religiosity inevitably needs to address. Questions such as: What does it mean to have a powerful religious life outside of a tradition? Suppose you feel a strong pull to engage with Spirit, yet feel no corresponding impulse to engage with one of the traditional religious communities? Do you re-christen your religious impulse, calling it "spirituality" or "yoga" or even "meditation?" Do you stick with (or return to) the religious tradition you were born into? Or find a tradition that seems more compatible?

Or do you, like the author of this most timely and useful book, explore your unique syncretistic path, combining elements of two or three traditions to create a worldview and a set of practices that can open you to genuine religious experience.

Patrick Mahaffey has spent a lifetime studying and practicing in three main spiritual traditions. Starting life as a Lutheran, he evolved into that most post-modern of figures, a true religious hybrid. As a scholar-practitioner of religion he has taught for many years at the Pacifica Graduate Institute, the renowned graduate school of depth psychology and mythology in Santa Barbara, California. Mahaffey describes himself as a Hindu-Buddhist-Jungian. His book offers us the fruits of his many years of study and practice in a form that will be immediately useful to anyone who suspects that though religion is crucial, it is never one-size-fits-all.

Many of us have suspected this for a while. Science, famously, has dismissed the metaphysical underpinnings of most traditional religions, including the existence of a "Great Chain of Being," the ancient assumption that reality includes a hierarchical relationship between a subtle Divine (at the top of the chain) and the physical world (at the bottom). Postmodernism has critiqued the traditions for being products of particular times and cultures, pointing out that many orthodox teachings are socially regressive by contemporary standards. And, of course, we are seeing a growing polarization even in religious communities. Fundamentalist Christianity and Islamism, ultra-orthodox Judaism, and even exclusivist Hinduism and Buddhism are on the rise around the world. Cultural liberals—even in academia—equate "religion" with religious fundamentalism. In the twenty-first century, many people on the cultural cutting edge describe themselves as "spiritual not religious," because so many of us have come to equate religion with repressive social attitudes and values.

For some major religious thinkers of the twentieth century, the answer to this dilemma was a form of religious pluralism. Religious pluralism is different from ecumenism, which a friend of mine once characterized as "Christians who don't believe in Christianity, getting together with Jews who don't believe in Judaism, and discovering that they have much in common." Ecumenical thinkers practice religious dialogue, but (as Mahaffey points out) their dialogues have often suffered from each party's assumption that their own religion is superior to anybody else's religion. Genuine pluralism is a different matter. A true pluralist recognizes that different religious paths open us to facets of Spirit. Therefore, a pluralist treats other people's paths not only respectfully, but sometimes with a willingness to practice another religion for a while before claiming to understand it. The pluralist vision intuits that the values and goals of someone else's religious tradition may be true even if they are different from our own, and that there are many names for the Mystery—of which "God" is only one.

Religious pluralism has an honorable—indeed, a spiritually powerful—history. Mahaffey traces its development through the lives and teachings of Christian thinkers such as John Hick; Hindu and Buddhist masters such as Ramakrishna Paramahamsa, Gandhi, and the Dalai Lama; and through the writings of scholars such as Huston Smith, Charles Taylor, and Karen Armstrong. But his true concern in this book is to discuss the possibilities of true religious syncretism—a path he has been engaging for many years, and which I believe is crucial for twenty-first century religious practice.

Given our modern education, we tend to dismiss much of the mythological underpinning of the traditions. Yet, as Jung intuited, and as Mahaffey understands, myth is not just fake history. Myth is a language that makes it possible to describe the indescribable, and therefore is an important part of any spiritual tradition. In the same way, just as someone who wants to take a physical journey needs a map, a person who wants to investigate the subtle worlds needs a set of descriptors that allow them both to transcend the ordinary and to make sense of it. The traditions offer such maps—sometimes in the form of stories, but just as often in the form of philosophies and creeds. And, as Mahaffey points out, each of the great traditions has "expertise" in certain areas. We could say that Christianity is particularly good at grace and charity, while Buddhism and Hinduism are especially skillful at contemplative practice. And, of course, one of Buddhism's strengths for modern practitioners is its basic non-theistic philosophy and emphasis on compassion, while Hinduism excels at making space for many different paths to the same truth.

Mahaffey's survey is deeply useful, and part of its power is his own deep experience with several different religious traditions. This is a man who has created his own syncretistic path by entering profoundly into these traditions. Thus, he can offer us much more than a survey on the ways different traditions support an integral perspective on religion. He is also able to suggest, from his own tested experience, the possibilities that emerge from taking an experimental approach to one's own religious life. Mahaffey discusses the possibility of what he calls "double belonging," in which, say, a Christian or Jew might engage with Hindu or Buddhist practice while maintaining their primary connection with the religion of their upbringing. He also describes a more radical and particularly post-modern approach to religion, in which we pursue what he and others have called an "integral" path, integrating metaphysics with science and postmodern ideas of social justice. This might mean that you deepen your connection to Jesus while practicing mindfulness or meditating with a Sanskrit mantra. You might maintain your Jewish heritage by studying Torah or keeping kosher, yet practice Vedantic self-inquiry. You can love Buddha's analysis of the Four Noble Truths, yet secretly adore a Hindu Goddess whose mythology expands your sense of what it means to experience the earth as your mother. You can study the integral map-making of Ken Wilber, or the insights of A. H. Almaas, while reserving the right to surrender all your maps—and even reason itself—into the mystery.

Reading this book can inspire you to look at the traditions in a genuinely integral way, and even to mine your own psyche for its deepest spiritual connections. Patrick Mahaffey has done this throughout a lifetime of study, teaching, and practice. As a result, he brings to his work a deep feeling for the traditions he engages, as well as for the questions that any postmodern religious practitioner must answer. His book points to, and helps us come to terms with, the central paradox of religion—that religions can be, at one and the same time, imperfect human creations, as well as sublime pointers to the mystery that lies beyond the human.

—Sally Kempton, a former swami in a Vedic tradition, is a teacher and author of several books, including *Meditation for the Love of It* and *Awakening Shakti: The Transformative Power of the Goddesses of Yoga*.

INTRODUCTION

This book is written for those who, like myself, desire a spirituality that is informed by religious traditions, Jungian depth psychology, contemplative yoga, and related modes of thought. While I do not conflate the aims and processes of psychotherapy and yoga's spirituality, I do explore how these two approaches to human development are complementary. I invite you to think anew and to journey with me on a quest to investigate our deepest existential questions and concerns. As a synthetic thinker, I look for converging insights that I can integrate into the fabric of my own thinking. I discuss the perspectives of writers who have deeply informed my spiritual quest. I believe their views will be useful to others who pursue psychological wholeness and spiritual awakening. The ideas of leading-edge theologians, religious philosophers, and depth psychologists are elucidated and integrated. Careful attention is also given to yogis, mystics, and contemplatives who embody insights and wisdom that align with and augment the theorizing of the academic authors discussed in the book. My conviction is that real change comes from inner work, one person at a time, and cumulative changes in our inner world shape the conditions of our shared social reality. Therefore, I have made the cultivation of interiority the primary focus of this book.

When I was nine years old I was concerned that my childhood friends across the street might not go to heaven because they were not baptized. With considerable urgency I asked my mother, "What will happen to my friends if they accidentally die?" Though she tried to answer my question reassuringly, I continued to feel troubled. The more I pondered the question, the more complex it became. "What happens to people born in countries where Christianity is not practiced?" and "What about people who lived before Jesus was born? God would not exclude them from heaven, would He?" While these were the simple questions of a child, they persisted into my adolescence and adulthood.

Later, my childhood questions morphed into more mature concerns, ones that continue to animate my academic career and my spirituality. How can religious pluralism flourish in a secular, postmodern world? How can the study of religious thinkers and contemplatives from different traditions inspire and inform one's spirituality? What is the nature of divinity? How does one's God-image relate to one's self-understanding? What is the relationship between psychological individuation and spiritual awakening?

My early religious experience was influenced by my family. I was born in Detroit and while my mother was a devout Lutheran, my father, with an Irish Catholic heritage, was agnostic and not very interested in religious matters. My earliest memories of the divine were often overwhelming. I experienced an immense power and silent presence that evoked fear and aloneness. I felt that I could not communicate these experiences to my parents or anyone else, believing that I would not be understood or that the experiences would be disavowed. Later, when I studied religion as an undergraduate, I realized in retrospect that I had experienced the *numinous* as described in Rudolf Otto's *The Idea of the Holy*. The numinous, he writes, is the *mysterium tremendum*—a tremendous mystery that evokes feelings of fear, urgency, and fascination.[1] My experiences were pervaded by the *tremendum* aspect, the fear and dread in the presence of the sacred that Otto characterized as "wholly other." Such an encounter, he says, entails "the emotion of a creature, submerged and overwhelmed by its own nothingness in contrast to that which is supreme above all creatures," and a primitive feeling of "daemonic dread."[2]

During this period, while lying in bed at night, I also had experiences of imagining heaven, which for me was more a state of consciousness than a visual landscape. This initially felt peaceful and safe, but it invariably changed into a condition that was unsatisfying and constrained. Consequently, I would need to imagine another heaven beyond the one I was in until that heaven also felt like a bound condition. I continued imagining still further heavens with the same result. These imaginings ended with a strong sense that the peace I sought could only come by ceasing to exist. I understand now that this feeling was not a death wish, but rather an early intuition that egoic existence is incomplete and ultimately becomes wearisome (which no heaven can resolve) and is something from which one needs to be released. In the language of the Buddha, the separate sense of self or ego needs to be extinguished for one to enter the realm of real freedom and joy called nirvana.

My spiritual quest began in earnest when I decided to major in religion. I was an undergraduate at Western Michigan University in Kalamazoo, one of the first public universities to have a department of religion. I was fascinated by the traditions I was studying and longed to find a spiritual path I could practice. While taking a course on Hinduism, I learned from a classmate that weekly meditation sittings were held at the home of Dr. Robert Shafer, a professor of English and Asian classical literature. I showed up at his home the following week. I enjoyed my first experiences of meditation and the conversations that followed as we drank tea together. Robert would typically read a letter he had received from his guru, Sri Raushan Nath, a Hindu yogi and meditation master, who lived with his family as a householder in New Delhi, India. One evening early on, I was quite surprised to learn that Nath-ji, as we called him, whom I had never met and who could have known nothing about me, had commented on my character and my presence in the group.

Nath-ji visited Kalamazoo that summer, and I met him for the first time at a retreat. When Robert introduced us, Nath-ji referred to me as a "lost child." I did not know what he meant, and I was too shy to ask. I later learned that he saw me as a person who was not at home with the family and culture into which I was born. He also saw that I had a restless desire to experience God.

From Nath-ji I received an initiation called *shaktipat*, a transmission of spiritual energy from a guru to a devotee. He chanted Om and touched me on the forehead. I felt the effect a few weeks later while meditating with Robert, when I was suddenly pervaded by a blissful energy. The experience was formless, yet personal. The energy felt like boundless love and conferred the feeling that I was completely acceptable and at home in the universe.

Shaktipat also led to profound, transpersonal experiences with Robert. A few weeks later while talking, we were spontaneously enveloped by a presence that left us silent and transfixed. There was a flow of spiritual energy (non-erotic) between and around us, and we experienced a loving presence. Robert's face morphed many times as I gazed at him. In that moment, I felt as though I had known him for many lifetimes.

We refrained from trying to analyze the experience; we both acknowledged that it was precious and numinous, a gift—an experience of grace—that came to us unbidden. Robert understood it to be what Jewish theologian Martin Buber describes as an I-Thou encounter. That characterization fit for me and is how I continue to understand relational mysticism. In the weeks and months that followed, whenever I saw Robert this powerful experience would happen spontaneously. Since these experiences were catalyzed by eye contact, I viewed them as *darshan*, a Hindu word that means seeing and being simultaneously seen by the divine. Given the mutuality entailed in these encounters, I believe we saw a divinity within one another that included—yet transcended—both of us. These experiences changed my relationship to the divine. Whereas my childhood encounters with the numinous evoked feelings of fear and estrangement, my experience of bliss in meditation and the I-Thou experiences with Robert were characterized by love, belonging, and wonder.

To continue my academic study of religion, I moved to California. At Claremont Graduate School I was a research assistant to Arabinda Basu, a visiting scholar from the Sri Aurobindo Ashram in Pondicherry, India. Basu, a direct disciple of Sri Aurobindo and his spiritual collaborator called The Mother (Mirra Alfassa), was the Director of the Sri Aurobindo Research Academy located at the ashram. The Center for Process Studies was scheduled to host a conference on Whitehead and Vedanta later in the year. My role was to work one-on-one with Basu and help him prepare his paper for the conference. Due to a problem with his vision, Basu had difficulty writing and typing. We met several times a week that year, and I served as his scribe. I marveled at how he dictated the paper in eloquent sentences that rarely needed revision. He worked without notes or texts and picked up effortlessly where he had left off during preceding sessions. A good deal of our work together entailed sidebar conversations about philosophy and spirituality. These discussions were precious to me and akin to the tradition of the Upanishads where students sit close to the teacher and receive instruction via intimate dialogue. From Basu I received a transmission of Sri Aurobindo's teachings that have deeply informed my views regarding the nature of divinity and my contemplative practice. The epigraph of Aurobindo's magnum opus, "All life is yoga," conveys the essence of his world-affirming, evolutionary mysticism that locates the divine in the world and in the body.

My year at Claremont was rich, but the school was not a good fit for me. Although I was enrolled in a department of religion, the School of Theology, which was a separate institution, was setting the agenda for my program as well. While I had respect for the liberal version of theology taught at Claremont (the leading-edge place to study process theology, based on the philosophy of Alfred North Whitehead and Charles Hartshorne), I was uncomfortable with the Christian context of these studies; instead, I longed to study with scholars who were specialists in Hindu traditions and the comparative philosophy of religion. I decided to enroll at the University of California, Santa Barbara, where I had the opportunity to study with Raimundo Panikkar, Gerald Larson, and Ninian Smart. Panikkar had recently published the *Vedic Experience*, an extensive commentary on the Vedas, as well as *Intrareligious Dialogue*, a book that advocated entering deeply into religious traditions to understand them. Larson had established himself as one of the foremost scholars of yoga and Indian philosophy. Smart, a leading-edge philosopher of religion, was largely responsible for establishing the field of religious studies in the United Kingdom. Deeply conversant with Hindu and Buddhist thought, he broadened the scope of traditional philosophy of religion by grounding it in the history of religions rather than limiting it to Christian theology. He characterized his comparative approach as the study of worldviews. In my dissertation, *Religious Pluralism and the Question of Truth*, I utilized his comparative approach to analyze Christian and Hindu religious thought. My own beliefs and practices, however, were undisclosed or *bracketed*, exemplifying the stance of an objective scholar.

Writing my dissertation was difficult, more for personal than academic reasons. I became stuck, like Sisyphus pushing his boulder up a mountain. Simultaneously, my first marriage was coming apart, and I sought help through marriage counseling. Later, my first experience of individual psychotherapy entailed a descent into melancholy. Completing my doctorate while grieving my divorce was a complex experience of death and rebirth. After navigating this transition, I remarried and experienced a new zest for life. I obtained a core faculty position at Pacifica Graduate Institute in a newly formed, interdisciplinary doctoral program in mythological studies that conjoins the study of religious traditions, literature, and depth psychology. For more than twenty years, I have taught courses on Hindu and Buddhist traditions and evolving God-images from the perspective of an "engaged scholar." In other words, instead of the bracketing required by my doctoral studies, I actively practice the traditions I teach. This stance aligns with the depth psychological ethos of Pacifica where the study of one's subjectivity, particularly the unconscious factors that shape and condition one's life, is of central importance. In this context, congruent with my own belief that each person must fashion a path to wholeness, C. G. Jung's concept of individuation—that unending process in which, as much as humanly possible, one gradually integrates the different and often fragmentary aspects of one's life—can be viewed as akin to a religious vocation.

Adjusting to the demands of my new position at Pacifica was challenging. Engaging in Jungian analysis helped with the transition and enabled me to better understand the depth psychological ideas taught at the institute. When my dreams signaled that the analysis was coming to an end, I felt compelled to revivify my meditation practice. I joined the local Siddha Yoga Meditation Center and made the first of several trips to the Shree Muktananda Ashram in the Catskills. On the first occasion, I received shaktipat from Gurumayi Chidvilasananda, the current guru of the lineage who succeeded Swami Muktananda. Muktananda transmitted the teachings of Siddha Yoga to the West.

For my first sabbatical, I traveled to India and made a pilgrimage to the places associated with the lineages of my spiritual teachers. I had dreams that foreshadowed the journey's significance for me. In one, I saw my face morph as I gazed into a bathroom mirror. Within the dream, I consulted an analyst who informed me that I would be another person when I returned. In a second dream, I encountered a giant Ganesha, the elephant-headed deity, and felt an intense influx of energy as he slowly extended his trunk towards my face. I placed my hands in the Namaste gesture and pronounced a mantra, "Om Ganesha," as the presence of this figure began to feel overwhelming. These dreams intimated that I was in the midst of a transformation of self-understanding. I visited the Sri Aurobindo Ashram and Auroville in Pondicherry; lived in Nath-ji-s household in New Delhi and participated in an annual festival in Jammu where he and his master's samadhi shrines are located; and spent several weeks at Gurudev Siddha Peeth in Ganeshpuri, the mother ashram for Siddha Yoga. I also traveled to the ashram of Sri Ramana Maharshi, a great twentieth-century Vedantic sage, and made a pilgrimage to Vaishno Devi, a goddess temple at the apex of a mountain in north India, where I made offerings to Lakshmi, Sarasvati, and Kali.

My first journey to India felt like a homecoming. My wife and I were graciously hosted by Nath-ji's family, and I was deeply touched by the warmth and generosity of the Indian people. I experienced the silent, luminous presence of the divine at many places: the tombs of Sri Aurobindo and The Mother; Sri Aurobindo's bedroom; the room where Ramana Maharshi had given darshan to devotees; and at the shrines for Nath-ji and his master. While I had long felt a deep affinity to Hinduism, my first sojourn to India confirmed that I am a Hindu, a Western yogi who feels deeply connected to several lineages of contemplative yoga.

The culminating event of my second sabbatical in India was a twenty-one day silent retreat at Gurudev Siddha Peeth. Upon its completion, I felt complete contentment with my life. Ironically, I soon experienced what Jung calls an *enantiodromia*, a situation that turns into its opposite. Once I returned home and resumed my meditation practice, I was repeatedly flooded with erotic energy so powerful that I could not contain it. Subsequently, I succumbed to a tryst with a friend that could have destroyed my marriage. The chaos that ensued was the opposite of contentment. In Jungian terms, I experienced an inflation and, unable to integrate the spiritual energy generated by the retreat, I projected it onto another and was forced to grapple with the consequences. While the meditation retreat was a peak experience, the therapeutic work that followed was a descent into the underworld. Through a second round of analysis, I retrieved the energy and qualities I had projected, and I was able to restore trust in my marriage. A dream revealed that the therapeutic work was complete. Henceforth, I engaged my *sadhana*, or spiritual practice, and my life in a more grounded and less naïve manner. By working through the inflation, I came to understand that the integration of masculine and feminine energies of the psyche, the alchemical *coniunctio*, must occur primarily within one's being.

My eight years of affiliation with Siddha Yoga were truly edifying. Weekly satsangs with fellow practitioners, weekend meditation intensives, and week-long retreats offered great support for my sadhana. I particularly loved the devotional chanting that is a core practice. During that period, I also deepened my understanding of yoga philosophy, especially the tantric teachings and practices of Kashmir Shaivism. After Gurumayi Chidvilasananda withdrew from public teaching, I established relationships with groups and Western Hindu teachers who belong to the lineage of Bhagavan Nityananda and Swami Muktananda. I studied with Swami Shankarananda, a former Siddha Yoga teacher, and visited his ashram in Australia several times, where my practice of his original form of Self-inquiry was enhanced. Along the way I also participated in a series of local Santa Barbara retreats led by B. Alan Wallace, scholar-practitioner of Tibetan Buddhism; while these deepened my meditation practice, they confirmed this realization: that my sensibility is deeply Hindu. Hinduism is the tradition in which I feel most at home.

Currently my teachers include several Western Hindu yogis. I receive spiritual direction from world-class spiritual teacher Sally Kempton, formerly a Siddha Yoga swami, who infuses meditation with contemplative practices that engage the archetypal energies of the Hindu goddesses of yoga. I sit regularly with meditation master Mark Griffin, a disciple of Swami Muktananda, and his sangha at the Hard Light Center of Awakening near Los Angeles.

I have been initiated into Neelakantha Meditation and study nondual Shaiva Tantra with Paul Muller-Ortega, a direct disciple of both Maharishi Mahesh Yogi and Gurumayi Chidvilasananda. He is a world-renowned scholar-practitioner of the philosophy of Kashmir Shaivism and the founder of Blue Throat Yoga.

I align with the Vajrayana Buddhist perspective that distinguishes between a practitioner's root guru and other teachers as one's sadhana unfolds. The Vajrayana tradition also speaks of the outer, inner, and secret guru. The outer guru initiates a person's practice and helps one establish a connection with the inner, archetypal guru. One may also receive periodic empowerments from outer gurus. The relationship to the inner guru may be cultivated through a devotion practice called deity yoga. Ultimately, one experiences the secret guru that is the luminosity of one's true nature. Viewed in this way, Nath-ji, who initiated my practice of contemplative yoga, was my root guru. Subsequent teachers have helped me refine particular aspects of my spirituality: meditation, contemplation, Self-inquiry, textual study, and devotional practices. (In this light, my Jungian analyst could be considered a kind of outer guru who helped me investigate my emotional complexes, dreams, shadow material, and relationship issues.) While the need for a guru is often debated among Western contemplative yogis, I personally have found the guidance of gurus to be essential.

In the first chapter, I examine how our worldviews are shaped by the *zeitgeist*, the spirit of the times in which we live. While we live in a secular age, in the wake of the death of God in the West, religion persists, as does our longing for a spirituality that gives our lives meaning and purpose. I assert that recovering spirituality involves cultivating a more inclusive mode of consciousness that embraces traditional/religious, modern/secular, and postmodern/pluralistic modes of being and knowing. Chapter 2 investigates the challenges posed by religious pluralism. Can more than one religion be true? Can I practice more than one? I also explore the relationship between religion, spirituality, and myth and view faith as a developmental process. Chapters 3 through 5 reveal ways in which exemplary Christians, Hindus, and Buddhists address these challenges, offering ways of envisioning ultimate reality and of engendering harmony among those who practice particular religions. Chapter 6 considers how C. G. Jung's depth psychology can function as a psychological mode of spirituality. Attention is given to Jungian perspectives concerning individuation, God-images, the divine feminine, and the chakra symbolism of kundalini yoga. Chapter 7 elucidates forms of contemplative yoga spirituality that have been effectively transmitted to the West, while Chapter 8 presents seminal ideas from the Integral Theory of Ken Wilber and the Diamond Approach of A. H. Almaas, two pioneering exemplars of contemporary spirituality who integrate spiritual awakening and psychological development. In the final chapter, I discuss my credo and the practices that comprise my form of integrative spirituality.

While this book is written for a general audience, it contains a number of specialized terms associated with particular religions. For instance, Chapters 4 (Hinduism) and 7 (Contemplative Yoga) contain many Sanskrit terms. To make the text more user-friendly, I have avoided diacritical marks, italicizing the transliterated terms except for words such as karma, yoga, and nirvana, which are now commonly used in English discourse. Similarly, I have italicized Christian and Buddhist words that convey meanings essential to these traditions. Hindu tradition and Jungian psychology both use the word Self (upper case) though the meanings are somewhat different in these respective modes of thought. The Self, for Hindus, refers to the true nature of a human being, said to be the birthless/deathless witness of all experience. For Jung and Jungians, the Self refers to the regulating center of the psyche that includes ego awareness and the unconscious, also described as the archetype of wholeness. In both cases, the Self is distinct from the ego or personality. Although the translators of *The Collected Works of C. G. Jung* allow the context to determine when self refers to the ego personality and when it refers to the archetype, I follow the convention of many contemporary writers who use upper case to clearly distinguish the archetype of wholeness from the ego.

My heartfelt wish is that this book will deeply inform and empower your unique path of spirituality. May your journey to psychological wholeness and spiritual awakening be a path with a heart—one that benefits not only yourself but all sentient beings.

Notes

1 Rudolf Otto, *The Idea of the Holy: An Inquiry into the Non-Rational Factor in the Idea of the Divine and its Relation to the Rational*, 2nd ed. London: Oxford University Press, 1950, 12–13.
2 Ibid., 9–10; 15–16.

1

THE SPIRIT OF THE TIMES

With advancements in scientific knowledge and methods, industrial capitalism, and the decline of traditional religious authority, modernity flourishes in Western civilization. By the end of the nineteenth century, influential philosophers and writers of the day turned away from the comforting absolutes of European culture. The age of relativism dawned and with it came a sense of meaninglessness. As Friedrich Nietzsche famously proclaimed about the impact of modernity on religion:

> Have you not heard of that madman who lit a lantern in the bright morning hours, ran to the market place, and cried incessantly, "I seek God! I seek God!" . . . "Whither is God?" he cried. "I shall tell you. We have killed him—you and I. All of us are his murderers. But how have we done this? How were we able to drink the sea? Who gave us the sponge to wipe away the entire horizon? What did we do when we unchained this earth from its sun? . . . Do we not smell anything yet of God's decomposition? Gods too decompose. God is dead. God remains dead. And we have killed him."[1]

For Nietzsche, the basic assumptions of art, philosophy, science, and religion are without any ultimate foundation. Without absolutes, the products of human culture, including religions, are little more than useful fictions or constructed realities to serve particular social functions and address deeply felt personal needs for security and certainty.

The *zeitgeist*, or the spirit of the times in which we live, shapes our worldviews. To understand our own time, we need to step back and observe it within a larger historical context. This chapter considers how different worldviews, engendered by traditional, modern, and postmodern periods of history, condition the ways in which humans find meaning and purpose in their lives.

Secularization and the persistence of religion

We live in a secular age; paradoxically, religions persist. Secularization, a key concept in the sociology of religion, is closely related to both the concept of modernity and the fundamentalist reactions against it. Within the secular thinking that has come to dominate the West, the historical development of religion is linear. Social science, born in nineteenth-century evolutionism, presupposes this notion and contributes many of the master terms used in contemporary discourse about social change: industrialization, modernization, rationalization, and urbanization. All these imply one-directional processes and, taken together, constitute the basis for the secularization thesis—the idea that society moves away from some sacred conditions toward those in which the sacred evermore recedes.[2]

The resurgence of religion, including fundamentalism, during the past three decades belies this thesis and requires a theory of religion that can account for so dramatic a change. As Mark C. Taylor observes:

> You cannot understand the world today if you do not understand religion. Never before has religion been so powerful and so dangerous. No longer confined to church, synagogue, and mosque, religion has taken to the street by filling airways and networks with images and messages that create fatal conflicts, which threaten to rage out of control. When I began pondering these issues in the 1960s, few analysts or critics would have predicted this unexpected turn of events.[3]

The relationship between religion and secularization has been misunderstood. In this regard, as Taylor further asserts, critics fail to appreciate the intricate relationship between secularity and the Western religious and theological tradition: "Religion and secularity are not opposites; to the contrary, Western secularity is a *religious* phenomenon."[4]

Secularists misinterpret religion as much as believers misunderstand secularism. Religion is not a separate domain; it pervades our culture and has an important impact on every aspect of society. We need an alternative to the either/or perspective or binary thinking that serves as the conventional wisdom for understanding religion and its secular and atheistic critics. One of the most pressing dangers we face today is the conflict between the competing absolutisms that divide the world. Such ardently opposed worldviews can never be mediated, Taylor argues.

All major religious traditions contain some fundamentalist elements. Evidence of this can be seen in the literalists' interpretations of scripture and reactions to aspects of modernity and secular culture. Taylor describes this phenomenon as a worldwide rise in neofoundationalism. He understands this development as a symptom and a response to the process of globalization. In his view, while modernism is correlative with industrialization, postmodernism is inseparable from the emergence of the postindustrial network culture.[5]

Network culture creates a world in which *to be* is *to be connected.* As connectivity spreads, the human landscape with its dependence on technology becomes increasingly complex, causing instability and uncertainty to grow. These developments, Taylor observes, lead to a longing for simplicity, security, and certainty. Neofoundationalism, in its abundant guises, ranging from the scriptural literalism of Christian evangelicals and some Islamists to the genomic logocentrism and neurophysiological reductionism of some of today's most sophisticated scientists, represents an effort to satisfy this longing. These disparate forms of belief are alternative versions of a religiosity that attempts to banish doubt by absolutizing relative norms and dividing the world into exclusive opposites: good/evil, sacred/profane, religious/secular, Western/Eastern, white/black, and Christian/Muslim.[6]

Canadian philosopher Charles Taylor, in *A Secular Age*, among the most profound inquiries into secularization, provides a map of the existential terrain of late modernity in Western Culture.[7] Our epoch is a haunted moment of history, he contends. We live in immanence and the twilight of the gods. But their ghosts have refused to depart, and every once in a while we might be surprised to find ourselves tempted by belief, by intimations of transcendence.[8] Taylor refers to this as the "immanent frame," a circumscribed world that precludes transcendence, a spiritual dimension of reality that exists beyond or within the world.[9] Even as faith endures in our secular age, believing does not come easily. Faith is fraught with an inescapable sense of its contestability. We do not simply believe (as opposed to doubting); we believe *while* doubting.[10] Most of us live in this cross-pressured space, where both our agnosticism and devotion are mutually haunted and haunting.

A Secular Age persistently asks two questions: "How did we move from a condition where, in Christendom, people lived naively within a theistic construal to one in which . . . unbelief has become for many the major default option?" and "Why was it virtually impossible not to believe in God in, say, 1500 in our Western society, while in 2000 many of us find this is not only easy, but even inescapable?"[11] These questions are concerned less with what people believe than with what is believ*able*. Taylor carefully differentiates between three meanings of the term *secular* (secular$_1$, secular$_2$, secular$_3$):

- Secular$_1$. In the classical and medieval accounts, *secular* amounts to something like "the temporal"—the realm of "earthly" politics or mundane vocations. The priest, for instance, pursues a "sacred" vocation, whereas others engage in "secular" pursuits. This is secular$_1$.[12]

- Secular$_2$. In the modern period, particularly in the wake of the Enlightenment, *secular* refers to a nonsectarian, areligious space or standpoint. This public sphere is secular insofar as it is (allegedly) nonreligious; schools are secular when they are no longer parochial; hence, public schools are thought to be secular schools. Similarly, in the late twentieth century, people describe themselves as secular, meaning they have no religious affiliation or beliefs. This notion is assumed by both the secularization theory and normative secularism.

Secular*ism* is always secular$_2$. And, secularization theory is usually a confident expectation that societies will become secular$_2$—that is, characterized by decreasing religious beliefs and participation.[13]

• Secular$_3$. It is the third meaning of *secular*, however, which Taylor stresses in *A Secular Age*. A society is secular$_3$ insofar as religious belief or belief in God is understood to be one option among others, and thus contestable (and contested). At issue here is a shift in "the conditions of belief." The shift to secularity in this sense indicates "a move from a society where belief in God is unchallenged and indeed, unproblematic, to one in which it is understood to be one option among others, and frequently not the easiest to embrace."[14] It is in this respect that we live "in a secular age," even if religious participation might be visible and fervent. The emergence of the secular in this sense makes possible the emergence of an "exclusive humanism"—a radically new option in the marketplace of beliefs, a vision of life in which anything beyond the immanent is eclipsed. As Taylor observes: "For the first time in history a purely self-sufficient humanism came to be a widely available option. I mean by this a humanism accepting no final goals beyond human flourishing, nor any allegiance to anything else beyond this flourishing. Of no previous society was this true."[15]

A secular$_3$ society could undergo religious revival in which vast swaths of the populace embrace religious beliefs. But this could never turn back the clock of secularization; we would always know that we *used* to believe something else, that there are other plausible visions of meaning and significance. We could also hold beliefs amidst the secular$_3$ condition; indeed, conversion is a response to secularity, not an escape from it.

Taylor also describes the *nova effect* in contemporary culture—the explosion of different new options for belief and meaning in a secular$_3$ age, produced by the concurrent cross-pressures of our history—as well as the concurrent pressure of immanentization and echoes of transcendence. Immanentization is the process whereby meaning, significance, and fullness are sought within an enclosed, self-sufficient, and naturalistic universe without any reference to transcendence. The newly emergent options for finding spiritual meaning are alternatives to conventional religious beliefs and secular disavowals of religion.

A third way—that of integrated spirituality—is put forward in this book, an approach that is open to the promise of transcendence offered by spiritual traditions while embodying the immanent conditions of our psychological and historical existence.

Worldviews and ways of knowing

Religion is a complex, adaptive network of symbols, myths, rituals, and structured patterns of feeling, thinking, and acting that lend purpose and meaning to life.[16] Put another way, religions are worldviews that provide ways of seeing and interpreting the world. Secular worldviews locate meaning entirely within immanent frames of nature, culture, and history. The shift from the sacred to the secular can be viewed within the context of three historical epochs—pre-modern or traditional; modern; and postmodern—and the epistemologies or ways of knowing associated with each. These epochs, however, are also attitudes or sensibilities that co-exist—often quite contentiously—in contemporary culture; each encodes values that set it apart from the others.

Huston Smith's writings on philosophy and religion have deeply influenced my thinking about worldviews. Unlike most of his contemporaries, Smith retained a passionate interest in metaphysics to which he refers as *worldview* or *Big Picture* (he uses these three terms interchangeably, as I do in this book). A worldview, Smith explains, resembles peripheral vision; it gets overlooked precisely for being peripheral. What we see is always affected by its background. Accordingly, life's problems press so heavily upon us that we seldom take the time to reflect on the ways in which our unconscious attitudes and assumptions about the nature of things affect how we perceive what is directly before us.[17]

Our need for a worldview is deeper and more fundamental than are our needs for sexuality, social power or possessions; we crave a kind of knowledge that orients us to reality, to the whole of things. There is a fundamental dis-ease within us that renders us incapable of being fully at peace, yet the desire for that peace and fulfillment resides in the deep recesses of our souls. "Whether we realize it or not," says Smith, "simply to be human is to long for release from mundane existence with its confining walls of finitude and mortality."[18] Therein lies our need for a worldview that truly nourishes our soul amidst the unending distractions that abound at the surface level of life.

Smith contrasts two worldviews, traditional and scientific, holding the former to be existentially superior to the latter. The traditional worldview is preferable to the one that now encloses us as it allows for the fufillment of the basic longing that lives in the depths of the human heart.[19] For Smith, the reality that excites and fulfills the soul's longing is God by whatsoever name. While this conviction may seem nostalgic, I share Smith's view. I admire him for boldly arguing the value of religion in a nuanced manner that responds to the contemporary worldviews that dismiss it.

Smith surveys the historical periods that have brought us to where we are now, highlighting the accomplishments and deficiencies of each. Wherever and whenever they live, he observes, people find themselves faced with three inescapable problems: how to obtain food and shelter from their natural environment (the problem nature poses to us); how to get along with one another (the social problem); and how to relate to the total scheme of things (the religious problem). These problems can be viewed within the context of three main periods of human history: the traditional period (from human beginnings to the rise of modern science); the modern period (from the rise of modern science to the first half of the twentieth century); and the postmodern era (which Nietzsche anticipated, but that did not take hold until the second half of the twentieth century). Each of these periods, according to Smith, pours energy into addressing one of these inescapable problems. Modernity gives us our view of nature that new discoveries continue to refine; postmodernity grapples with social injustices more resolutely than people ever had before; but when it comes to worldviews or metaphysics, the accomplishments of our ancestors in the traditional period remain unsurpassed.[20]

In the sixteenth and seventeenth centuries Europe developed the scientific method, a new way of knowing derived from observing nature and asking questions or forming hypotheses to be tested and analyzed, to produce measureable and reproducible results. Brick by brick an edifice was erected from evidence-based truths; the edifice became the scientific worldview.[21] Because this mode of knowing focuses only on the natural or material world, supernatural or immaterial realities at first drop from view and then, as the worldview hardens, are denied existence.[22] Modernity's Big Picture is materialism or, in its most plausible version, naturalism, which acknowledges the existence of non-physical things—thoughts and feelings, for instance—while insisting these depend entirely on matter.[23] When science is regarded as the only way of knowing all that can be known, it becomes scientism, a worldview that claims unique authority for knowing what is real.

Postmodernism opposes the very ideas that comprise the Big Picture. It begins by critiquing the worldview of the Enlightenment but comes to argue the more radical position that worldviews are misguided in principle. In *The Postmodern Condition*, Jean François Lyotard defines postmodernism as "incredulity towards metanarratives," a synonym for metaphysics.[24] In Smith's view the incredulity takes three forms that have become increasingly shrill: *postmodern minimalism* points out that we do not have a consensual worldview because we do not have any maps, nor do we know how to make them; *mainline postmodernism* adds, "and never again will we have a consensual worldview," such as the one that prevailed in the Middle Ages; and *hardcore postmodernism* carries the trajectory of thought to its logical limit by adding, "good riddance!"

Worldviews are said to totalize by marginalizing minority viewpoints; they are inherently oppressive and should be resolutely resisted.[25] Smith refutes this postmodernist conclusion, which prevails merely because it reflects widely occurring examples of oppression. What it fails to demonstrate, Smith argues, is the impossibility of a worldview that builds into its foundations, as essential building blocks, the rights of minorities. Actually, whether or not we have a worldview is not a choice. The only choice we have, Smith maintains, is to be consciously aware of our own worldviews and those in our midst. We can either criticize them where needed or let them work on us unconsciously and acquiesce to living unexamined lives. Our challenge, from Smith's perspective, is not to disavow worldviews that differ from our own nor to discard them altogether, but to extract the gold from each historical period and let the rest sink back into the sands of history. Modernity's gold—science—is certain to remain important in the third millennium, and postmodernity's focus on justice stands a good chance of continuing. In jeopardy is the traditional worldview that requires rehabilitation if it is to survive.[26]

Wisdom traditions delineate states of expanded awareness and subtle dimensions of reality that may be experienced through contemplative practices. The wisdom traditions typically conceptualize reality as "the Great Chain of Being," characterized more recently by integral philosopher Ken Wilber as "the Great Nest of Being," wherein the chain is imagined as nested levels of reality. Spirit, impelled by a creative impulse, manifests a universe through involution. Spirit first becomes soul, a stepped-down and diluted reflection of itself. Soul then steps down into mind, mind into life, life into body, and body into matter. These levels in the Great Nest are all forms of Spirit, but the forms become less and less conscious of their source. Each greater level goes beyond and envelops or contains its lesser ones without being reduced nor explained by them.[27]

Involution, or the infolding of Spirit, must occur before evolution, or the unfolding of Spirit, can happen. Conversely, in the wisdom traditions, evolution is the unfolding of Spirit, in which the higher levels emerge out of the lower ones. For example, life appears to emerge out of the matter into which it was first deposited by involution. As Wilber explains, "You cannot get the higher out of the lower unless the higher were already there, in potential—sleeping, as it were—waiting to emerge. The 'miracle of emergence' is simply the Spirit's creative play in the fields of its own manifestation."[28] Figure 1.1 depicts the emergent stages in evolution as (A), (A + B), (A + B + C), and so on. The addition signs mean that something is emerging or being added to manifestation. Spirituality, in this context, is an evolutionary process. "That which was dis-membered, fragmented, and forgotten during involution," says Wilber, "is re-membered, reunited, made whole, and realized during evolution."[29]

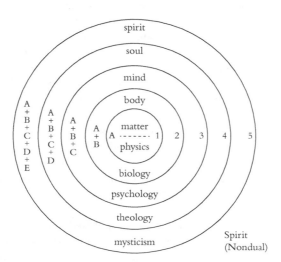

FIGURE 1.1 The traditional Great Chain of Being

Figure from *Integral Spirituality*, by Ken Wilber. Copyright © 2006. Reprinted by arrangement with The Permissions Company, Inc. on behalf of Shambhala Publications.

The Great Chain of Being, pejoratively labeled *metaphysical* to mean speculative and non-empirical, and thus unreal, has long been negated as a view of reality by modern and postmodern modes of thought. Many contemporary thinkers such as Smith and Wilber consider the dismissal of the non-material dimensions of Being a great loss for humanity and would like to retrieve or incorporate the Great Chain worldview into modern and postmodern thinking.

Modernity is associated with social developments, such as the rise of science and political democracy, as well as dramatic breakthroughs in understanding empirical reality through scientific inquiry. Immensely positive aspects of modernity include the ideals of equality, freedom, and justice, irrespective of race, class, creed, or gender; modern medicine, physics, biology, and chemistry; the end of slavery; the rise of feminism; and the affirmation of universal rights for humankind.[30] These gains were achieved through the differentiation of the three cultural value spheres: art, morals, and science.

Pre-modern cultures certainly possessed art, morals, and science but, as Wilber explains, these spheres tended to be relatively undifferentiated. In the Middle Ages, for example, Galileo could not freely look through his telescope and truthfully report the results because the morals of the Church defined what science could—or could not—do. Later, with the differentiation of these spheres of inquiry, an astronomer could report findings without fear of being charged with heresy or treason. Art, morals, and science could pursue their own truths. Artists could then paint nonreligious themes without fear of reprisal, and moral theorists could pursue inquiry into the good life whether it agreed with the Bible or not. These differentiations, according to Wilber, are the *dignity* of modernity.[31]

These achievements are the good news of modernity, but there is also the bad news. Critics of modernity lament a long list of disastrous effects that include the death of God and Goddess, commodification of life, leveling of qualitative distinctions, brutalities of capitalism, replacement of quality with quantity, loss of value and meaning, fragmentation of the natural world, existential dread, rampant and vulgar materialism—which, taken together, create "the disenchantment of the world."[32] In other words, the modern world is soulless, devoid of spiritual radiance and depth.

The problem, Wilber observes, is that the wonderful differentiations of modernity went too far, resulting in dissociation, fragmentation, and alienation. Science became *scientism*—a scientific materialism and imperialism. The dominant worldview of modernity pronounced that the other value spheres were unscientific or illusory. Wilber aptly summarizes the implications:

> The Great Nest of matter, body, mind, soul, and spirit could be thoroughly reduced to systems of matter alone; and matter—whether in the material brain or material process systems—would account for all of reality, without remainder. Gone was mind and gone was soul and gone was Spirit—gone, in fact, was the entire Chain, except for its pitiful bottom rung—and in its place, as Whitehead famously lamented, there was reality as a "dull affair,

soundless, scentless, colorless; merely the hurrying of material, endlessly, meaninglessly." And so it came about that the modern West was the first modern civilization in the history of the human race to deny the substantial reality of the Great Nest of Being.[33]

Disenchanted indeed! Wilber describes this modern view of reality as a "flatland"—the cosmos reduced to its external and measurable surfaces.[34]

Recovering the spiritual

C. G. Jung's depth psychology emerged in the wake of Nietzsche's proclamation and after his break from Sigmund Freud, just before the outbreak of the First World War. Jung describes these chaotic times and his personal crisis of meaning as a struggle between *the spirit of the times* and *the spirit of the depths*.[35] The former phrase describes the loss of soul that characterizes modernity, while the latter is the deeply personal path that leads to its recovery.

As predicted, the rational and scientific worldview gained strength in European culture. Many intellectuals, including Freud, anticipated that the importance of religious faith, even for the masses, would fade away and finally disappear altogether. Science would eventually explain what religions had sought to account for with their mythologies and theologies. The need for myth would diminish, and humans would be free to live purely rational and meaningful lives without reference to anything beyond the material world as measured by science and as celebrated by consumerism. Modernity finally achieved a type of consciousness that no longer depended on or needed myths or symbols. This was the state of mind reflected in Jung's account of his personal crisis in 1913, and it was this perception of the soulless condition of modernity—as a worldview, sensibility, and attitude—that pushed him to leave the spirit of the times and follow the spirit of the depths.[36] The result was *Liber Novus* (*The Red Book*), Latin for "The New Book," his deeply personal work that exemplifies the path of individuation—a psychological mode of spirituality that draws upon the mythic and symbolic riches of the world's religions without being constrained by them—as an alternative to both scientific materialism and traditional religion.

Rational consciousness, so highly esteemed by modern science and secular critics of religion, may be considered a form of attachment to a habituated way of being in the world. Rational consciousness revolves around the dichotomy between our ego and the world in which we experience ourselves as separate from everything and everyone.[37] As cultural philosopher Jean Gebser explains, this way of experiencing ourselves is divisive, atomizing, and ultimately destructive; this is the ruling structure of consciousness in Western culture. The opposition between the *experiencing subject* and *experienced object* has intensified to the point that we experience ourselves as estranged from the world in which we live. Because of this alienation, we are sick at heart and our world is fractured.[38]

Characterizing this strongly ingrained habit of dualistic perception as an addiction, yoga historian Georg Feuerstein delineated a process of spiritual recovery, akin to twelve-step programs, that can reconnect us to the same spirit of the depths that attracted Jung and enabled him to recover his soul. Several steps in the process follow, each providing an antidote to the reigning worldview of materialism that pervades modern and postmodern culture.

The first step is to stop denying there is anything wrong with our ordinary state. By labeling our ordinary state, the *consensus consciousness*, as "normal," we dismiss and disempower all other states of consciousness. The fact that we call them "altered" states means they are regarded as merely modifications of the ordinary waking state.[39]

Another step counters the conviction inherent in the disempowering feeling that there is nothing we can do to change our situation. We refuse to consider the possibility that the world may actually be comprised of dimensions of reality that transcend the mundane world. We disallow ourselves the possibility of inner or spiritual growth because our view of human potential is limited to the capacities of the rational mind.[40]

One of the most crucial steps in recovery is to understand the nature of existential suffering. Whenever we exaggerate our independence as individuals, we cut ourselves off from others, we regard the world as an enemy to be conquered, and we become our own source of suffering. This suffering is superimposed on any adversity or pain we may experience as human beings. A psychological malaise takes hold from which we may recover only when we have realized that our habit of egoic self-encapsulation is artificial and self-inflicted, resting upon a denial of the essential interconnectedness and interdependence of everything.[41] This realization is at the heart of Buddha's Four Noble Truths.

Feuerstein's spiritual recovery process closely aligns with Jung's depth psychology. While Freud's writings about the psychopathology of everyday life offer a glimpse into the ways in which ordinary life is based on an impoverished and distorted view of reality, he does not look deeply enough, asserts Feuerstein. If he had, he would have seen that the dichotomizing rational consciousness itself is the root of our malaise, for the rational consciousness creates the unhealthy split of the ego from the id or of consciousness from the unconscious.

Freud's work was the first effort within modern rationalistic psychology to reintegrate the unconscious with the conscious part of the human psyche and culture. His concept of the unconscious is still, however, largely subject to the constraints and prejudices of rational consciousness itself. He was unable to move beyond his concept of the unconscious as a dumping ground and therefore failed to appreciate the rich texturing of other forms and states of consciousness and philosophies based on experiences of "non-ordinary" reality.[42] C. G. Jung took the next step by discovering the deeper dimension of the unconscious and its capacity to engender meaning and wholeness in individuals through inner work.

When viewed in this way, spiritual life can be regarded as a gradual recovery from the addiction to the peculiar type of awareness that splits everything into subject and object. This primary addiction is the source of all secondary addictions. The latter are possible only because the ego is confronted by objects it tries to control or by which it feels controlled. The secondary addictions are substitutes for the bliss that inheres in our depths, a teaching that is at the heart of Hindu and Buddhist philosophies and spiritual practices. Secondary addictions are desperate and mistaken attempts to remove the primary addiction. Spiritual recovery is an uncovering of the spiritual dimension hidden by the self-divided ego personality functioning under the influence and constraints of rational consciousness.[43]

Structures of consciousness

Although rationality engenders a sense of separation between ordinary egoic awareness and the world, it is a great achievement. Gebser distinguishes five structures of consciousness that have emerged during the long course of human cultural history—*archaic, magic, mythic, mental,* and *integral*—each providing a distinct mode of perceiving and understanding reality.[44] Combs provides a gloss of these five structures that underlie cultural evolution. The archaic structure of consciousness that emerged during the transition from ape to human was our animal, instinctual heritage organized around basic physiological needs such as food, water, warmth, and shelter. The magic structure arose in the first major human societies that consisted of hunters and gatherers, and continued in later horticultural societies. The spiritual life of magical cultures most likely centered on local shamans who acted as guides and healers in service to the spiritual and physical well-being of their communities, and who typically relied on power animals and spirits to achieve their goals. The mythic structure dawned with the agricultural revolution. Here the focus of spirituality shifted to grand mythic themes involving gods and goddesses and stories about the creation and fate of the world; this developed further with urbanization and the formation of civilizations and the world's great religions. The mental structure of consciousness, which I designate as *rational*, first appeared in the West in the pre-Socratic philosophers who applied reason to the older mythic ideas, gradually leading to new and more logically systematic theories about the physical cosmos. While the rational structure tended to dominate the ancient Greek and Roman worlds, it was largely lost in the West during the Middle Ages, when a mythic Christian worldview prevailed in Europe, until the coming of the Renaissance.[45]

With the Renaissance and Enlightenment in the West came the flowering of the rational structure of consciousness, distinguished by objective evidence-based scientific inquiry. Rational thought entails the capacity to take a third-person perspective—the ability to step back and look at one's self and society—and to ask questions that give rise to the possibility of new forms of organizing society. What would it be like if slaves were free? What's fair for all people? Consequently, the rational worldview engenders representative democracy, the end of slavery, and the beginning of integrating women throughout society.[46]

Postmodernity brought another structure of consciousness that may be characterized as relativistic and pluralistic, a capacity to rise above third-person perspectives in order to reflect on them and critique their adequacy. Reflecting critically upon the rational thinking of modernity, postmodern thought views all knowledge, including science, as being conditioned by our subjectivity, socially constructed, and culturally embedded. The pluralistic form of rational consciousness is more multicultural in scope as it includes spirituality, ethics, aesthetics, and the truths of other cultures, and it attempts to include previously excluded or marginalized cultures and people. Feminism, the civil rights movement, and the environmental movement are all products of postmodern pluralism.

While these structures of consciousness emerged in different historical epochs, this does not mean that during each epoch everyone experienced the same worldview. The epochs overlap considerably and within each there have always been differences. The dominant structure in much of the world today is the rational worldview.[47] However, large numbers of people continue to live within the mythic and even magic worldviews, which helps explain why contemporary society is comprised of people with widely divergent belief systems, from religious fundamentalists to rationalist critics who decry religion as a childish anachronism. The intense conflict between worldviews is aptly referred to as "the culture wars." The main clashes in this fight today are between individuals and groups who hold three discrepant worldviews: traditional religious; modern scientific; and postmodern pluralist. Proponents of each regard theirs to be the only valid view.

Rational consciousness reached its zenith during the modern period. Postmodernity may be seen as a transitional epoch in which the limitations of modern ways of knowing are revitalized. Postmodern thought has greatly enhanced our appreciation for cultural diversity and dethroned grand theories that impose the hegemonic values of the West upon Eastern and indigenous cultures. Yet, as important as this breakthrough is, it does not in itself overcome the divisions and conflicts that prevail in our contemporary world. What is called for, in my view, is an integral mode of consciousness that engenders inclusion and harmony within our vision of reality, promotes our understanding of personal and cultural differences, and allows us to embrace traditional/religious, modern/secular, and postmodern/pluralistic modes of being and knowing.

Notes

1 Friedrich Nietzsche, *The Gay Science, with a Prelude of Rhymes and an Appendix of Songs*, trans. Walter Kaufman. New York: Random House, 1974, 95–96.
2 Phillip E. Hammond, introduction to *The Sacred in a Secular Age: Towards Revision in the Scientific Study of Religion*, ed. Phillip E. Hammond. Berkeley: University of California Press, 1985, 1.
3 Mark C. Taylor, *After God*. Chicago: University of Chicago Press, 2007, xiii.
4 Ibid.
5 Ibid., 3.
6 Ibid., 4.

7 Charles Taylor, *A Secular Age*. Cambridge, MA: The Belknap Press of Harvard University Press, 2007.
8 James K. A. Smith, *How (Not) To Be Secular: Reading Charles Taylor*. Grand Rapids, MI: William E. Eerdmans Publishing Co, 2014, 3–4.
9 Ibid., 141. While I agree with Taylor's characterization of Western modernity, his distinction between transcendence and immanence overlooks the fact that these binaries need not be opposed. Transcendence can be experienced as present within the body, nature, and the world. His transcendence/immanence distinction, however, does reflect how most theologians and philosophers think about divinity in the West.
10 Ibid., 4.
11 Taylor, *A Secular Age*, 14, 25.
12 James K. A. Smith, 20–21.
13 Taylor, *A Secular Age*, 25, 14.
14 Taylor, 3.
15 Ibid., 18.
16 Mark C. Taylor, *After God*, 12.
17 Huston Smith, *Why Religion Matters: The Fate of the Human Spirit in An Age of Disbelief*. San Francisco: HarperSanFrancisco, 2001, 25.
18 Ibid., 28.
19 Ibid., 28.
20 Ibid., 11–12.
21 Ibid., 12–13.
22 Ibid., 19–20.
23 Ibid., 20.
24 Jean François Lyotard, *The Postmodern Condition: A Report on Knowledge*, trans. Geoff Bennington and Brian Massumi. Minneapolis, MN: University of Minnesota Press, 1984, xxiv.
25 Huston Smith, *Religion Matters*, 21.
26 Ibid., 21–22.
27 Ken Wilber, *Integral Spirituality: A Startling New Role for Religion in the Modern and Postmodern World*. Boston: Integral Books, 2006, 213–16. See Arthur O. Lovejoy, *The Chain Chain of Being*. Cambridge, MA: Harvard University Press, 1964, for the definitive study of this idea.
28 Ibid., 216.
29 Ibid., 218.
30 Ken Wilber, *The Marriage of Sense and Soul: Integrating Science and Religion*. New York: Random House, 1998, 11.
31 Ibid., 12.
32 Ibid., 11.
33 Ibid., 13.
34 Ibid., 10, 56–57, 235.
35 C. G. Jung, *The Red Book: Liber Novus: A Reader's Edition*, ed. Sonu Shamdasani, trans. Mark Kyburz, John Peck, and Sonu Shamdasani. New York: W.W. Norton, 2009, 119.
36 Murray Stein, *Minding the Self: Jungian Meditations on Contemporary Spirituality*. London: Routledge, 2014, 76.
37 Georg Feuerstein, *The Deeper Dimension of Yoga: Theory and Practice*. Boston: Shambhala, 2003, 89.
38 Ibid. Feuerstein draws upon Jean Gebser's *The Ever-Present Origin, Part One: Foundations for the Aperspectival World*. Athens, OH: Ohio University Press, 1986, to elucidate distinguishing characteristics of rational consciousness.
39 Ibid., 89–90.
40 Ibid., 90.
41 Ibid., 91.
42 Ibid., 91–92.
43 Ibid., 92–93.

44 Alan Combs, *Consciousness Explained Better: Towards an Integral Understanding of the Multifaceted Nature of Consciousness*. St. Paul, MN: Paragon House, 2009, 61. Combs provides a concise gloss of Gebser's theory of the five structures of consciousness that underlie cultural evolution.

45 Ibid., 63–69.

46 These observations correlate with Wilber's analysis of the positive aspect of modernity discussed earlier in this chapter.

47 Ibid., 62.

2

RELIGIOUS PLURALISM, SPIRITUALITY, AND STAGES OF FAITH

> Be then, within yourself, a receptacle for the forms of all beliefs, for God is too vast and too great to be confined to one belief to the exclusion of the other.
>
> —*Ibn al-'Arabi*

Our awareness of the variety of religions and their diverse beliefs and practices poses a challenge to the authority and self-understanding of particular traditions. It provides a new horizon for religious thought and practice. Adherents of current day religion must reflect upon questions that religious people of the past—secure in more self-contained and homogeneous communities and societies—rarely had to face. Why are there so many religions? Why do I belong to one religion rather than another? Can more than one religion be true? And, if so, are they equally true? How should my religion relate to the others? Religious pluralism is equally challenging for those who do not align with a particular tradition but who, nevertheless, feel religious longings and seek spiritual experiences within the context of secular culture.

Philosophers of religion characterize the challenge of religious pluralism as the problem of conflicting truth claims. In the past the different religions of the world often developed in relative isolation from one another. There were occasions when great movements of expansion brought two faiths into contact, but their interactions generally entailed discord rather than dialogue. Only during the last one hundred years or so does the scholarly study of religions make possible an appreciation of the faiths of other peoples. This increase in knowledge reveals differences that distinguish religions as alternative visions of life. As one prominent philosopher observes:

> If I had been born in India, I would probably be a Hindu; if in Egypt, probably a Muslim; if in Sri Lanka, probably a Buddhist; but I was born in England and am, predictably, a Christian. These different religions seem to say different and incompatible things about the nature of ultimate reality, about the modes of divine activity, and about the nature and destiny of the human race. Is the divine nature personal or nonpersonal? Does deity become incarnate in the world? Are human beings reborn again and again on earth? Is the empirical self the real self, destined for eternal life in fellowship with God, or is it only a temporary and illusory manifestation of an eternal higher self? Is the Bible, or the Qur'an, or the Bhagavad Gita the Word of God? If what Christianity says in answer to such questions is true, must not what Hinduism says be to a large extent false? If what Buddhism says is true, must not what Islam says be largely false?[1]

Inherent in these questions is a challenge to the claims of all traditions. How can all religions, with their divergent beliefs about these matters, be true? A more disturbing possibility confronts the reflective person—perhaps none of them are true.

How do religious philosophers and theologians respond to this new context of multiple options for belief? Three responses predominate:

- The first entails reasserting the authority of religious tradition in the face of modern secularity; thus, playing down the challenges of traditional religious beliefs in order to hold as tenaciously as possible to the faith as it has been historically understood. This approach often attempts to separate the concerns of religion from those of science and other forms of secular discourse. When successful, this kind of religious thought minimizes doubt and cognitive dissonance in the faithful. On the other hand, this kind of religiosity can be rigid, defensive, and conducive to fundamentalist beliefs.

- Another response is to reinterpret religious beliefs in secular terms. Rather than resist, one embraces modernity as a basis for making sense of reality. The best example of this approach is the program of "demythologizing" Christian doctrine. Rudolf Bultmann, for instance, replaces mythical interpretations of reality, such as the three-decker vision of heaven, earth, and hell, with ideas appropriated from modern existentialism. God is understood as the Ground of Being and faith is construed as authenticity. This strategy has the advantage of reducing cognitive dissonance in the self-conscious believer, but the religious content of the tradition tends to dissolve in the process of translation.

- A third response is to ground religious affirmations in experience. This style of religious thought tends to be non-dogmatic and empirical in character, focusing on experiences that underlie religious doctrines. C. G. Jung's depth psychology, for example, places great emphasis on experience by positing a religious function of the psyche. He offers us a way to appreciate our common humanity through the diverse symbols that issue forth from a collective unconscious. Jung's approach is discussed in detail in Chapter 6.

Religion, spirituality, and myth

The religious options available to contemporary people raise questions about the meaning of religion, spirituality, and myth. *Religion* is a complex cultural phenomenon that contains many interrelated components: sacred texts, myths, rituals, doctrines, architectural structures (churches, temples, shrines), iconography, and social organizations. *Spirituality*, by contrast, refers to a direct experience of the sacred in the myriad forms in which it may manifest. Some people experience this as a divinity, others as the formless absolute, and still others in natural phenomena such as mountains, rivers, or caves. Spiritual practices help us to experience the sacred. Historically, spirituality described the contemplative aspect of religious traditions associated, though not exclusively, with the lifestyle and practices of persons living in monastic communities. The term is now used more broadly to include the pursuits of laypeople who seek a more experience-based religious life or to describe the values and practices of those who no longer identify with traditional religions. Examples of the latter include those who have embraced Eastern forms of meditation; shamanistic practices of indigenous traditions; the goddess-centered practices, largely but not exclusively, of women and neo-Pagan groups; as well as psychological techniques associated with the human potential movement. Religion is a broad category while spirituality focuses on the experience of the sacred whether it occurs in a religious context or not.

Myth, in contemporary culture, is often regarded to be an untruth. I use the term in its more traditional, affirmative sense. Ancient Greek philosophers distinguished mythos from logos: from mythos came intuitive narrations; from logos, reasonable explanations. Mythos is comprised of stories that express subjective truths about the mystery of life that cannot be articulated in ordinary language. Myths are a subdivision of the broader category of stories. As Wendy Doniger says, all myths are stories, but not all stories are myths; myths raise *religious* questions.[2] Myths are stories that are sacred to and shared by a group of people wherein they find their most important meanings. Depth psychologists regard myth as a source of archetypal themes and images that express the deepest truths about the psyche—truths that can only be expressed through symbol and metaphor.

Religion and myth both express worldviews or visions of life. Joseph Campbell's writings and public lectures on mythology, which reveal how myth addresses people's enduring need to find meaning in their lives, ignited a renewed interest in the subject. Myth, in his view, serves these four important functions:

- First and foremost, myth evokes a sense of awe at the mystery of being. Myth opens the world so that it becomes "transparent to transcendence," making possible an experience of the numinous beyond speech or language.[3]

- Second, myth provides us with an image of the universe that supports our sense of awe "before the mystery of a presence and the presence of a mystery."[4]

- Third, myth supports the social order and validates its guiding principles of morality. While this purpose provides the basis for the cohesiveness of a society, myth can also be oppressive for some groups within that society.[5]

- Myth's fourth function is psychological and liberating: to initiate the individual into the realities of her own psyche, thereby guiding her toward spiritual enrichment and realization.[6] Put another way, this function supports the individuation process that is at the heart of both spirituality and Jung's depth psychology.

Science and spirituality

There is good reason for the incongruity between our scientific and spiritual worldviews. As Deepak Chopra observes, "Either reality is bounded by the physical universe, or it isn't. Either the cosmos was created from an empty, meaningless void, or it wasn't."[7] Science and spirituality differ in significant ways. Science, he explains, has set humanity on a mission to unravel the secrets of nature, harness natural forces, and develop new technologies, using reason and observation as the means for uncovering the truth of things. Spirituality looks to an invisible, transcendent realm discovered within the self. Science explores the world as it is offered to the five senses and the brain; spirituality considers the universe to be imbued with meaning.

The challenge for spirituality, in Chopra's view, is to offer something that science cannot provide. As sages and seers declare, you must go back to the source of religion, to God within, and there you will find the source of everything— your own awareness.[8] Spirituality is the means by which we discover this source within our being. The inner journey takes us into a deeper reality that is not about objects "out there" or feelings and thoughts "in here." Eventually, Chopra affirms, those two worlds meld into one state of being. But how do the inner and outer express a singularity? He turns to the *Isha Upanishad* for an answer: "*That* is complete, and *this* is also complete. *This* totality has been projected from *that* totality. When this wholeness merges in that wholeness, all that remains is wholeness."[9] Chopra further clarifies the meaning of this passage: *that* is the state of pure consciousness, while *this* is the visible universe.

For four centuries science has been satisfied with exploring the visible universe. The spiritual worldview concerns the hidden wholeness that underlies all of creation. It is this invisible wholeness, Chopra insists, that matters most, though we do not have to choose between the inner and outer worlds. Instead, he offers a truly integral perspective on the matter: "The dispute between science and religion has persuaded almost everyone that either you face reality and deal with the rough questions of everyday life (science), or you passively retreat and contemplate a realm beyond everyday life (religion)."[10] That either/or choice is forced on us when religion fails to deliver its promises. But, Chopra explains, spirituality—the deeper source of religion—can meet science face-to-face, offering answers to the great questions of human existence that are consistent with the most advanced scientific theories. Through its first-person methods of meditation and contemplative inquiry, spirituality gives us access to the interior domains of consciousness where the meaning and purpose of life can be discerned.

Religious truth

Science tells us what *is*, not what should be or ought to be. It does not inform us about good and bad, wise and unwise, desirable or undesirable. Science offers us truths about the phenomenal world, but it is mute about how to use that truth wisely; that is not what it was designed to do. In the midst of this silence, religion speaks. Human beings are destined to seek meaning—to find value, depth, worth, and significance in their everyday lives. For billions of people around the world, religion provides basic meaning and useful guidelines for ethical living. In other words, it offers a different kind of truth.

Religious truth can be characterized as knowledge or wisdom imbued with the power to effect self-transformation. Religious traditions have expressed this life-changing transformation in phrases such as the movement from darkness to light; illusion to insight; bondage to freedom; or sin to salvation. By knowing the truth, one becomes aligned with what is real or enters into the right relationship with it—not how things typically appear to be, but how they actually are. This understanding of truth cannot be limited to a relationship between words or ideas and things, even though words, ideas, and mental images may evoke the quality of truth in the consciousness of a person who responds appropriately to the reality of what is.

Philosophers of religion clarify the meaning of religious truth by pointing out how language is used. Religious language serves a variety of purposes. Some scriptural statements are revelatory as they aim to disclose reality and are deemed true when they fulfill that aim. The Hebrew Bible announces, "Hear, O Israel: The Lord is our God, the Lord is one!" The Gospel of John declares, "In the beginning was the Word, and the Word was with God, and the Word was God." In Hindu tradition, four "great sayings" (*mahavakyas*) in the Upanishads evoke the essence of the Veda: "That thou art"; "Consciousness is Brahman"; "I am Brahman"; and "The Self is Brahman." A Mahayana Buddhist text, the *Prajnaparamita Heart Sutra*, discloses the nature of reality in paradoxical terms: "Form is emptiness; emptiness is form." All of these statements invite the person who hears or reads them to attune to the truth that is being revealed. The language articulates an order of experience, a state of being, from the inside out; it is not so much a matter of *pointing to* as it is of *standing out from*. Truth, in revelatory language, is not a matter of correspondence between a statement and some state of affairs; it requires discernment and recognition. Revelatory truth is self-certifying; criteria from other areas of experience are not appropriate for verifying its veracity.[11]

Another type of religious language, used to point the way for other purposes, is teaching language. Advisory, exhortative, and celebrative utterances are intended to inspire the hearer to follow some inner or outer path. Language serving these functions is not addressed *to* a person but *for* a person; it requires attentiveness to the person being addressed and must be easy to understand. The language can only be provisionally true as the truthfulness of such language involves pragmatic efficacy. Unlike the language of revelation, language that aims to teach or persuade is dependent on a variety of external conditions, is open to falsification, and may prove to be inadequate or inaccurate.[12] Some sermons or religious discourses edify the audience that hears them; others do not.

Still another kind of religious language is primarily intellectual. It is used to interpret experience conceptually, to draw out the implications of spiritual experience for other areas of life and, when employed within a theological context, it transmits a religious tradition in creedal and systematic terms. Such language communicates religious meanings and values, aims to inform consciousness in relation to reality, and is true to the extent that it accomplishes that purpose.

A theology or religious philosophy articulates an entire perspective or vision of reality. This is where religious disagreements may come into play. For instance, the Christian claim that God exists is opposed to the Buddhist denial of a creator God, a Prime Mover or First Cause that is the basis for creation. In contrast, Buddhists teach the doctrine of dependent origination, the notion that all things arise from an interconnected network of causes and conditions; no being (not even God or the gods, if such exist) has independent existence or can be said to be the sole cause of other beings or events. However, such disagreements need not be dead ends and may serve as opportunities to converse in religious language that can lead to more adequate apprehensions of reality. Buddhist and Christian philosophers have, in fact, engaged in fruitful dialogues regarding their respective views on the nature of ultimate reality. The Buddhist concept of emptiness (*shunyata*) has helped some Christian theologians better understand their own tradition's doctrine of *kenosis*, the "self-emptying" nature of Christ. Conversely, Buddhists have come to appreciate how the Christian concept of God promotes the cultivation of love, forgiveness, and service to others.

Religions can be a source of peace, justice, and harmony, or a source of division, oppression, and discord. Are there criteria for distinguishing between life-enhancing and destructive forms of religion? John Hick, a Christian philosopher of religion, asserts that we must differentiate between the value and validity of religious doctrines and practices. The most significant religious figures, the founders and reformers of great traditions, have invariably been deeply critical of some of the religious ideas and practices surrounding them. Gautama, the Buddha, rejected the caste system and the doctrine of an eternal soul or *atman*, ideas that were integral to the religious thought of India in his time. The great Hebrew prophets criticized mere outward observances and sacrifices, proclaiming instead that the Lord requires justice and righteousness. Jesus rebuked the formalism and insincerity of some of the religious leaders of his day. Muhammad rejected the polytheism of his contemporary Arabian society. Martin Luther in Europe and Guru Nanak in India attacked much in the accumulated traditions into which they were born. These religious leaders emphasize that some kind of critical assessment of religious belief or behavior is a corollary of authentic religiosity and openness to the divine.[13] But by what criteria can this assessment be made?

The basic criterion of judgment is the extent to which a religion promotes or hinders the aim of all religious life. Religions exhibit a common soteriological structure; that is, they offer a transition from a radically unsatisfactory state to a limitlessly better one. Each speaks in differing ways of the wrong, distorted, or deluded character of present human existence in its ordinary condition—a fallen life lived in alienation from God (sin); a life caught in illusion (*maya*); or a life pervaded by suffering (*duhkha*).

Religions profess many claims about the nature of ultimate reality—that it is a loving or merciful God; an infinite Being-Consciousness-Bliss of Brahman; or the further shore of nirvana. Accordingly, each religion offers its own way to the ultimate—through faith in response to divine grace; by total submission to God; or through contemplative disciplines that lead to enlightenment. In each case, salvation or liberation is a new and limitlessly better mode of existence that occurs in the transition from self-centeredness or egocentricity to Reality-centeredness.[14]

Additional criteria for assessing religion can be discerned from an analysis of how human beings respond to the founders of religious traditions, such as Gautama, Confucius, Jesus, Muhammad, Guru Nanak, Baha'ullah, and other exemplary figures who serve as mediators of the divine. One criterion is the moral character of the mediator. This quality must be recognized as genuine and consistent with their teachings. Another requirement is that a new and commanding vision of reality be revealed in such compelling terms that people feel called to embrace it. A further criterion of religious truth is that the people who decide to live in accordance with this vision are, in fact, transformed themselves, whether suddenly or gradually, as direct assurance that reality has been mediated to them.[15]

While religious phenomena can in principle be assessed and judged by these criteria, it is impossible to judge religions as totalities. The history of a religious tradition is inevitably marked by high periods of flourishing and creativity as well as periods of stagnation and decline. Each tradition demonstrates a mix of good and evil embodied in the lives of saints and sinners, sometimes forming liberating— but more often oppressive—social structures, and giving birth to both human nobility and human corruption, justice and injustice, and beauty and ugliness.[16] Religious traditions are too internally diverse for us to be able to comparatively judge their merits as systems of salvation or liberation.[17] Nevertheless, I propose five additional criteria that may be helpful for reflecting critically on religious worldviews, one's own tradition as well as others'—experience of the sacred; social and ethical efficacy; adaptability; persuasiveness; and inter-religious under-standing.

Experience of the sacred

Experience of the sacred is one of the core dimensions of religion, perhaps the most important of all. Direct experience is the hallmark of spirituality and the central theme of this book. The academic study of religion clearly delineates many forms of religious experience—prophetic, mystical, visionary, and shamanic. In addition, the differing temperaments of people are expressed in different forms of spirituality. Hindu tradition, for example, supports several ways to approach the divine—the path of devotional love for deeply feeling people who revel in images of the divine (*bhakti yoga*); selfless service for active or vital persons (*karma yoga*); discriminating wisdom for intellectuals (*jnana yoga*); and meditation for contemplative persons (*raja yoga*). These temperaments are common in most cultures. If a tradition fails to offer various modes of religious experience, individuals may feel unable to resonate with it, and may either withdraw or seek to fulfill their religious needs through another religion or some other alternative. In recent decades, for example, many Christians and Jews have left their inherited traditions in search of mystical states thought to be more available through the practices of Eastern religions.

Social and ethical efficacy

Another closely related criterion is the efficacy of experience. Religions may be judged on the basis of the actions and effects of their practitioners; in the language of the New Testament, "By their fruits you shall know them" (Matthew 7:1). A religion needs to demonstrate that it has the capacity to produce the kind of behavior it values. Admittedly, judging the moral effects of religious worldviews is a complex matter and there will be differing valuations across and within traditions. Some traditions value social action and service while others favor the cultivation of contemplative peace and quietude. Even so, a particular tradition can be judged by how well it fulfills its intentionality. Do forms of Engaged Buddhism or liberation theologies in Christian communities effectively promote social justice in the societies in which they are practiced, or not?

Adaptability

A religious worldview needs to account for the beliefs and values of secular society. As scientific knowledge changes, religious worldviews need to effectively adapt themselves without diminishing their capacity to evoke the sense of the sacred and transmit the values that inspire people to live meaningfully. Religious worldviews that are capable of integrating scientific knowledge are more adequate than those that are not. His Holiness the Dalai Lama perhaps best exemplifies this criterion of religious truth. In *The Universe in a Single Atom: The Convergence of Science and Spirituality*, he writes: "My confidence in venturing into science lies in my basic belief that as in science so in Buddhism, understanding the nature of reality is pursued by means of critical investigation: if scientific analysis were conclusively to demonstrate certain claims in Buddhism to be false, then we must accept the findings of science and abandon those claims."[18] Sponsored by The Mind and Life Institute for over two decades, he has participated in collaborative dialogues with Western psychologists, neuroscientists, and philosophers as a means of generating more integral understanding of complex and important issues such as addiction, ethics, neuroplasticity, destructive emotions, and economics.[19]

Persuasiveness

The philosophies and theologies of religions present varying assessments of the human condition—the root cause of human suffering and how it may be ameliorated; basic human nature (loving or aggressive); human agency (free or determined); the embodiment of the soul (one life or multiple lives); and the postmortem condition (heaven or hell, merging with the divine, extinguishment). In the age of science and technology, the cogency of a religion's philosophy or theology makes a difference for many people. We must ask ourselves if the teachings of our tradition are persuasive. Developments in the social sciences have changed how we understand ourselves and provide new ways for addressing our problems. Psychotherapeutic methods, in particular, provide alternative ways for people to cope with existential suffering and to find meaning. A religious worldview that takes into account these developments is more credible than ones that do not.

Religions also contain psychological insights and techniques that may complement secular therapies. Many Western psychotherapists, for example, have been attracted to forms of Buddhism owing to its sophisticated psychological theories regarding mental and emotional states, as well as its effective techniques for cultivating optimum mental health. The empirical attitude of the Buddha and subsequent Buddhist traditions are also attractive to many people. Buddha's teaching claims to be a "come and see" matter, that is, the practices can be tested through direct experience. People drawn to Buddha's teachings can discover for themselves whether they are true or efficacious.

Inter-religious understanding

Clearly, religious pluralism challenges the self-understanding of religions. The need to understand and respect others who have beliefs and values different from our own has never been more urgent. The clash between segments of the Islamic world and the West is but one powerful case in point. Each tradition in a global world needs to develop a perspective that takes into account the values and beliefs of other religions. Thus, the capacity of a religion to accurately understand other religious worldviews may also be regarded as a criterion of religious truth.

The prevailing model for truth in the West is grounded in the Aristotelian principle of non-contradiction. According to this principle, two divergent propositions cannot be affirmed. One must be true and the other false. Truth, therefore, is defined through exclusion. This is what the word *"de-finition"* means—to determine the limits, to set off one thing from another. Defining religious truth in this way gives it an absolute quality. For something to be true it has to be, in its category, the only or absolute truth. One can know it is true by showing how it excludes all other alternatives or, conversely, how it absorbs and includes all other alternatives. Another model of truth is relational. What is true reveals itself by its ability to be related to other expressions of truth and to grow through those relationships.[20] Pluralistic religious thinkers (described in Chapters 3–5) who engage in inter-religious dialogue or comparative theology are exemplary in this regard. By deeply considering the views of others, a Christian or Hindu, for example, may gain a more nuanced understanding of the nature of ultimate reality.

Stages of faith

In his pioneering book *Stages of Faith*, James Fowler advanced a structural-developmental theory of faith, an account of how faith unfolds as individuals mature during the life cycle (childhood, adolescence, and adulthood), incorporating the work of developmental theorists such as Jean Piaget (cognitive development), Erik Erikson (psychosocial development), and Lawrence Kohlberg (moral development). Fowler also drew upon the work of William Cantwell Smith, a historian of religion, who carefully distinguished between faith and belief and who avowed, "Faith is deeper, richer, more personal."[21]

Faith, for Fowler and Smith alike, is engendered by a religious tradition and its doctrines, but it is a quality of the person, not the system. It is an orientation of the personality to one's self, one's neighbor, and the universe, that is, a total response—a way of seeing whatever one sees and of handling whatever one handles; a capacity to live at more than a mundane level; to see, feel, and act in terms of a transcendent dimension.[22] On the other hand, belief involves "the holding of certain ideas." Belief, at least in religious contexts, arises out of the effort to translate experiences of transcendence into concepts or propositions. Belief may be one of the ways faith expresses itself, but one does not have faith *in* a proposition or concept.

Smith demonstrates that the language dealing with faith, in the classical writings of the major religious traditions, never speaks of it in ways that can be translated into the modern meanings of belief or believing. Rather, faith involves an alignment of the heart or will, a commitment of loyalty and trust. His treatment of the Hindu term for faith, *shraddha*, perhaps says it best—"It means, almost without equivocation, *to set one's heart on*."[23]

This characterization of faith is eloquently expressed in the Hindu *Bhagavad Gita*. Here Lord Krishna tells his disciple, "Our faith conforms to our nature, Arjuna. Human nature is made of faith. A person is what his shraddha [faith] is" (17:3). The Hebrew (*āman* he' mîn, 'munah), the Greek (pistuō, Pistis), and the Latin (*credo*, *credere*) words for faith parallel those from Buddhist, Muslim, and Hindu sources. They do not mean belief or believing in the modern sense.

The Latin term *credo*, usually translated in Christian creedal statements as "I believe," conveys a more accurate understanding of the classical and biblical declarations of faith: "The first meaning . . . in classical Latin had been and its primary meaning continued to be 'to entrust, to commit, to trust something or someone.'" A secondary meaning in secular usage is "to trust upon" or "to place confidence in."[24]

Until the early modern period (sixteenth century), *believe* carried much the same range of meaning as that associated with "to set the heart upon." As Smith discerned, "Literally and originally, 'to believe' means 'to hold dear': virtually, to love." Modern German usage of *belieben* still means "to cherish" or "to hold dear."[25] Gradually, after the sixteenth century, especially in the seventeenth and eighteenth centuries, secular usage of the words *belief* and *believe* began to change. By the nineteenth century the change was virtually complete. So pervasive was the impact of the secularizing consciousness that religionists and people of faith even now tend to reduce *belief* to acceptance of a set of propositions or a commitment to a belief system.[26]

Fowler saw four implications of this understanding of faith. First, faith, rather than belief or religion, is the most fundamental category in the human quest for relationship to transcendence. Faith, it appears, is generic, a universal feature of human living, recognizably similar everywhere despite the remarkable variety of forms and contents of religious practice and belief. Second, in each of the major religious traditions, faith involves an alignment of the will and a resting of the heart in accordance with a vision of transcendent value and power, one's ultimate concern. Third, faith, as it has been classically understood, is not a separate dimension of life. It is an orientation of the total person, giving purpose to one's hopes, strivings, thoughts, and actions. Finally, the unity and recognizability of faith, despite myriad variants of religions and beliefs, support the struggle to develop a theory of religious relativity in which religions are seen as relative apprehensions of our relatedness to that which is universal.[27] The exemplary writers I discuss in subsequent chapters articulate viewpoints that achieve this pluralistic aim. Based on extensive field research interviews, Fowler conceptualized six stages of faith:

- Stage 1: Intuitive-Projective
- Stage 2: Mythic-Literal
- Stage 3: Synthetic-Conventional
- Stage 4: Individuative-Reflective
- Stage 5: Conjunctive
- Stage 6: Universalizing

An overview of each stage reveals that faith moves from literal and exclusive attitudes to increasingly symbolic and inclusive modes of understanding of the self and the world we share with others.

Stage 1: Intuitive-projective faith

The intuitive-projective stage of faith, typical of children from ages three to seven, is a fantasy-filled, imitative phase. A child can be powerfully and permanently influenced by examples, moods, actions, and stories of the visible faith of parents and other influential adults. The imaginative processes underlying fantasy are unrestrained and uninhibited by logical thought. The child is egocentric with little concern for the perspectives of others.[28]

Stage 2: Mythic-literal faith

The mythic-literal stage of faith is characteristic of a school-aged child, though this structure is sometimes found in adolescents and adults. A person begins to assimilate the stories, beliefs, and observances that symbolize belonging to the community. Beliefs are adopted with literal interpretations, as are moral rules and attitudes. Symbols are taken as one-dimensional and literal in meaning. Story becomes an influential source of meaning. People at Stage 2 can be affected deeply and powerfully by symbolic and dramatic content, but they do not step back from the flow of stories to formulate reflective, conceptual meanings. At this stage, the meaning is both carried by and trapped in the narrative.[29]

Stage 3: Synthetic-conventional faith

With the emergence of synthetic-conventional faith, a person's experience of the world now extends beyond the family. A number of spheres demand attention: family, school, work, peer relationships, society, media, and perhaps religion. Faith must now synthesize values and information and provide a basis for identity and outlook. This stage typically develops during adolescence, but for many adults it becomes a permanent place of equilibrium. It is a conformist stage in the sense that it is acutely tuned into the expectations and judgments of significant others; one does not yet have a sure enough grasp on one's own identity and autonomous judgment to construct and maintain an independent perspective. Beliefs and values are deeply felt but only tacitly held. A person at Stage 3 has an ideology and a more or less consistent clustering of values and beliefs, but has not objectified these for examination and is therefore unaware of having them. At this stage, a person would be open to receiving direction from those in traditional authority roles or valued face-to-face groups.[30]

Stage 4: Individuative-reflective faith

Individuative-reflective faith emerges in young adulthood. However, Fowler notes, this does not occur for many adults and, for a significant group, happens only in the mid-thirties or forties. The self, previously sustained in its identity and faith compositions by an interpersonal circle of significant others, now claims an identity no longer defined by the composite of one's roles or value to others. To sustain this new identity, the self composes a meaning frame conscious of its own boundaries and inner connections. One's identity and worldview are differentiated from those of others and become acknowledged factors in the reactions, interpretations, and judgments one makes on the actions of oneself and others. Stage 4 translates symbols into conceptual meanings, which makes it a "demythologizing" stage. Here the capacity for critical reflection on self and world is strengthened. However, a limitation inheres in this strength—an excessive confidence in the conscious mind and in critical thought, as well as a kind of secondary narcissism in which the now clearly-bounded reflective self over-assimilates reality and the perspectives of others into its own worldview.[31]

Stage 5: Conjunctive faith

Conjunctive faith integrates into the self and outlook much that is suppressed or unrecognized in Stage 4's self-certainty and conscious, cognitive, and affective adaptation to reality. In this stage, symbolic power is reunited with conceptual meaning. A person becomes able to reclaim and rework one's past. Conjunctive faith also requires one to be open to the voices of the deeper self with a critical recognition of one's social unconscious—the myths, ideal images, and prejudices built deeply into the self-system by virtue of one's conditioning within a particular class, religious tradition, or ethnicity. A person at this stage appreciates paradox, the truth in apparent contradictions, and strives to unify life's opposites. There is a willingness to engage the strange truths of those who are "other." In this stage of faith, one's commitment to justice is freed from the confines of tribe, class, religious commitment, or nation.

The new strength of this stage is the capacity to discern one's most powerful meanings while simultaneously recognizing that they are relative, partial, and inevitably distorted apprehensions of transcendent reality. Conjunctive faith can appreciate symbols, myths, and rituals (its own and others') because it grasps, to some degree, the depth of reality to which they refer. It also sees the divisions of the human family vividly because it apprehends the possibility of an inclusive community of being. Yet, Fowler explains, a person at this stage remains divided. One lives and acts in an untransformed world while holding onto a vision of a world free from divisiveness and fragmentation.[32] Because it entails the development of symbolic/metaphorical consciousness (*mythic-symbolic*, in sharp contrast to the *mythic-literal* consciousness of Stage 2), I regard conjunctive faith to be an exemplification of Jung's depth psychology.

Stage 6: Universalizing faith

Universalizing faith emerges from grappling with the paradoxical aspects of Stage 5. Now, as Fowler elucidates, those with conjunctive faith can see injustice in sharply etched terms because they have an enlarged awareness of the demands of justice and their implications. Having a more comprehensive vision of truth, one can recognize partial truths and their limitations. Able to perceive the depth of reality to which symbols refer, we can better understand and cherish myths and rituals. Able to envision the possibility of an inclusive commonwealth of being, we see the fractures and divisions of the human family with vivid pain. Stage 5 remains paradoxical or divided, however, because the self is caught between a universalizing vision of life and the need to preserve its own well-being. The transition to Stage 6 involves overcoming this paradox. Heedless of the threats to self, primary groups, and the institutional arrangements of the present order that are involved, Stage 6 becomes a disciplined, activist incarnation—a making real and tangible— of the imperatives of absolute love and justice that Stage 5 faith envisions.

Individuals at Stage 6 typically exhibit qualities that call into question our usual criteria of normalcy. As Fowler expounds, their heedlessness to self-preservation and the vividness of their taste and feel for transcendent moral and religious actuality give their actions and words an extraordinary and often unpredictable quality. Their leadership initiatives, often involving strategies of nonviolent suffering and ultimate respect for being, constitute affronts to our usual notions of relevance. For this reason, Stage 6 persons frequently become martyrs for the visions they incarnate. Fowler notes that attaining Stage 6 is exceedingly rare. Those best described by it have cultivated a felt sense of an ultimate environment, inclusive of all being. They have become embodiments and actualizers of the spirit of an inclusive and fulfilled human community. Fowler considers Mahatma Gandhi, Martin Luther King, Jr., Mother Teresa of Calcutta, Abraham Heschel, and Thomas Merton to be exemplars of universalizing faith. Interestingly, Fowler insists that persons who exemplify the qualities of Stage 6 are not perfect; nor, he adds, are they necessarily self-actualized persons or fully functioning human beings. Greatness of commitment and vision often coexist with great blind spots and limitations.[33]

The stages of faith condition how people understand religious truth. Religious traditions exhibit three different responses to the beliefs and truth claims of other religions.

- *Exclusivists* deny that other religions are alternative ways to salvation or liberation—the only valid tradition is one's own. Consequently, exclusivists often attempt to convert others who are regarded as non-believers or believers in erroneous teachings. The intent is to negate otherness.

- *Inclusivists* attempt to incorporate other religions into their own scheme of salvation. Other religions are seen as partially valid or as incomplete versions of one's own religion. One projects one's self-understanding onto the other.

- *Pluralists* affirm that one's own religion is one of many valid ways to salvation or liberation. Other traditions are acknowledged as being different from one's own, but can be encountered and understood in ways that enrich or deepen one's self-understanding.

Pluralists, in my view, express the most accurate understanding of other traditions and convey the most useful attitude for promoting goodwill and harmony among religions. Pluralists, however, can also be partial in one respect. Since they formulate their perspective within the conceptual framework of a particular tradition, their theologies primarily serve the needs of those who identify with and are fully contained by their own tradition. Thus, some of their viewpoints fail to address the needs of those who do not confine their allegiance to a particular tradition nor identify with any religious community. Since my own path embraces two religious traditions, Hinduism and Buddhism, as well as psychological forms of spirituality, my response to religious pluralism aligns with the perennial philosophy and the integral worldview that has emerged from it. This perspective seeks to include and integrate wisdom and transformative practices from all traditions, religious or not, and to serve the psychological and spiritual needs of individuals regardless of affiliation.

The next three chapters exemplify Christian, Hindu, and Buddhist responses to religious pluralism, focusing on leading-edge perspectives from exemplary thinkers from each tradition. In each case, the exemplar's faith develops towards a greater capacity to understand and affirm traditions different from their own.

Notes

1 John Hick, *Philosophy of Religion*, 3rd ed. Englewood Cliffs, NJ: Prentice-Hall, 1983, 107–08.
2 Wendy Doniger, *The Implied Spider: Politics and Theology in Myth*. New York: Columbia University Press, 1998, 2.
3 Joseph Campbell, *The Masks of God: Occidental Mythology*. New York: The Viking Press, 1964, 519. For commentary on Campbell's phrase, "transparent to transcendence, see Joseph Campbell, *The Hero's Journey: Joseph Campbell on His Life and Work*, ed. Phil Cousineau, Novato, CA: 1990, 40.
4 Campbell, *The Masks of God: Occidental Mythology*, 519.
5 Ibid., 520.
6 Ibid., 521.
7 Deepak Chopra and Leonard Mlodinow, *War of the Worldviews: Science vs. Spirituality*. New York: Harmony Books, 2011, 10.
8 Ibid., 4.
9 Quoted in Chopra and Mlodinow, 8.
10 Chopra and Mlodinow, 8.
11 Eliot Deutsch, *On Truth: An Ontological Theory*. Honolulu: University Press of Hawaii, 1979, 49–51.
12 Ibid., 53.
13 John Hick, "On Grading Religions." *Religious Studies* 17 (1981): 451.
14 Ibid. 453.
15 Ibid., 458–60.
16 Ibid., 461.
17 Ibid., 467.
18 Dalai Lama XIV, *The Universe in a Single Atom: The Convergence of Science and Spirituality*. New York: Morgan Road Books, 2005, 2–3.
19 See, for example, Daniel Goleman, *Destructive Emotions: How Shall We Overcome Them? A Scientific Dialogue with the Dalai Lama*. New York: Bantam Books, 2003.

20 Paul F. Knitter, *No Other Name? A Critical Survey of Christian Attitudes Toward the World Religions*. Maryknoll, NY: Orbis Books, 1985, 217–19.
21 Wilfred Cantwell Smith, *Faith and Belief*. Princeton, NJ: Princeton University Press, 1979, 12.
22 James W. Fowler, *Stages of Faith: The Psychology of Human Development and the Quest for Meaning*.San Francisco: Harper & Row, 1981, 11. See also Wilfred Cantwell Smith, *Faith and Belief*, 135.
23 Fowler, 11 and Wilfred Cantwell Smith, 61.
24 Wilfred Cantwell Smith, 76.
25 Fowler, 12.
26 Ibid., 13.
27 Ibid., 14–15.
28 Ibid., 133.
29 Ibid., 149.
30 Ibid., 172–73.
31 Ibid., 182–83.
32 Ibid., 197–98.
33 Ibid., 199–201.

3

CHRISTIANITY

> Things known are in the knower according to the mode of the
> knower.
>
> —*Thomas Aquinas*

In my view, each person must work out a response to religious pluralism. Doing this is an act of religious or spiritual individuation. My own religious individuation has taken place gradually over four decades. The impetus, which began with my earliest childhood questions, was amplified during my undergraduate years when I plunged into a wide-ranging study of religious traditions. I also engaged in some experimentation with Christian churches, attending the campus ministry services for Lutherans, Catholics, and Unitarians, as well as a brief dalliance with a group of charismatic Christians. While each of these diverse communities had something attractive to offer, I did not feel at home with any of them. Nevertheless, I studied Christian theology in depth as a means of engaging my inherited tradition. I agree with those who argue, as Jung did, that people attracted to a religion from another culture must grapple with the one into which they were born. Otherwise they disavow an important aspect of their psyche, pushing it into the unconscious, and they are likely to project fantasies and expectations upon the religion they embrace in its stead. In this chapter, I consider theological understandings of Christianity that were troublesome for me insofar as they reject or devalue other religions. I then present the views of Christians who I find exciting and exemplary, pluralistic perspectives that align with my conviction that all religions contain valuable truths that are complementary rather than contradictory.

The biblical story of the life, death, and resurrection of Jesus has had the greatest impact on Western civilization of any myth in our collective history. Approximately one-third of the people in the world today identify as Christian. Although there are myriad versions of Christianity, summarizing the heart of Jesus' teachings in a way that most Christians can affirm is possible. Christianity is based on the story of a humbly born man whose gentle presence teaches his followers a new way to think about life and community. A radical visionary, a prophet, and an avatar of love, Jesus' central message contrasted radically with the aggressive and dominating values of his time. Teaching his followers to love their enemies, turn the other cheek, and practice forgiveness of trespassers, Jesus modeled compassion as an alternative to judgment, thereby collapsing the stratifications of a classist and sexist society into a new community of social equality.[1]

In the myth that grows out of his brief thirty-three year existence, Jesus, the product of an immaculate conception between a divine father and a virginal human mother, is regarded as both human and divine. He purportedly claimed his own divinity with the statement, "I and the Father are one" (John 10:30), and told his followers that they, too, were gods (John 10:34). A rebel who challenged the values of his time, he ignored Jewish law by working on the Sabbath, and broke social taboos by associating with tax collectors, lepers, and whores; disparaged the greed of money changers; preached that salvation is available to everyone, Jew or gentile, rich or poor, slave or master; and welcomed the participation of women into the community as equals, a radical act for that time. Further, in a hierarchical world of haves and have-nots, he leveled the playing field with a kind of equal-opportunity spirituality, inviting the poor to join in and break bread with those of higher classes, a practice that violated strong social taboos. Jesus required only faith and love from his followers—faith that the individual would find salvation in the Kingdom of God and that love was God's divine gift to be shared unconditionally. Seeing scarcity turn to plenty, water turn into wine, diseases healed, eyesight restored, and even the dead being raised, his followers believed that the miracles he performed demonstrated his love and divine powers.[2]

Christian exclusivism

While the purpose of this chapter is to highlight how exemplary Christian pluralists invite us to appreciate and respectfully appropriate the wisdom of other religions, their views are a radical departure from the traditional, exclusivist attitudes that have dominated Christian thought. Jesus teaches a gospel of God's universal love for humanity, but the dominant institutional and theological voice in Christianity, often referred to as "the church," has denied that other religions are valid paths to salvation from sin. For Christians, sin has traditionally meant a fundamental separation from God, due to guilt, alienation or meaninglessness. It is a condition that requires redemption through grace. The roots of this view have prevailed throughout Christian history and can be traced to the New Testament. Two paradigmatic examples convey this attitude in unequivocal terms. First are the words of Peter in the Book of Acts—"And there is salvation in no one else, for there is no other name under heaven given among men by which we must be saved" (4:12). Second are words attributed to Jesus in the Gospel of John—"I am the way, and the truth, and the life; no one comes to the Father, but by me" (14:6). These New Testament texts recapitulate the first commandment of the Hebrew Bible (or Christian Old

Testament) from the book of Exodus, "Thou shalt have no other gods before me" (20:3). Yahweh's demand for supremacy in this commandment eventually became a theological conviction that there are indeed no other real gods. A polytheistic pantheon, with one god asserting supremacy, was turned into a monotheistic conviction. Consequently, the "other gods" disappeared altogether, except as threatening temptations or tempters, and the biblical view or myth that Yahweh rules all—as the creator, sustainer, and redeemer for the whole world—continued.

Exclusivist views toward other religions, though problematic, can provide believers with a sense of security and certainty in a complex world fraught with ambiguity and change. Like the fundamentalism discussed earlier, exclusivism is a reaction against the fear of a meaningless world, an understandable response to the age-old human longing for something fixed and certain that one can depend upon.

Exclusivism in Christian theology is rooted in the Christological doctrines formulated at Nicea and Chalcedon in the fourth century. The Chalcedonian definition declares, "Jesus Christ is unique in the precise sense that while being fully man, it is also true of him and him alone, that he is also fully God, the second person of the co-equal trinity."[3] The corresponding ecclesiological doctrine is that the church alone is the way of salvation for all humankind. This traditional Roman Catholic teaching is enshrined in the axiom, "Outside the Church no salvation," which, until recent times, played a decisive role in the Roman Catholic Church's relations with other religions.

Exclusivism is not confined to the pronouncements of the Roman Catholic Church. The Protestant equivalent is conveyed in the firm conviction that outside Christianity there is no salvation. This attitude is expressed in "the theology of the Word," which proclaims the revelatory and saving acts of God. Karl Barth, a Swiss Reformed theologian regarded as one of the most important Protestant theologians of the twentieth century, best exemplifies this mode of thinking, as well as its exclusivist response to religious pluralism. Barth maintains that the task of theology is essentially one of preaching the words of Christ.

Barth distinguishes Christian revelation from religion. Religions, in his view, are human constructions that are incapable of providing human salvation. Christian revelation, in his estimation, is entirely God's initiative. Christianity alone has been created and elected by God as the one and only true religion. It alone has the authority and responsibility to be a missionary religion. From this perspective, knowledge of other religions is of limited value, and dialogue with persons from different religious faiths is useful only insofar as it provides a more effective basis from which to preach the gospel. Barth's concept of God is also emblematic— God is the "wholly Other"—the One who is qualitatively different from creaturely and fallen human beings, who must be saved and redeemed by the saving grace available through Christ.[4]

Other Protestant theologians influenced by Barth express more positive views regarding God's presence in other faith traditions, though they are seen as lacking the crucial element, that being God's decisive revelation in Christ. As Emil Brunner, also a Swiss Reformed theologian, expressed it:

> From the standpoint of Jesus Christ, the non-Christian religions seem like stammering words from some half-forgotten saying: none of them is without the breath of the Holy, and yet none of them is the Holy. None of them is without its impressive truth, and yet none of them is the truth; for their Truth is Jesus Christ.[5]

Likewise, Hendrik Kraemer, a prominent figure in the Dutch Reformed Church, acknowledged that God's presence is revealed to humankind in the moral law of the creation, but that it is distorted through sin and blindness to God.[6] The revelation of Christ is required to overcome this deficiency in human nature and to confer reconciliation with God. These evangelical theologians regarded knowledge of other religions to be important, but only for missionary work to be effective.

Exclusivist attitudes toward non-Christian religions persist among conservative evangelicals. The influential Frankfurt Declaration, approved by a theological convention of evangelicals in 1970, states that "salvation is due to the sacrificial crucifixion of Jesus Christ, which occurred once and for all and, therefore, rejects the false teaching that non-Christian religions and worldviews are ways of salvation like belief in Christ."[7] In addition, the declaration refutes the ideas that a mere "Christian presence" among the adherents to the world religions and a "give-and-take dialogue" with non-Christians can substitute for a proclamation of the gospel. Non-Christians, it maintains, must be freed from their former ties and false hopes and, through belief and baptism, enter the church of Christ.[8] The basic message of this declaration was affirmed at an International Congress of World Evangelization held at Lausanne, Switzerland in 1974. This event, regarded as the most important evangelical meeting of the twentieth century, was a reaction against the liberalizing trends toward syncretism and universalism within the World Council of Churches and its diminished commitment to evangelism. The congress declared that Jesus Christ, being the only God-man, is the only mediator between God and humanity.[9]

Some exclusivist theologians believe that Christians "know in part" and must not give the impression that they have a monopoly on religious truth. Accordingly, Christians must be prepared to learn from other faiths as they encounter each other. The role of the Christian in such dialogue is to be a witness to Jesus Christ. In this process, the church learns something new about Jesus when a stranger to the gospel is converted. However, such dialogue is self-serving and lacks genuine mutuality because the aim is to convert the other, to make him or her like oneself. The Christian conviction that Jesus is the sole source of salvation prevails. As one evangelical theologian affirms, "For the human sickness there is one specific remedy, and this is it. There is no other."[10] Christian exclusivists exemplify a deductive approach to other religions and an either-or view of religious truth. Doctrine dictates what is true. If Christianity rests on true revelation, then by logical inference, the other faiths must be false or illusory.

These responses also distinguish between revelation and religion, describing religion as a human construction. Although Christianity is acknowledged to be a religion, it differs from all others since it alone embodies the influence of the revelation of Christ. However, the non-Christian could reverse the argument. A Hindu, for example, could argue that all religions are human constructions except Hinduism since it has its source in the Vedas. Hindus do, in fact, maintain that their religion has no historical origin; it is viewed as *santana dharma*, the eternal religion.

The problem with the revelation/religion distinction is that there can be no revelation apart from its manifestations in cultural and religious forms. The exclusivists' belief that faith is unmediated is untenable. Attempts to distinguish the pristine gospel from the empirical history of the church ignore the fact that Christian faith is mediated through a tradition of scripture, sacrament, and ritual, as well as doctrine formulated in particular, historical contexts. Likewise, exclusivists wrongly assume that the gospel is unencumbered by theological interpretations and that the Bible simply presents the witness of prophets and apostles without theology. To the contrary, all understandings of the biblical texts are based on interpretation, as are all transmissions of the Christian gospel when it is preached. Finally, Christian exclusivism precludes genuine dialogue; its value is based primarily on the extent to which it enables Christians to bear witness to adherents of other religions solely with intent to convert them to the Christian faith.

Christian inclusivism

Christian inclusivism expresses a much more affirmative view of non-Christian religions—as the fulfillment of what is best and true in the others—while regarding Christianity as the completion of all other religions. Although Christian inclusivism appears to be a recent theological development, it dates to the early roots of the Christian tradition. A paradigmatic source of inclusivism in the New Testament is Paul's speech on the Areopagus, described in the New Testament (Acts 17:22–31). In this passage, Paul acknowledges the authenticity of the Athenians' worship at their altar "to an unknown God" by conferring a name on the God whom they already worship but do not truly recognize. By being so inclusive, their religion is brought to completion.

In the twentieth century, inclusivism was more typical of Catholic theology than of Protestant thought. Documents formulated during the second Vatican Council in the 1960s moved away from the exclusivist doctrine of "no salvation outside the Church." Karl Rahner, one of the most influential Catholic theologians of the past century, developed the notion of "salvation history" to account for the fact that the Christian gospel had not reached people who, through no fault of their own, lived before or subsequent to New Testament times. God offers grace to those who have never properly encountered the gospel, which is mediated through the non-Christian's religion; God's presence is implicit in other faiths' traditions. Rahner regards virtuous non-Christians to be "anonymous Christians."[11]

Hans Küng, another influential Catholic theologian, offers a more liberal and affirmative view on non-Christian religions:

Every human being is under God's grace and can be saved: whether he be of this or that nation or race, of this or that caste or class, free or slave, man or woman, or even inside or outside the Church of Christ. Every human being can be saved, and we may hope that everyone is . . . Every world religion is under God's grace and can be a way of salvation: whether it is primitive or highly evolved, mythological or enlightened, mystical or rational, theistic or non-theistic, a real or only a quasi-religion. Every religion can be a way of salvation, and we may hope that every one is.[12]

Küng, however, also stresses the uniqueness of Christianity. Christians, he believes, are challenged by both the great world religions and secular humanisms. Jesus, he argues, is not merely one of the many archetypal religious personalities who have founded world religions; he is uniquely different and normative for all others.[13] By *normative*, Küng means that Christ is the definitive standard for what is true or valid; *archetypal*, by contrast, refers to a model, a recurring symbol, or an image from the collective unconscious. Küng insists that Christ must be more than an archetype, for he cannot merely be one among many exemplary beings that embody the path to salvation or liberation.

Küng asserts that Christianity is the necessary *critical catalyst* for all other faiths. Without Christ's revelation, the religions cannot really understand and appropriate the salvation at work within them. Moreover, without Christ, religions cannot really adapt their spirituality to modernity, to the demands of a world-affirming technological age. Without the gospel, they are caught in "unhistoricity, circular thinking, fatalism, unworldliness, pessimism, passivity, caste spirit, social disinterestedness."[14] Küng dismisses worldviews that posit cyclical time, such as Eastern traditions and those that entail a belief in karma and reincarnation or rebirth. He implies that non-Christian religions, unless catalyzed by the normative revelation in Christ, lack something essential. By contrast, Christianity possesses the potential for a synthesis of religious truths; it can bring together and to full realization that which is isolated and scattered, fragmented and sporadic, and distorted and disfigured through mutual critical questioning and genuine dialogue with other religions. The attitude this approach engenders "would be neither arrogant absolutism, not accepting any claim, nor a weak eclecticism accepting a little from everything, but an inclusive Christian universalism claiming for Christianity *not exclusiveness, but certainly uniqueness*."[15]

Although Küng stresses the historical uniqueness of Jesus, he initiated a pioneering project called *Weltethos* (Global Ethic) that focuses on what the world religions have in common, proposing rules of behavior that everyone can accept. His vision of a global ethic is embodied in *Towards a Global Ethic: An Initial Declaration*, which was signed by religious and spiritual leaders from around the world at the 1993 Parliament of the World's Religions. Küng's project later culminated in the United Nations *Dialogue Among Civilizations*. One of Küng's core convictions is that there can be no peace among nations until there is peace among religions.[16] Küng's progressive views regarding traditional teachings, most notably his critique of the doctrine on papal infallibility, put him into conflict with his church. Although he is still regarded as "a Catholic priest in good standing," the Vatican rescinded his authority to teach Catholic theology, an action that has not impeded his tireless efforts to promote causes such as his global ethic project.

Protestant versions of inclusivism are also based upon a concept of salvation history and often draw upon Logos Christology as a means of incorporating non-Christian religions into the Christian way of salvation. John Farquhar, a Scottish Protestant missionary who served his church in India, used the evolutionary thinking in vogue at the time to support his claim that Christ fulfills and brings to completion the spiritual aspirations of Hindu traditions. In Farquhar's evolutionary view, a lower stage does not develop into a higher one; instead, it is replaced by a higher stage through a conscious choice. A Hindu, for example, who is brought into contact with Christianity and Western civilization, is introduced to something higher. Thus a Hindu, confronted by the challenge of the gospel of Christ, must abandon Hinduism once he or she recognizes the superiority of Christianity. It is the person's duty—for the person's own sake and that of his nation—to choose Christianity, *duty* being the term often used for *dharma*, the Indian word closely approximating the Western concept of religion. Otherwise, the Hindu impedes the work of God. As Farquhar puts it, "This dying to all that impedes the work of God includes for the Hindu a dying to Hinduism. . . . Hinduism must die in order to live. It must die into Christianity."[17] Fulfillment, for Farquhar, entails three distinct but related processes. First, Hinduism is fulfilled in the sense that it is replaced by Christianity. Second, the truths of Hinduism are fulfilled by reappearing in a higher form in Christianity. Finally, Christ fulfills the quests of Hinduism by providing an answer to its questions, a resolution of its problems, and a goal for its religious strivings.[18]

But in what way does Christianity fulfill Hinduism? How do Christian rituals fulfill Hindu rituals or Christian doctrines fulfill Hindu doctrines? Did Farquhar or those who continue to adopt a similar approach really understand the needs and quests of a Hindu? Eric Sharpe, a comparative religion scholar, aptly criticized the fallacy of this kind of Christian inclusivist theology, declaring:

> The Christian may very well believe that Christ has brought to completion the human life entrusted to his care, and has fulfilled all the legitimate longings that the human mind and heart has ever felt. But are those longings always and in every case the same? The Christian may want to say, for instance, that Jesus Christ saves man from the guilt and power of sin. Suppose, though, that the Hindu has simply no notion of what this form of words means, and longs instead for what he has come to understand as the goal of all human striving, *moksha*, release from the continual rebirth brought about by *karma* and *samsara*. For this quest the Christian message can offer no remedy. And it is impossible to avoid the conclusion that the Christian is here offering the Hindu an answer to a question he has never asked, the fulfillment of a need he does not feel, while the need he *does* feel

remains either unanswerable, or answerable only from within his own religious tradition.[19]

Hindus, like individuals from all cultures, engage in a quest for meaning and purpose in life that accords with the mythos that informs their culture. A *mythos* is a worldview that includes a notion of how the universe is constituted (a cosmology) and the corresponding behaviors that put one in accord with it (rituals and spiritual practices). Inclusivists who wish to incorporate others into their religious vision of life, however well-intentioned they may be, mistakenly assume that the others' underlying worldviews are the same as their own when, in fact, they are not.

John A. T. Robinson, a New Testament scholar and former Anglican Bishop, was a major force in shaping liberal Christian theology. In his view, religious truth is "two-eyed," a bifocal metaphor that refers to two modes of religious experience—the prophetic and the mystical. While these two types of religious experience may occur in a single religious tradition, the former is usually associated with the traditions of the West and the latter with the East. Robinson's inclusivism contends that these two centers are complementary. In other words, a viewpoint that reflects only one of these centers is one-eyed or incomplete; when pressed to its limits, it leads to a serious distortion of even its own truth.

Robinson sees the need for mutual correction and complementarity in relation to the prophetic and mystical perspectives on human existence. Like Hans Küng, he acknowledges the need for mutual exploration of religious truth by means of critical questioning of one another's traditions through open dialogue. Ultimately, however, Robinson believes that an individual must make a choice between religious views that are incompatible, a decision one makes after due consideration of the perspective offered through the other eye of truth.

Our existential situation remains either-or, to use Soren Kierkegaard's phrase; that is, one cannot embrace both views simultaneously. As a Christian, Robinson asserts that Christ defines the reality of God, but insists that this affirmation need not have exclusivist implications, avowing, "To believe that God is best defined by Christ is not to believe that God is confined to Christ."[20] While this theologizing repudiates an exclusivist stance towards other religions, it stops short of affirming a pluralist position by invoking traditional Logos Christology: "The God who discloses himself in Jesus and the God who discloses himself in Krishna must be the same God, or he is not God—and there is no revelation at all. *Ultimately* for both sides there are not 'gods many and lords many' but one God, under whatever name, and indeed one Christ or *Logos*, however various the faces of his appearing."[21]

The doctrine of anonymous Christians is a pseudo-solution to the challenge of religious pluralism. It would be just as easy to label devout Christians as anonymous Muslims, or Hindus and Muslims as anonymous Christians. At best the designation "anonymous Christian" is an honorary status granted unilaterally to people who express no desire for it. The inclusivist initiatives in Catholic thought, that move from a church-centered (ecclesiocentrism) to a God-centered (theocentrism) perspective, are nonetheless Christ-centered (Logos-centered) modes of theology. While some theologians of this kind may no longer assert that Christ is the source of all salvation, they still regard Christ and the church as normative for whatever revelation and grace is found in other religious traditions.

Christian inclusivism imposes itself on other religions by incorporating them into its scheme of salvation. Clearly, an analogous move has been made by non-Christian religions. Hindus, for example, often include Christianity and Buddhism within their scheme for liberation from suffering while glossing over the doctrinal differences that clearly distinguish these traditions from their own teachings. From a Hindu's perspective, Christ and the Buddha are regarded as incarnations of Vishnu. While this willingness to regard others' religions as versions of one's own is far more charitable than the rather tribal views of exclusivists, it fails to appreciate the other as *other*. In this view, there is really nothing to be learned from another tradition; one's own religion already contains the truth that is latent in the others.

Christian pluralism

To my mind, pluralistic religious thinkers are the leading-edge representatives of their respective traditions. They are exemplary models for individuals who are maturing into the conjunctive and universalizing states of faith. I turn now to the Christian pluralists who have most inspired my thinking and spirituality. Each one articulates God-images that engender inter-religious harmony and emergent forms of integrative spirituality.

Paul Tillich

Paul Tillich, one of the most influential Protestant theologians of the twentieth century, began his career as a professor in Germany, where he lectured until his public speeches brought him into conflict with the Nazi movement. When Hitler became the German Chancellor, Tillich was dismissed from his position. He immigrated to America where he taught in prominent universities and completed his major works. There, grappling with the experiences of anxiety, meaninglessness, and alienation so prevalent in modern society, he found the symbols of Christian revelation useful in addressing pressing existential issues. Although he rejects Barth's exclusivist perspective on the revelation of Christ, Tillich develops his own critique of religion and its tendencies toward idolatry. He is particularly critical of the nationalism, fascism, and communism that function like quasi-religions in secular society. At the same time, he rejects relativism by positing a criterion by which Christianity can judge other faiths and ideologies, as well as itself.

Tillich's critique of religion, as expressed in the Protestant Principle, protests against the tendency to make absolute claims for what is relative and finite, through the application of a paradoxical criterion. He believes that true bearers of revelation and of symbols of faith should both express the ultimate and deny their own ultimacy. For Tillich, this criterion of self-negation is realized in the cross of

Christ. The cross represents the denial that the Holy can be contained and manipulated; it is the symbolic representation of the God who refuses to be tied down to any particular manifestation. As Tillich says:

> What is particular in him is that he crucified the particular in himself for the sake of the universal. This liberates his image from bondage both to a particular religion—the religion to which he belonged has thrown him out—and to the religious sphere as such; the principle of love in him embraces the cosmos, including both the religious and secular spheres. With this image, particular yet free from particularity, religious yet free from religion, the criteria are given under which Christianity must judge itself and, by judging itself, judge also the other religions.[22]

Although Tillich connects his understanding of the symbols of faith and the critique of idolatry to the cross of Christ, the criterion of paradoxical form need not be tied to that particular Christian symbol. Since paradox is part of the structure of all religious expression, the criterion can be applied both within and beyond the Christian tradition.

In *The Encounter of Christianity with the World Religions*, Tillich points out that Christianity developed into a specific religion through a critical process of receiving elements from all the other religions it had encountered. This is the vital power of Christianity in its early formative centuries. However, the openness and receptivity that were once its glory were gradually lost with the strengthening of hierarchical authority, until "the tradition ceased to be a living stream," becoming a "sum of immovably valid statements and institutions."[23] This stagnation and self-absorption lasted through the medieval period and the Reformation until the rise of modern secularism. In the contemporary world, Tillich feels, the relationship between religions ought to be characterized by self-criticism and dialogue. The goal is neither the mixing of religions nor the victory of one religion over the others; rather, it is to penetrate to the depths of one's own religion. Paradoxically, this approach allows each particular religion, including Christianity, to break through its own particularity to an apprehension of the ultimate ground of the world's pluralistic religious heritage.[24]

Tillich's critique of the idolatrous tendencies inherent in religions, springing from his understanding of religious symbols, is an important precursor to most contemporary Christian responses to pluralism. I am profoundly appreciative of Tillich's critique, partly due to his being a Lutheran, the tradition into which I was confirmed during my adolescent years. I still own Tillich's autobiographical writing, *On The Boundary*, which was gifted to me from the personal library of my pastor at that time, though I later crossed the boundary that once contained me within the Christian tradition.

Dissatisfied with traditional theistic conceptions, Tillich argues that God is not a Being, but is a Being-Itself or the Ground of Being. He moves away from theism and affirms "a God above God," a modern conception of God that answers our existential needs. He expresses this beautifully in the closing words of *The Courage to Be*, one of his most influential works.

> One can become aware of the God above the God of theism in the anxiety of guilt and condemnation when the traditional symbols that enable men to withstand the anxiety of guilt and condemnation have lost their power. When "divine judgment" is interpreted as a psychological complex and forgiveness as a remnant of the "father-image," what once was the power in those symbols can still be present and create the courage to be in spite of the experience of an infinite gap between what we are and what we ought to be. The Lutheran courage returns but not supported by the faith in a judging and forgiving God. It returns in terms of the absolute faith which says Yes although there is no special power that conquers guilt. The courage to take the anxiety of meaninglessness upon oneself is the boundary line up to which the courage to be can go. Beyond that is mere non-being. Within it all forms of courage are re-established in the power of the God above the God of theism. *The courage to be is rooted in the God who appears when God has disappeared in the anxiety of doubt.*[25]

These words are profoundly psychological and quite liberating for anyone who struggles to find meaning in a world in which traditional symbols fail to speak to one's experience. However, they are expressed from within a Christian worldview that presupposes concepts like sin (a fundamental separation from God or the Ground of Being), human guilt, divine judgment, and the need for redemption— even if these are interpreted in a psychological sense.

The boundary I crossed that separated me from Christian tradition pertained mostly to Christology, the teachings centering on the nature of Christ and his unique or normative function in human history. Another reason for my departure from Christianity concerned traditional teachings about human nature. I could not accept the idea that humans are innately sinful, unless that is simply taken to mean that we tend to be self-centered or egocentric. To be sure, human beings do exhibit such behaviors and attitudes, but I believe this is how we begin our human journey—it is not what we are condemned to be until such time as we receive the grace of Christ. Thus, my views regarding divinity and human nature are outside the frame of traditional Christian theology and modern reinterpretations of its core doctrines.

The writings of Tillich, a pioneering liberal thinker, were written within the context of Christian theological and Western philosophical traditions. In his later years, he visited Japan, held extensive dialogues with Zen philosophers in Kyoto, and opened his mind to an even more radical range of possibilities. In one of his last public lectures, he disclosed that if he could re-live his career, he would re-think his entire theology on a multi-faith basis.

Raimundo Panikkar

Born in Barcelona to a Spanish Roman Catholic mother and an Indian Hindu father, Raimundo Panikkar became a Catholic priest and theologian, as well as a historian of religions. An advocate for ecumenism who strove for unity among world religions without denying or compromising diversity, he believes the basis for unity is found in the mystery that underlies every authentic religious experience. His theological writings focus on the link between divinity and the world, realizing that each religion attempts to explain and to name the symbol that best reveals the mystery, such as Christ, Veda, or Dharma. He identifies this mediator or link as Christ, but insists that this name not be identified exclusively with Jesus.[26]

Here again we encounter a Logos Christology. While a Christian believes "Jesus is the Christ," this is not the same as "Christ is Jesus," nor should the Christian say, "Christ is *only* Jesus."[27] Christ is one name for the principle, person, or Logos that other religious traditions call by a variety of names. For example, in the context of the encounter of Christianity and Hinduism, Panikkar correlates Christ with *Ishvara*, a Sanskrit word that means "Lord," ascribed to Rama and Krishna, incarnations of the god Vishnu.[28]

Panikkar, a passionate advocate of dialogue between religions, insists that we understand religions on their own terms. Dialogue, in his view, is both *intra-religious*—an interior process—and *inter-religious*—between persons of different faiths. He believes it is important to enter the subjectivity of other traditions, as a kind of conversion experience, and insists that it take place at a level much deeper than that of comparing doctrines. This process achieves a "fusion of horizons"— one's perspective or horizon of understanding co-mingles with that of the other. For example, Panikkar argues that a Christian will never fully understand another's religion, such as Hinduism, unless he is "converted" to that tradition. Conversely, a Hindu will never fully grasp Christianity unless he becomes a Christian. He expresses this beautifully, as an encounter in the human heart:

> Religions meet in the heart rather than the mind . . . The meeting of two differing realities produces the shock of the encounter, but the place where the encounter happens is one. This place is the heart of the person. It is within the heart that I can embrace both religions in a personal synthesis. And it is also within the heart that I may absorb one of the two religions into the other. In actuality, religions cannot sincerely coexist or even continue as living religions if they do not "co-insist"—that is, penetrate into the heart of the other.[29]

This is not merely a matter of *assimilating* or *incorporating* another religion into the Christian path of salvation; this is an encounter that mutually transforms each religion and affirms each one's evolving particularity. Panikkar describes his own religious identity as evolving from such a process, one that took place over many years as he studied Hindu and Buddhist texts, affirming, "I 'left' as a Christian,

I 'found' myself a Hindu, and I 'return' a Buddhist, without having ceased to be a Christian."[30] Entering the subjectivity of another tradition and trying empathetically to imagine what deep-seated longings and fears it addresses for others can be a profoundly intimate experience that expands one's self-understanding in ways that would not otherwise be possible.

Panikkar's pluralism strongly affirms the particularity of each religious or spiritual path. "It is not simply that there are different ways leading to the peak, but that the summit itself would collapse if all the paths disappeared. The peak is in a certain sense the result of the slopes leading to it."[31] Similarly, religious symbols are understood to be singular and irreducible. Thus, Panikkar rejects the concept of the one God (or ultimate) that exists over and above the names of the various religions, and avers: "It is not that this reality *has* many names as if there were a reality outside the name. This reality *is* many names and each name is a new aspect, a new manifestation and revelation of it. Yet each name teaches or expresses, as it were, the undivided Mystery."[32] The plurality may be celebrated as refractions of light that shade into one another through creative contact and interaction.

> The different religious traditions . . . are like the almost infinite number of colors that appear once the divine or simply white light of reality falls on the prism of human experience: it refracts into innumerable traditions, doctrines, and religions. Green is not yellow, Hinduism is not Buddhism, and yet at the fringes one cannot know, except by postulating it artificially, where yellow ends and green begins. Even more, through any particular color—through any particular religion—one can reach the source of the white light . . . If two colors mix, they may sire another. Similarly, with religious traditions, the meeting of two may give birth to a new one. In point of fact, most of the known religions today are results of such mutual fecundations.[33]

Paul Knitter

The rainbow metaphor brings us to what I regard as one of the most leading-edge responses to religious pluralism, exemplified in the life and writings of Paul Knitter, a contemporary American Catholic theologian. Knitter argues that the traditional model for truth in the West is grounded in Aristotle's principle of non-contradiction—two divergent propositions cannot be affirmed, one must be true and the other false. Truth, therefore, is defined through exclusion, wherein *de-fined* means having determined the limits or having set off one thing from another. Defining truth in this way gives it an absolute quality. For something to be true, it not only has to be true in its category, it has to be the only, or absolute, truth. One can know it is true by showing how it excludes all other alternatives— or, how it absorbs and includes all other alternatives.[34] Knitter's alternative model posits that truth is relational, defined not by exclusion but by relation. As he explains, "What is true will reveal itself mainly by its ability to be related to other expressions of truth and to grow through these relationships."[35] This model recognizes that no truth can stand alone, as no truth can be totally unchangeable.

In *Without Buddha I Could Not Be a Christian*, Knitter provides an autobiographical account of his evolving religious identity. As a theologian who works dialogically, he gradually discovered his need to be religious in an *inter-religious* manner by engaging with the way other people—including Jews, Muslims, Hindus, and Native Americans—live and understand their religious lives. His closest other-religion friends are Buddhists, including his spouse, and he himself has practiced a form of daily Zen meditation for many years. In this book, he describes his journey of *double belonging*—his life as a Buddhist Christian—in which he wrestles with the question of whether such a life amounts to a kind of religious promiscuity. One's religious identity, he notes, is analogous to a committed relationship such as marriage. Critics, including his theological colleagues, may well argue that Christians who try to identify and nourish themselves with another tradition are likely to end up either diluting or shifting their religious commitments, and that they are, in effect, Christians having an affair. Knitter disagrees. He does not believe that double-belonging is tantamount to religious infidelity. Speaking experientially, he asserts that his relationship with Buddha does not diminish his relationship or commitment to Jesus and the teachings of his church and tradition.[36]

There is another way to think about double-belonging or what others call *inter-spirituality*. Knitter observes that our religious self—like our social or cultural self—is, at its core and conduct, a hybrid:

> Our religious identity is not purebred, it's hybrid. It's not singular, it's plural. It takes shape through an ongoing process of standing in one place and stepping into other places, of forming a sense of self and then expanding or correcting that sense as we meet other selves. There is no such thing as a neatly defined, once-and-for-all identity.[37]

Put simply, we change as we interact with others who are different from us. The etymological meaning of *promiscuity*, from the Latin *miscere*, is the inclination to "mix it up." In a sense, Knitter observes, all of us are promiscuous and cannot be otherwise. We have an identity, but that identity changes and remains vital only through mixing it up with others.[38]

A religious hybrid may still give primacy to some relationships over others; some relations are more influential than others. Knitter acknowledges that Christ has a certain primacy for him over Buddha. Most double-belongers, he observes, have a core religious identity—typically, the tradition in which they grew up—that enters into a hybrid relationship with another religious identity and tradition. While Knitter's core identity as a Christian is profoundly influenced by his engagement with Buddhism, he notes there is a depth he finds with Christ that he does not find elsewhere, similar in a way to the special feelings he has for his wife.[39] The devotion he feels for Christ, however, does not diminish the power of what he discovers through his interreligious journey. To the contrary, he believes it enhances his ability to engage other traditions:

> I believe I have discovered something that I suspect characterizes religious experience in whatever tradition or historical context: the more *deeply* one enters into the core experience that animates one's own tradition, the more *broadly* one is able and perhaps moved to enter into the experience of other traditions. The more deeply one sinks into one's own religious truth, the more broadly one can appreciate and learn from other truths.[40]

In his own case, Knitter asserts that double-belonging has become a necessity: he can only be a Christian by also being a Buddhist. For this reason, after careful consultation with his Buddhist teacher, he decided to "take refuge" (the formal way in which one becomes a Buddhist) and pronounced the bodhisattva vows as part of the Dzogchen community in the United States.[41] While he wonders whether he is on the outer- or leading-edge of his Christian community, he believes it is the latter. In my view, he is an inspiring model for people who feel compelled to "mix it up" with others as they seek greater spiritual fulfillment in their lives.

John Hick

While Knitter crossed the boundaries of his tradition by experimenting with belonging to two traditions, John Hick, an English philosopher of religion and a Protestant theologian, was the most pioneering of all Christian pluralists and the Christian exemplar that has most influenced my views on religion and spirituality. His life presented a striking example of how a Christian's views can develop and change through a lifetime of sustained reflection. As a university student he converted to evangelical Christianity, which was a shift from the fundamentalist Christian background in which he was raised. As a philosopher and theologian, he continued to question and reformulate his beliefs. While teaching at the University of Birmingham in England, he founded a group called All Faiths for One Race. Later at Princeton Seminary, he began to question the literalness of many traditional doctrines, including his own Christology, a process that led to his extensive writings on religious pluralism.

Hick's innovative thinking on religious pluralism has been liberating for some Christians and controversial for others. In the United States he received strong opposition and resentment from many fundamentalists and evangelicals. While teaching in the United States, two attempts were made to exclude him from the ministry of the Presbyterian Church—first at Princeton over the Virgin Birth doctrine, and later at Claremont, California, over his pluralist attitude regarding the validity of other religions. Hick's concern for the development of inter-faith, inter-ethnic, and inter-cultural human relations was practical as well as theoretical. Having friends of different faiths in many parts of the world and involvement in inter-religious dialogue, particularly Jewish-Christian-Muslim and Buddhist-Christian dialogue, he gradually developed a personal faith, in his own words, of "a more universal than exclusively Christian kind." During the latter years of his life, he practiced Buddhist mindfulness meditation and attended both United Reform Church services and Quaker meetings for worship.[42]

The epistemology of faith

Throughout his career, Hick's concerns about the epistemology of faith and the validity of religious experience led him to argue that the universe is religiously ambiguous, as it may be interpreted intelligently and experientially from both religious and naturalistic perspectives. He also found arguments for and against the existence of God inconclusive. Engaged in ongoing interpretations, usually operating in unconscious and habitual ways, we form hypotheses about our environment's character and practical meaning that we then test in our behavior. In this way, Hick maintains that all conscious experience is *experiencing-as*.[43] We experience something as important or not, as beautiful or not, as religious or not.

Both the religious and naturalistic ways of construing the world arise, in Hick's view, from a fundamental cognitive choice he calls *faith*, which is continuous with the interpretative element within our experience of the physical and ethical character of our environment.[44] Thus, Hick defines faith as *the interpretative element in religious experience*.[45] It is rationally appropriate, Hick argues, for those who experience life in relation to the transcendent to trust their own experience—together with the stream of religious life in which they participate and the great figures who are its primary exemplars—and to proceed to live on that basis. It is likewise proper, he adds, for those who do not participate in a religious way of experiencing life, to reject a belief in the transcendent.[46]

The incarnation of Christ as myth and metaphor

Hick gradually came to believe that Christology, as formally adopted at the Council of Chalcedon, expresses an unwarranted deification of Jesus, and that a literal understanding of the incarnation has led to attitudes of exclusivity and triumphalism towards non-Christians. Hick argues:

> If Jesus was literally God incarnate, and if it is by his death alone that men can be saved, and by their response to him alone that they can appropriate that salvation, then the only doorway to eternal life is Christian faith. It would follow from this that the large majority of the human race so far have not been saved. But is it credible that the loving God and Father of all men has decreed that only those born within one particular thread of human history shall be saved? Is not such an idea excessively parochial, presenting God in effect as the tribal deity of the predominantly Christian West?[47]

This query, albeit rhetorical for Hick, answers the urgent question that kept me up at night as a boy. In his theology, I see a Christian who acknowledges and thoughtfully responds to the fact that there have always been, and no doubt always will be, many valid religions and forms of religious life.

For Hick, the traditional Christian attitude toward other religions must be seen as egocentric and ethnocentric. His view closely aligns with mythologist Joseph Campbell's reflections on religion as an expression of metaphor and myth:

> From the point of view of orthodoxy, myth might be defined simply as "other people's religion," to which an equivalent definition of religion would be "misunderstood mythology," the misunderstanding consisting in the interpretation of mythic metaphors as references to hard fact: the Virgin Birth, for example, is taken to be a biological anomaly; or the Promised Land as a portion of the Near East to be claimed and settled by a people chosen by God; or the term "God" is understood as denoting an actual, though invisible, masculine personality, who created the universe and is now resident in an invisible, though actual, heaven to which the "justified" will go when they die, there to be joined at the end of time by their resurrected bodies.[48]

Campbell bluntly asks how a modern mind is to make sense of such nonsense. He suggests that we understand that myths are productions of the human imagination that, like dreams, contain narratives and images that are psychologically symbolic. They must be read not literally, but as metaphors.[49]

Incarnational language, in Hick's view, is mythic and metaphorical. The doctrine of the incarnation of Christ is a powerful metaphor for the divinity inherent in human beings. He distinguishes between two aspects of a religion—its central affirmations about the nature of reality (truth claims), and its mythology of poetic elaborations and concrete cultic expressions. The former primarily factual aspect is ultimately true or false or, more probably, partly true and partly false. The latter non-factual aspect of myth, symbol, and poetry is not in the same sense true or false. Hick applies this distinction to Christianity by viewing the "God incarnate" interpretation of Jesus as metaphorical and mythological. He explains how the Christian tradition turned the poetic image "Son of God" into prose, so that the metaphorical son of God became a metaphysical God the Son, the Second Person of a divine Trinity. The problem is this: while the symbols of Jesus as Son of God, God the Son, God incarnate, and Logos made flesh served their purpose for centuries of Christian history, the resulting doctrine of a unique, divine incarnation has poisoned the relationships between Christians and both Jews and Muslims, perpetrating the history of Christian imperialism elsewhere in the world. Within the present pluralistic context, Hick argues that it is essential for Christians to become conscious of both the optional and mythological character of traditional language.[50]

Hick's pluralistic hypothesis

Hick describes his theocentric alternative to traditional Christology ("God-centered" rather than "Christ-centered") as a Copernican revolution in theology. Analogous to the shift from Ptolemy's earth-centered cosmology to Copernicus' sun-centered one, Hick argues that the old Ptolemaic theology propped up an increasingly implausible system with the Church, Christ, or Christianity at the center of the universe of faiths. His model places God at the center, with all religions (including Christianity) revolving around this center.[51] Since a wide range of terms is used for the transcendent reality affirmed by various religious traditions, a relatively neutral term is needed. Options include the transcendent, the ultimate, ultimate reality, the divine, the One, the Eternal One, and the Real. While there is no right choice among these, and people legitimately differ in their preferences, the terms "the divine" and "the Eternal One" are theistically colored. Hick opts mostly for "the Transcendent" and "the Real." Personally, as a pantheist, I often use the word "divine" and also the "ultimate" or "ultimate reality" when I am thinking in a broader context that includes the perspectives of non-theistic traditions like Buddhism.[52]

Hick's thinking has been deeply influenced by Immanuel Kant, a philosopher who maintained that we cannot directly experience the world as it is, but only by way of its phenomenal appearance to us. This idea was also conveyed in a statement from the theology of Thomas Aquinas—"Things are known in the knower according to the mode of the knower."[53] Hick applies this idea to religious experience, distinguishing between the divine reality or the Real—which from our human viewpoint is ineffable or inexpressible—and that which we experience through the conceptual systems and images of different religious traditions.

Different forms of religious experience justify different and often incompatible sets of beliefs. Hick addresses this issue with what he calls *the pluralist hypothesis*: people from different cultures conceive, experience, and respond differently to the infinite Real that, in itself, is beyond the scope of concepts. The Real, perceived and conceptualized by human beings, produces the experience of divine *personae* (such as Jahweh, the heavenly Father, Allah, and Vishnu) and metaphysical *impersonae* (such as Brahman, the Tao, the Dharmakaya, and Sunyata) to which human beings are oriented from their respective faith traditions. The function of religion in either case is to provide contexts for salvation/liberation that, in various forms, consist of the transformation of human existence from self-centeredness to Reality-centeredness. *Salvation* is the term used in Christianity; *liberation* is the analogous term used in Eastern traditions such as Hinduism and Buddhism. Both terms, for Hick, describe the transformation from a state of alienation to a radically better state in harmony with the Real. The basic criterion by which to assess particular religious phenomena and religious systems as totalities is *soteriological* (the capacity to confer salvation or liberation). Salvific transformation is most readily observed by its moral consequences, which can be identified by means of the ethical ideal of *agape/karuna* (love/compassion) common to all great traditions.[54]

From this perspective, the different streams of religious life need not be regarded as competitive or incompatible with one another. Instead, they are better understood as different phenomenal experiences and conceptions of the one divine noumenon.[55] These phenomenal experiences and conceptions are images of the Real, and the plurality of such images reflects the various ways in which the Real has impinged on human consciousness in its different historical and cultural circumstances.

Our religious awareness is continuous with our awareness of other aspects of the environment; we are selectively aware of certain aspects while we shut out others. This need to shut out certain aspects of reality in order to live as the finite creatures we are also applies to our consciousness of the transcendent. Accordingly, Hick describes religion as a system for filtering out divine reality and reducing it to forms with which we can cope. "This system is religion, which is our resistance (in a sense analogous to that used in electronics) to God. The function of the different religions is to enable us to be conscious of God, and yet only partially and selectively, in step with our own spiritual development, both communal and individual."[56] Although their religious traditions, perceptions, and experiences may differ, people often share similar apprehensions regarding encounters with the one infinite reality. Thus, we have to seriously consider the probability that all accounts of the Real may be true even if expressed in human analogies, but that none of them are the truth, the whole truth, and nothing but the truth.[57]

Interpreting the problematic aspect of human existence

As noted earlier, one of the reasons I left Christianity pertains to its conception of human nature as inherently sinful, a doctrine that evokes guilt and the need for justification or redemption. Hick is critical of the traditional reading of human existence that Augustine inscribed in Catholic theology and that Martin Luther and John Calvin, the architects of the Reformation, inscribed in Protestant thinking. Religions do, in fact, presuppose that life, as ordinarily experienced, entails a sense of incompleteness or is unsatisfying in character, and therefore they proclaim a path to a limitlessly better mode of existence. However, there are significant differences in how the problematic aspect of the human condition is interpreted.

In the Semitic religions, the sense of incompleteness, or unsatisfactory quality of life, has a primarily moral focus: human nature contains an evil inclination which we have to resist or overcome (Gen. 6:5); or we are fallen beings, bearing within us the original sin of Adam and Eve because of whom the whole human face fell (I Cor. 15:22); or we are made out of the dust of the earth (Qur'an 3:59), and are self-centered and prone to disobey God's commands (Qur'an 96:6–7). In Eastern traditions, the focus has been less on sin and guilt and more on false consciousness. This is expressed metaphysically in the Hindu concepts of spiritual ignorance (*avidya*) and illusion (*maya*), whereas the more psychological and moral aspects of false consciousness are expressed in the Buddha's basic teachings as summarized in the Four Noble Truths.

The first of the Four Noble Truths is the truth of *duhkha*, variously translated as unsatisfactoriness, suffering, or unhappiness. Its source is our self-centered way of participating in the process of life. Originating from a biological instinct for self-preservation, it consists in seeing and valuing everything primarily as it affects oneself. This produces a distrust of strangers, worries about what the future may bring, and a fear of death—all building up into a pervasive angst that deprives us of peace and the deep joy of inner freedom. This leads to greed, cruelty, jealousy, untruthfulness, and collective forms of suffering entailed by war, slavery, and institutionalized injustices. According to the Buddha, all this human misery flows from a false consciousness that renders us fundamentally insecure, so that we safeguard ourselves by grasping at power and possessions. What we lack is awareness of our Buddha-nature, an awareness that would release us from the constant defensive self-concern that makes life a danger, the future a threat, and the human world a jungle of competing interests.[58]

Hick derived an alternative Christian perspective on human existence from a strand of early Hellenistic thought. Irenaeus, in the second century, depicted Adam and Eve as immature, childlike creatures who fall because of an understandable error rather than a cosmic crime.[59] In this view, we may outgrow our immaturity and gradually experience the grandeur of our true nature and destiny. Deification (*theiosis*) is one of the main metaphors used by Christian mystics, particularly in the Eastern church, as influenced by Neoplatonism. Plato seems to have thought of the soul as naturally divine, so that the process of divinization is a return to one's original state. Clement of Alexandria, also from the second-century, wrote that "the Word of God became man, that thou mayest learn from man how man may become God."[60]

Hick, like these early Christian thinkers and other mystics from subsequent traditions, understands the human journey in terms of a distinction between the image (*eikon, imago*) and the likeness (*homoiosis, similitudo*) of God. In modern terms, Hick explains, "the image of God is our existence as intelligent ethical animals with a spiritual nature capable of responding to our creator. As such, however, we are only at the beginning of a long process of development towards the 'likeness' of God, which is our perfecting by the Holy Spirit. It is this perfecting that is called in the eastern Christian tradition deification or divinization."[61] While this alternative Christian view on human existence is not identical to the Hindu and Buddhist views described above, it is much closer to these Eastern traditions than to the traditional Augustinian-Calvinist teachings on sin and the need for redemption. It is a move in the direction I needed to go as I reformulated my religious identity.

Exemplars of spirituality

There is a final aspect of Hick's thinking that also aligns with the unfolding of my religious individuation. Hick calls as much attention to contemporary exemplars of spirituality as to the founders of great traditions. He acknowledges that while the word *saint* is a distinctly Christian term, other great traditions also recognize special

individuals who serve as exemplars of an authentic response to the transcendent: the
rishi (Vedic sage), *jivanmukta* (liberated soul), *mahatma* (great soul), and *guru* (teacher)
of Hinduism; *the arahant* (one who has attained nirvana) of Theravada Buddhism,
the *bodhisattva* (who remains in the world to help others), and the *roshi* (Zen master)
of Mahayana Buddhism; the sage (*shen*) of Confucianism; the *tsaddiq* (just man) and
other exemplary figures of Judaism; and the *wali* (friend of God) of Islam, particularly
for Sufis. Such exemplars fulfill what I refer to above as the soteriological function
of religion. In Hick's words, they are the "men and women of all traditions who
are much more advanced than the rest of us in the transformation from natural self-
centeredness to a re-centering in God, the Real, the Ultimate."[62]

In my own spiritual journey, I also came to appreciate that exemplary human
beings did not simply exist long ago, in the distant past; these individuals have lived
century after century in all the great, as well as the lesser-known, smaller-scale indigenous traditions. Moreover, these exemplars live among us now. Thus, I turn to
them in my own spiritual quest. A glimpse into one such pioneering figure follows.

Karen Armstrong

Karen Armstrong is an influential British independent scholar of religion who, at
the age of seventeen, entered a Roman Catholic convent, eager to meet God.
She was convinced that she was embarking on a spiritual quest to find the infinite
and ultimately satisfying mystery that we call God, in the course of which she
would lose the confusions of her adolescent self. For her, God would no longer
be a remote, shadowy reality, but a vibrant presence in her life. She would become
serene, joyful, inspired, and inspiring, perhaps even a saint.[63] Instead, she discovered
that the convent was not what she expected, and after seven years she left. She
entered religious life at a particularly inauspicious moment during which her
superiors, involved in a painful period of change, were trying to decide what
exactly it meant to be a nun in modern society. During her first few months
in the convent, the Second Vatican Council was convened in Rome, summoned
by Pope John XXIII, to open the windows of the church and let the fresh air of
modernity sweep through the musty corridors of the Vatican. But the reforms set
in motion by the Vatican Council came too late for her.[64]

Prior to leaving the convent she enrolled in Oxford University. Although
she loved her studies, her life soon fell apart. As a nun she felt torn in two—her
academic work at the university was changing her as much or more than her
religious training, and the two systems seemed irreconcilable. Within a year
she broke down completely and applied for a dispensation from her vows, trying
to put the convent completely behind her and hoping to erase the damage and
transition to a wholly secular existence.[65] However, she never managed at that
time to integrate fully with the world. As she explains in her memoir:

> I predicted that I would in some sense be a nun all my life. Of course, it is
> true that in superficial ways, my present life is light-years away from my

convent experience. I have dear friends, a pretty house, and money. I travel, have a lot of fun, and enjoy the good things of life. Nothing *nunnish* about any of this. But although I tried a number of different careers, doors continually slammed in my face until I settled down to my present solitary existence, writing, thinking, and talking almost all day and every day about God, religion, and spirituality.[66]

In this passage, we see an example of a contemporary woman who discovers a path of integrative spirituality. In the language of her memoir, it is a long, winding ascent from darkness by means of a spiral staircase. In other words, Armstrong exemplifies the individuation process, which Jung describes as circumambulation, an inner journey in which one circles one's life again and again, in a movement that leads from fragmentation to wholeness. In her words:

For years it seemed a hard, Lenten journey, but without the prospect of Easter. I toiled round and round in pointless circles, covering the same ground, repeating the same mistakes, quite unable to see where I was going. Yet all the time, without realizing it, I was slowly climbing out of the darkness. In mythology, stairs frequently symbolize a breakthrough to a new level of consciousness. For a long time, I assumed that I had finished with religion forever, yet in the end, the strange and seemingly arbitrary revolution of my life led me to the kind of transformation that—I now believe—was what I was seeking all those years ago, when I packed my suitcase, entered my convent, and set off to find God.[67]

Taking a new path—her path

Armstrong's decision to write *A History of God: The 4,000 Year Quest of Judaism, Christianity and Islam* changed her life radically, as it was the first step along the path that led her in a wholly unexpected direction. She anticipated that the book would follow a skeptical line of reflection:

God does not exist, but I would show that each generation of believers was driven to invent him anew. God was simply a projection of human need; "he" mirrored the fears and yearnings of society at each stage of its development . . . but increasingly, in the clear light of rational modernity, people were learning to do without this divine prop.[68]

Why, she asks herself, go on producing religious books of little interest in predominately secular Britain? Furthermore, she often declared that she was finished with God and was much the better for it. Yet, despite the evidence she amassed to the contrary, she realized, at some inchoate unconscious level, that this was not the case.[69]

While working on the book, she began to focus on her inner life. She was about to "turn again" and experience what the Greeks call *metanoia*, or conversion, though it was the last thing she wanted. The insight that dawned on her was that, in most traditions, faith is not about belief, but about practice. As she puts it, "Religion is not about accepting twenty impossible things before breakfast, but about doing things that change you. It is a moral aesthetic, an ethical alchemy. If you behave in a certain way, you will be transformed."[70] She found that the religious quest is not about discovering "the truth," but about living as intensely as possible in the here and now. Viewed in this way, archetypal figures such as Muhammad, the Buddha, and Jesus become icons of fulfilled humanity. In the past, her practice of religion diminished her, whereas true faith, she comes to feel, makes one more human than before.[71]

Through her research, she discerned that all of the world's faiths put suffering at the top of their agenda and teach a spirituality of empathy—wherein the faithful relate their own suffering to that of others—a principle enshrined in the Golden Rule. As the great Rabbi Hillel taught, you must look into your own heart, find out what distresses you, and then refrain from inflicting similar pain on other people. That, he insisted, is the Torah, and everything else is commentary. This, Armstrong discovered, is the essence of the religious life.[72]

God-image

I have included Armstrong in this chapter on Christianity though she is no longer a traditional Christian. By immersing herself in the study of the world's religions, her identity expanded beyond that label, though this is not to say she would disavow it. Like Tillich, she discovered the God above God, a God-image that transcends traditional theism but that nevertheless accords with the insights of eminent Jewish, Christian, and Muslim theologians and mystics. She discovered that God is not an objective fact, not another being, not an unseen reality like an atom whose existence can be empirically demonstrated.[73] "The reality we call God," she realized, "is transcendent—that is, beyond any human orthodoxy—and yet God is also the ground of all being and can be experienced almost as a presence in the depths of the psyche."[74]

For Armstrong the notion of a personal God is a symbolic way of speaking about the divine, but it cannot explain the far more elusive reality. The writings on faith by Wilfred Cantwell Smith, the historian of religion discussed in Chapter 2, supported her return to a viable form of spirituality. Faith, she came to understand, is "the cultivation of a conviction that life has some ultimate meaning and value, despite the tragic evidence to the contrary."[75] As the medieval theologian St. Anselm of Canterbury wrote, *credo ut intelligam*, "I believe in order that I can understand."[76] In contemporary terms this phrase could be translated, "I commit myself in order that I may understand." First you must live in a certain way, Armstrong elaborates, and then you will encounter a sacred presence which monotheists call God, but which others call the Tao, Brahman, or Nirvana. From this perspective, the only test of a valid idea, doctrinal statement, or devotional practice is that it must lead directly to practical compassion. Your understanding of the divine must make you kinder, more empathetic, and better able to express this sympathy in concrete acts of loving-kindness.[77] Hers, then, is a pragmatic faith. A personalized God, she acknowledges, might work for other people, but not for her.

Utilizing empathy in the study of religion

Another turning point in Armstrong's life was her decision to write a book about the prophet Muhammad. She wrote it in the wake of the Ayatollah Khomeini's fatwa that condemned Salman Rushdie to death for publishing *The Satanic Verses*, a novel that includes a portrait of the prophet Muhammad that many Muslims find blasphemous.[78] The fatwa was an example of the cruel religious certainty she came to loathe. She firmly believed Rushdie had the right to publish whatever he wished. Yet, the raw pain experienced by the more thoughtful Muslims, who condemned the fatwa and book burning and who tried to explain why the novel evoked such outrage, also moved her. She pondered the Golden Rule and asked herself, "If I had felt this type of pain, I should not inflict it on others. How would we in the West like our traditions misrepresented in this manner? *The Satanic Verses* itself was a brilliant and sympathetic study of the way this kind of prejudice turned people into monsters. And I felt a pang of fear for the future."[79] Through her writing, she sought to counter the inaccurate Western depictions of Islam as a bloodthirsty religion and the Qur'an as a text that preaches a God of vengeance.

Her book began as a polemic; she wanted to set the record straight. But during the writing, something else happened. To her surprise, she found herself strongly drawn to Muhammad, and her research took on a more contemplative character. While writing his biography, she had to make a constant, imaginative attempt to enter empathetically into the experience of another. This was a kind of ecstasy, an experience of standing outside of herself. Even though she was not a believer, she came to think within a religious frame of reference and entered the mind of a man who believed that he was touched directly by God. Unless she was able to make that sympathetic leap, she would miss the essence of Muhammad. As she explains, "Writing his life [is] in its own way an act of *Islam*, a 'surrender' of my secular, skeptical self, which [brings me], if only at second hand and at once removed, into the ambit of what we call the divine."[80] The book introduced her to a different world. She began to receive invitations to interfaith gatherings, and was surprised and moved—as a woman and non-Muslim—to be invited to speak to Muslims on the occasion of their Prophet's birthday. Would Christians, she wondered, be willing to invite a Muslim to address their congregation on Christmas, the birthday of the prophet Jesus, who is, in fact, greatly revered in Islam?[81]

In subsequent books, as she continued to write about the Abrahamic traditions, she did not see any one of them as being superior to the others and was struck by their profound similarity. She was equally delighted by the insights of Jewish, Muslim, and Christian thinkers, discovering that, while working in isolation from each other and often in a state of deadly hostility, they had come to remarkably similar conclusions. The unanimity, she discerned, suggested their being onto something real about the human condition. Her studies became grounded in what Islamist Louis Massignon calls the science of compassion. Compassion, Armstrong insists, does not mean to feel pity or to condescend, but to *feel with*. It demands what St. Paul calls *kenosis*, an emptying of self that leads to an enlarged and enhanced perspective. It is not enough to understand other people's beliefs, rituals, and ethical practices intellectually; one must feel them, too, and make an imaginative, though disciplined, identification.[82]

The practice of compassion

While writing a biography of the Buddha, Armstrong realized she could never be a serious practitioner of formal meditation. As the Buddha teaches, the practice of compassion can also affect "the release of the mind" from the toils of self-seeking that is synonymous in the Buddhist scriptures with the supreme enlightenment of Nirvana. Translated into monotheistic terms, this compassion, she understood, could bring one directly into the presence of God. Compassion, she concluded, has been advocated by all the great faiths because it has been found to be the safest and surest means of attaining enlightenment. In her words, "It dethrones the ego from the center of our lives and puts others there, breaking down the carapace of selfishness that holds us back from an experience of the sacred."[83] It fulfills the soteriological function of religion described by John Hick in the preceding section of this chapter—the shift from an ego-centered life to one that is oriented towards the Real.

Since the September 11, 2001 bombings of the World Trade Center, Armstrong has redoubled her efforts to quell the discord engendered by different worldviews. Our task, she believes, is to mend our broken world. What the world needs now, she maintains, is not belief, not certainty, but compassionate action, and practically expressed respect for the sacred value of all human beings, even our enemies. Currently, she spends most of her time trying to share her understanding of Islam and fundamentalism, viewing this work as a form of ministry. She sees "the September apocalypse" as a revelation—an "unveiling" of a reality that has been there all the time, but which had not been seen clearly enough: we live in one world. The study of other people's religious beliefs is no longer merely desirable, but necessary for our survival.[84]

The Compassion Charter

In 2007 Armstrong received and used the TED (Technology, Entertainment, Design) Prize to facilitate the formulation of the Charter of Compassion, a project based on her studies in the history of religion. Focusing on the Abrahamic traditions with their long history of conflict, she found common ground that could serve as a basis for cooperation rather than strife. Armstrong asserts that compassion is the true test of religiosity and that each of the world's religions has put the Golden Rule at the core of its ethical teachings. Religions insist that you cannot confine compassion to your own group; we are enjoined, instead, to love our enemies and welcome the stranger. Any ideology that does not foster global understanding is failing the needs of our time.

Although Armstrong was once deeply disillusioned by religion, she has come to believe that it can be a force for harmony in the world. On the basis of that conviction, she used her award money to work with religious leaders from many traditions to establish the Charter of Compassion. Thousands of people from around the world contributed to a draft charter on a multilingual website, in Hebrew, Arabic, Urdu, Spanish, and English. Their comments were presented to the Council of Conscience, a group of notable individuals from six faith traditions (Judaism, Christianity, Islam, Hinduism, Buddhism, and Confucianism), who met in Switzerland to compose the final version. The Charter for Compassion, unveiled to the world on November 12, 2009, in sixty different locations throughout the world, is now enshrined in synagogues, mosques, temples, and churches, as well as in secular institutions like the Karachi Press Club and the Sydney Opera House. The text of the charter reads as follows:

> The principle of compassion lies at the heart of all religious, ethical and spiritual traditions, calling us to always treat others as we wish to be treated ourselves.
>
> Compassion impels us to work tirelessly to alleviate the suffering of our fellow creatures, to dethrone ourselves from the center of our world and put another there, and to honor the inviolable sanctity of every single human being, treating everyone, without exception, with absolute justice, equity and respect.
>
> It is also necessary in both public and private life to refrain consistently and empathetically from inflicting pain. To act or speak violently out of spite, chauvinism or self-interest, to impoverish, exploit or deny basic rights to anybody, and to incite hatred by denigrating others—even our enemies—is a denial of our common humanity. We acknowledge that we have failed to live compassionately and that some have even increased the sum of human misery in the name of religion.
>
> We therefore call upon all men and women
> * to restore compassion to the center of morality and religion;
> * to return to the ancient principle that any interpretation of scripture that breeds violence, hatred or disdain is illegitimate;
> * to ensure that youth are given accurate and respectful information about other traditions, religions and cultures;
> * to encourage a positive appreciation of cultural and religious diversity;
> * to cultivate an informed empathy with the suffering of all human beings—even those regarded as enemies.[85]

Through her books, the Charter of Compassion initiative, and interfaith activities, Armstrong has become an exemplary advocate of religious pluralism by struggling with her own religious past and courageously climbing out of the darkness of her loss of faith. Hers is a powerful story of individuation for people from any tradition or from none at all—and it points us to the common ground of all forms of authentic spirituality.

Insights for integrative spirituality

Christian pluralists offer constructive and innovative responses to the challenge of religious pluralism, though their perspectives are—and will no doubt remain— controversial to many traditional Christians. While there are differences among them, the exemplary figures discussed share many views in common that create new possibilities for Christians and people from other religious traditions:

- In the preceding chapter, *faith* is distinguished from *belief*. Faith is a quality of a person within a system; it is an orientation of the personality to oneself, one's neighbor, and the universe. It involves seeing, feeling, and acting in relation to a transcendent dimension of existence. Furthermore, it may be understood as the interpretative element of religious experience. Thus understood, as Hick maintains, faith enables one to experience the ambiguity of the universe through a religious or spiritual lens; it is a rational response to the Real or Transcendent. In Armstrong's pragmatic terms, faith is about doing things that change you; it is a moral aesthetic, an ethical alchemy. If you behave in a certain way, you will be transformed.

- Authentic religion engenders a spirituality of empathy and compassion. "By their fruits ye shall know them" (Matt. 7:20). Hick and Armstrong both insist that the criterion by which to assess religion and spirituality is the degree to which a person engenders love and compassion toward others. The Charter of Compassion embodies this principle and enjoins persons of all faith traditions to make compassion the center of morality and religion, to promote appreciation for cultural and religious diversity, and to cultivate an informed empathy for the suffering of all human beings.

- Christian pluralists help create the possibility for religions to peacefully co-exist, thereby promoting peace among nations, as well as for individuals within faith traditions to conceive their faith more freely. Positive relationships between religions may be cultivated through inter-religious dialogue when the aim is to foster mutual understanding and respect rather than to convert or persuade others to change their beliefs.

- From the perspective of Hick's pluralist hypothesis, religions are diverse human responses to the Real. The Real is filtered, so to speak, through the language, images, and concepts of particular cultures and religious traditions. Furthermore, knowledge of the Real, which is ineffable and beyond concepts, is partial in all faith traditions. Religious truth need not be assessed with the criterion of non-contradiction (a given view is either true or it is false); instead, religious truths may be seen as different, though overlapping or complementary, perspectives on ultimate reality or the Real. Christians no longer need to regard other traditions as competing rivals, but rather as partners in a common quest for truth. Furthermore, the Real may be experienced through personal or non-personal God-images, thereby validating temperamental differences among individuals. Devotional people, for example, are predisposed to worship Christ, whereas more philosophical individuals are inclined to experience the Real as Being itself, the formless Godhead affirmed by some Christian mystics and modern theologians, such as Paul Tillich.

Some Christian pluralists go further and affirm other possibilities rarely thought possible in the past:

- Traditional doctrines can be understood in a more symbolic manner. The incarnation of Christ, for example, may be seen as a myth that animates faith and a powerful metaphor for the divinity inherent in all beings. Likewise, other religious figures, such as Muhammad and the Buddha, may be regarded as icons of fulfilled humanity.

- Christians who are edified by teachings and practices from other religions are free to develop hybrid religious identities, allowing them to belong or participate in another tradition.

The Christian pluralists discussed in this chapter exemplify how faith may change during one's lifetime. One person may find it necessary to embrace and incorporate ideas or practices from another religion to retain their tradition (Knitter). Another might move from a fundamentalist or conservative, evangelical version of their religion to a liberal, pluralistic form of faith (Hick). Still another might become disillusioned by their immersion in a religious community to the extent of losing faith altogether, yet discover a new form of faith inspired by an empathetic and comparative study of religions (Armstrong).

Notes

1 Anodea Judith, *The Global Heart Awakens: Humanity's Rite of Passage from the Love of Power to the Power of Love.* San Rafael, CA: Shift Books, 2013, 132–34.
2 Ibid., 135–36.
3 Quoted in Maurice Wiles, "Christianity Without Incarnation," *The Myth of God Incarnate*, ed. John Hick. Philadelphia: Westminster, 1977, 1.
4 Karl Barth, "The Revelation of God as the Abolition of Religion," in *Christianity and Other Religions*, ed. John Hick and Brian Hebblethwaite. Philadelphia: Fortress Press, 1980, 32–51.
5 Emil Brunner, *Revelation and Religion*, trans. Olive Wyon. Philadelphia: Westminster, 1947, 270.

6 Hendrik Kraemer, *The Christian Message in a Non-Christian World*, 3rd ed., Grand Rapids, MI: Kregel Publications, 1956, 126.
7 "The Frankfurt Declaration," *Christianity Today* 14 (1970): 844–46.
8 Ibid.
9 Waldron Scott, "No Other Name—An Evangelical Conviction" in *Christ's Lordship and Religious Pluralism*, eds. Gerald H. Anderson and Thomas F. Stransky. Maryknoll, NY: Orbis, 1981, 59–60.
10 Gerald Anderson, *Christianity and World Religions: The Challenge of Pluralism*. Downer's Grove, IL: Inter-Varsity Press, 1984, 205.
11 Karl Rahner, *Theological Investigations*, trans. Karl-H Kruger, vol. 5. Baltimore: Helicon, 1966, 118–33.
12 Hans Küng, "The Freedom of Religions," in *Attitudes Toward Other Religions*, ed. Owen C. Thomas. New York: Harper & Row, 1969, 216.
13 Hans Küng, *On Being a Christian*, trans. Edward Quinn. New York: Doubleday & Co., 1976, 123–24.
14 Ibid., 110.
15 Ibid., 112.
16 Hans Küng, "No World Peace Without Religious Peace," in *Christianity and the World Religions: Paths of Dialogue with Islam, Hinduism, and Buddhism*, by Hans Küng, Josef van Ess, Heinrich von Stietencron, and Heinz Behert, trans. Peter Heinegg. Garden City, NY: Doubleday & Co, 1986, 443.
17 Quoted in Eric Sharpe, *Not to Destroy but to Fulfill: The Contribution of J. N. Farquhar to Protestant Missionary Thought in India Before 1914*, Uppsala: Gleerup, 1965, 334–39.
18 Ibid., 339.
19 Eric Sharpe, *Faith Meets Faith: Some Christian Attitudes to Hinduism in the Nineteenth and Twentieth Centuries*. London: SCM Press, 1977, 29.
20 John A. T. Robinson, *Truth is Two-Eyed*. Philadelphia, PN: Westminster, 1979, 120.
21 Ibid., 98.
22 Paul Tillich, *Christianity and the Encounter of the World Religions*. New York: Columbia University Press, 1963, 81–82.
23 Ibid., 83.
24 Ibid., 97.
25 Paul Tillich, *The Courage to Be*. New Haven, CT: Yale University Press, 1952, 189–90.
26 Raimundo Panikkar, *The Unknown Christ of Hinduism: Towards an Ecumenical Christophany*, rev. ed. London: Darton, Longman & Todd, 1981, 48–49.
27 Ibid., 14.
28 Ibid., 27.
29 Ibid., 43.
30 Raimundo Panikkar, *The Intrareligious Dialogue*. New York: Paulist Press, 1978, 1.
31 Panikkar, *The Unknown Christ of Hinduism*, 24.
32 Ibid., 29.
33 Panikkar, *Intrareligious Dialogue*, xix–xx.
34 Knitter, *No Other Name?*, 217.
35 Ibid., 219.
36 Paul F. Knitter, *Without Buddha I Could Not Be a Christian*. Oxford: Oneworld, 2009, xii–xiv; 213–14.
37 Ibid., 214.
38 Ibid., 215.
39 Ibid.
40 Ibid., 215–16.
41 Ibid., 216.
42 John Hick, *An Autobiography*. Oxford: Oneworld, 2002, 321–23.
43 John Hick, *An Interpretation of Religion: Human Responses to the Transcendent*, 2nd ed. New Haven, CT, 2004, 12.

44 Ibid., 13.
45 Ibid., 158–60.
46 Ibid., 13.
47 John Hick, "Jesus in the World Religions," in *The Myth of God Incarnate*, ed. John Hick. Philadelphia, PN: Westminster, 1977, 180.
48 Joseph Campbell, *The Inner Reaches of Outer Space: Metaphor as Myth and as Religion*. New York: Harper & Row, 1986, 55.
49 Ibid.
50 Hick, "Jesus and the World Religions," 173–80.
51 John Hick, *God and the Universe of Faiths*. Glasgow: Collins, 1977, 131.
52 Hick, *An Interpretation of Religion*, 10–11.
53 Quoted in Hick, *An Autobiography*, 69.
54 Hick, *An Interpretation of Religion*, 10–14. Hick's conjoint term, agape/karunā, indicates that he regards the Christian emphasis on agape (love) to functionally equivalent, ethically speaking, to karunā (compassion), the Sanskrit word for compassion extolled for this virtue by Hindu and Buddhist traditions.
55 John Hick, *God Has Many Names*. Philadelphia: Westminster, 1982, 92–94.
56 Ibid., 112.
57 Hick, *God and the Universe of Faiths*, 140.
58 John Hick, *The Fifth Dimension: An Exploration of the Spiritual Realm*. New York: Oneworld, 1999, 6–7.
59 Ibid., 131.
60 Quoted in Hick, *The Fifth Dimension*, 148.
61 Hick, *The Fifth Dimension*, 149.
62 Ibid., 174.
63 Karen Armstrong, *The Spiral Staircase: My Climb Out of Darkness*. New York: Anchor Books, 2004, xiii.
64 Ibid., xi–xiii.
65 Ibid., xvi–xvii.
66 Ibid., xviii.
67 Ibid., xx.
68 Ibid., 265.
69 Ibid., 267.
70 Ibid., 270.
71 Ibid., 271.
72 Ibid., 272.
73 Ibid., 291.
74 Ibid., 292.
75 Ibid.
76 Ibid., 292–93.
77 Ibid., 293.
78 Ibid., 273–74.
79 Ibid., 274.
80 Ibid., 279–80.
81 Ibid., 282
82 Ibid., 289–90.
83 Ibid., 296.
84 Ibid., 304.
85 Karen Armstrong, *Twelve Steps to a Compassionate Life*. Toronto: Alfred A. Knopf, 2011, 6–8.

4

HINDUISM

> The Real is one, the sages call it by various names.
> —*Rig Veda*

> As they approach me, so I receive them. All paths lead to me.
> —*Bhagavad Gita*

I have a somewhat inexplicable predilection for Indian culture. I love the mythology, philosophy, music, and cuisine, and I feel deep respect and affection for Indian people. It should come as no surprise, then, that I love Indian spirituality, too, which embodies the values and sensibility of the culture. Perhaps it is a matter of *samskaras*, impressions from past lives; in any case, becoming a Western Hindu has been an essential aspect of my individuation process. For me, Hinduism is the ultimate both-and religion; it is a broad confluence of teachings and practices that holds the tension between many of the contrary tendencies inherent in religiosity—logos and mythos, contemplation and devotion, formless and personified mysticism, renunciation and desire, world-negating and world-embracing attitudes toward nature and the body, homelessness and family values. More than any other religion, Hinduism combines myriad forms of religiosity into a unity that embraces diversity.

Hinduism is an abstract designation for a diverse family of religions that primarily includes the Vaishnava, Shaiva, and Shakta traditions. Vaishnavas worship Vishnu or one of his *avatars* or incarnations, especially Rama and Krishna; Shaivas worship Shiva, often depicted as an ascetic yogi seated in a cross-legged posture in the Himalayas while absorbed in meditation; and Shaktas worship Shakti in the form of various goddesses who personify the feminine, creative power animating the phenomenal world. These traditions are sourced by sacred texts, including the ancient Vedas and Upanishads; the great Indian epics (*Mahabharata* and *Ramayana*); the *Yoga Sutras*; compendiums of myth and sectarian teachings (Puranas); and esoteric writings called Tantras. These texts provide spiritual aspirants with several paths for experiencing the divine, including those promoted in the well-known

Bhagavad Gita, often considered the bible of Hinduism. Containing Krishna's teachings on the paths of knowledge (*jnana yoga*), action (*karma yoga*), and devotional love (*bhakti yoga*), as well as instructions for meditation (*dhyana yoga*), the *Bhagavad Gita* exemplifies the synthetic nature of Hinduism and its recombinant powers.

Modern Hindu responses to religious pluralism are predominantly inclusivist, though there are Hindus who express exclusivist views that resemble their Christian counterparts. Hindu inclusivists are frequently praised for their acceptance and tolerance of other religions, although careful consideration of their views reveals a bias that other religions are less developed than their own. Full-fledged pluralism, in religious and secular modes of thought, is rare. As I explained in Chapter 1, pluralism is a hallmark of the structure of consciousness that emerged during postmodernity, a perspective characterized by multiculturalism and critique of hegemonic attitudes toward cultures different from one's own. The distinction between Hindu inclusivism and pluralism is subtle and hinges on the degree to which other traditions are studied or directly engaged. For instance, Hindus who consider the formless Brahman a higher truth than theistic or personified God-images are inclusivist rather than pluralist; they do not regard theism to be as valid as the non-theistic view of the divine. In my estimation, Hindu inclusivists approximate a full affirmation of other religions on their own terms and there is much we can learn from them.

Hindu exclusivism

Hindu exclusivism is rooted in traditional Hindu attitudes toward the Vedas. Hindus consider the Vedas to be eternal, impersonal (not sourced by a person or god), and the most perfect revelation of the divine truth from which all knowledge of *dharma* comes and without which *moksha* or liberation is impossible.

In the late nineteenth century Swami Dayananda Sarasvati established a Hindu reform movement, the Arya Samaj, in response to European colonialism and the Christian missionary presence in India. His movement responded aggressively to the challenge of other religions, particularly Christianity and Islam, and became part of the Hindu Renaissance that revitalized Indian culture and led to India's independence from Great Britain. Other great sages, writers, and political leaders, such as Sri Aurobindo, Rabindranath Tagore, and Mahatma Gandhi, were also catalysts for the dynamic changes that flowered in the twentieth century. Basing his reforms on purely indigenous sources, Dayananda differed from other reformers of the Hindu Renaissance. Born into a Brahmin family in a part of India relatively untouched by British cultural influence, he revolted against idol worship as a youth and ran away to avoid marriage by becoming a sannyasin. For the next fifteen years he lived as a wandering ascetic in jungles and places of pilgrimage in northern India. During his journey he was instilled with a deep reverence for the four Vedas and contempt for all later scriptures. Afterwards he lectured throughout India on the exclusive authority of the Vedas.[1]

Dayananda studied other religions, including their scriptures, for polemical purposes. When translations were unavailable, he had them privately translated into the languages he knew. His primary purpose for studying these texts, such as the Bible and the Qur'an, was to show their inherent inconsistencies and absurdities and to render their gods unworthy of human worship. But Dayananda's exclusive commitment to the authority of Vedic truth made it impossible for him to understand any religion other than his own.[2] He believed in the infallible authority of the Vedas and distinguished its revealed truth from that of other institutionalized religions. In this regard, his response to religious pluralism resembled a Christian exclusivist theologian like Karl Barth. Dayananda considered Jainism, Buddhism, Christianity, Islam, and various sectarian forms of Hinduism to be "the product of ignorance."[3] Ignorance, or not-knowing the truth (*avidya*), is the existential equivalent of sin in Christian tradition. Later, to protect Hindus from conversion by Christian missionaries, Dayananda strongly criticized Christianity in his public lectures, particularly the central tenets of Protestant evangelical thought dominant among the missionaries in India in the 1870s, and he introduced a strategy for reconverting Indian Christians to Hinduism. His purpose was to recover lost Hindus, convert new Hindus, and raise the status of the lower caste, including the untouchables.[4]

Bhaktivedanta Swami Prabhupada, a Vaishnava monk and influential teacher of Gaudiya Vaishnava theology in India, was influential in the West through his leadership of the International Society for Krishna Consciousness (ISKCON) that he founded in 1966. A key player in bringing his version of devotional Hinduism to the West, his stance was largely that of a missionary. In his view true religion is only bestowed by Krishna, the Supreme Personality of the Godhead, and people are discontent and suffer when unaware that they are an essential part of God. He believes the goal of life is to become aware of one's relationship with Krishna by taking up the chanting of the Hare Krishna mantra.[5] Critical of other Hindu traditions and non-Hindu religions, he repudiates pluralism: "In this present day, man is very eager to have one scripture, one God, one religion, and one occupation. So let there be one common scripture for the whole world—*Bhagavad-gita*. And let there be one God only for the whole world."[6] That God is Krishna, and the means of relating to him is through repetition of the mantra of his holy names.

Prabhupada's attitude toward other religions adhered to the principle of isolation—a devotee must avoid unholy association and listen exclusively to the recitation of the *Srimad Bhagavatam* and other Vaishnava texts. He told disciples not to study the doctrines of non-Hindu traditions. He believed that the entire world was originally one Vedic culture that divided into many countries, religions, and political parties that did not necessarily provide the unity and Truth found on the transcendental level. Ultimate unity is found only by transcending the phenomenal plane in which religions exist; one reaches a transcendental level by becoming a Vaishnava, by engaging in service to Krishna—in effect, by becoming part of the Krishna consciousness movement.[7]

Although Prabhupada's knowledge of Christianity was limited, he affirmed that the goal and teachings of Christianity and the Krishna consciousness movement are the same—to love God and obey his commandments. The main difference, he argued, is that Krishna teaches people how to achieve this aim. He asserted that Christ is merely a form of Krishna and the names are the same: "Christ comes from Christos, and Christos is the Greek version of the word Krsta. When an Indian person calls on Krishna, he often says Krsta. Krsta is a Sanskrit name meaning 'object of attraction.' So when we address God as 'Christ,' 'Krista,' or 'Krishna,' we indicate the same all-attractive Supreme Personality of Godhead."[8] The inference of identity (Christ and Krishna) was made not only to eliminate unnecessary conflict with Christians, but also to enlist their support for Prabhupada's mission. Accordingly, he enjoined Christian clergy to cooperate with the Krishna consciousness movement and taught Christians to chant the name of Christ or Christos and to stop condoning the slaughter of animals for food consumption.[9] Since Prabhupada viewed Krishna consciousness as the true religion, his response to religious pluralism was mostly exclusivist; however, his seeing Christ as a form of Krishna shaded into inclusivism. He also opened the door to dialogue, though his purpose was to enlist Christians to cooperate with the movement and experience Krishna consciousness, the only true and fully efficacious path to liberation.

The responses of Hindu exclusivists to religious pluralism parallel those of Christian exclusivists in several respects:

- First, Dayananda and Prabhupada judged other religions without sufficient knowledge of their beliefs and practices. Dayananda studied their scriptures primarily for polemical purposes. In Prabhupada's case, the principle of isolation meant he rarely read non-Hindu texts and discouraged the adherents of his movement from doing so; he rejected religious pluralism within and outside of the Hindu tradition since he had the fundamental conviction that the Krishna consciousness movement is the essence of religion and alone offers salvation.

- Second, the claim that Vedic revelation is eternal disregards the extent to which Hindu beliefs and practices, and those of other traditions, are historically conditioned. This is analogous to the distinction Barth and other Christian exclusivists make between Christian revelation and other religions. While these theologians argue that all other religions are human constructions, Hindu exclusivists reverse the argument.

- Third, Christian and Hindu exclusivists assume there is only one correct interpretation of their respective traditions and do not acknowledge a plurality of interpretations. Dayananda's interpretation of the Vedas is one of many; Prabhupada's interpretations of Hindu texts express a particular Vaishnava theological position.

- Fourth, the presuppositions of Hindu exclusivism preclude genuine dialogue; they function as polemical efforts to discredit other religions or convert new members to the faith. Dayananda's attitude toward other religions was a reaction to the presence of Christians and Muslims who converted Hindus to their faiths; his teachings intended to stop or reverse this. Prabhupada, by contrast, sought to establish his teaching outside of India, in the West, to persuade or convert others to his movement. Neither purpose is conducive to promoting mutual respect between religions or encouraging authentic inter-religious dialogue.

Hindu inclusivism

The paradigmatic source of Hindu inclusivism is the famous passage from the *Rig Veda*, "The real is one, the sages call it by various names" (1:164.46). Sayings scattered throughout Hindu religious literature convey the same idea, such as a frequently quoted verse from the *Bhagavad Gita* suggesting that all religions are included and accepted by Krishna—"As they approach me, so I receive them. All paths, Arjuna, lead to me" (4:11). Hindu inclusivists often view religions as having different, and sometimes conflicting, perspectives on the one divine or ultimate reality. A classic parable in the tradition sheds some light on this view: A number of blind persons encounter an elephant. Each describes their experience on the basis of touching various parts of the animal–the ears, trunk, feet, and so on. Each description is based on an actual encounter with the elephant, but varies considerably according to the part of the elephant described. In all cases, the part is mistakenly assumed to be an accurate account of the totality of the elephant. According to this logic, Hinduism should be tolerant and open to other religions because the more aspects of the divine we can perceive, the more complete our understanding. Within the tradition, devotees of the *avatars* or incarnations of Vishnu (especially Rama and Krishna), Shiva, or a goddess such as Kali or Durga, are tolerated. Likewise, six systems of Indian philosophy (*darshanas*) are accepted as orthodox, including the influential perspectives of Sankhya, Yoga, and Vedanta.

In the Hindu tradition, religious seekers start with whatever path matches their sensibility and is within reach by focusing their devotion on a chosen deity (*ishta-devata*). It is not so much the path that matters, but the goal—freedom or release from karma (action and its consequences) and from samsara (the cycle of birth, death and rebirth). Hindus often describe this ultimate destiny as God-realization or union with God.

Swami Vivekananda

Swami Vivekananda was Ramakrishna's greatest disciple and founded the Ramakrishna Math and Ramakrishna Mission in India, as well as the Vedanta Society in the West. (Since Ramakrishna, in my view, was a pluralist, I discuss him later in the chapter.) As the first Hindu swami to visit America, Vivekananda introduced the Indian philosophies of Vedanta and Yoga to the West and helped bring Hinduism into the status of a major world religion. Best known for his charismatic speech at the Parliament of World Religions held in Chicago in 1893, which helped establish the widespread impression that Hinduism's attitude to other religions is inclusive, hospitable, syncretistic, and above all, tolerant, he quoted from a hymn recalled from his earliest childhood, one which is repeated every day by millions in India—"As different streams having their sources in the different places all mingle their water in the sea, O Lord, the different paths which men take through different tendencies, various though they appear, crooked or straight, all lead to Thee."[10] In his talk, Vivekananda lamented "the sectarianism, bigotry, and fanaticism that have long afflicted our beautiful earth, filling it with violence, often drenching it in human blood, destroying civilization, and sending whole nations into despair." He passionately expressed the hope that the convention might be "the death-knell of all fanaticism, of all persecutions with the sword or the pen, and of all uncharitable feelings of persons wending their way to the same goal." He voiced the spirit of the assembly and gained widespread attention in the press. The *New York Herald* described Vivekananda as "undoubtedly the greatest figure in the Parliament of World Religions. After hearing him we feel how foolish it is to send the missionaries to this learned nation."[11] Though sectarianism and fanaticism have persisted since the time of the Parliament, I believe Vivekananda's signature speech initiated a new era in which religious spokespersons henceforth responded to the challenge of pluralism.

Vivekananda described the essence of Hinduism as Vedanta, the contemplative teachings expressed in the Vedas. The word *Vedanta* literally means "the end of the Veda," and it also refers to the texts called the Upanishads that express the deepest meanings contained in the Vedas. While other components of the Vedas comprise hymns and ritual elements, the Upanishads are introspective inquiries and dialogues between teachers and students that disclose the true nature of reality. These teachings convey the discovery of an all-pervading principle, Brahman, present in the cave of the human heart. The core teachings are summarized in *mahavakyas*, or great sayings, such as *tat tvam asi*, which means "That Thou Art." In other words, the inmost soul of a person, the Atman or Self, is identical in nature with Brahman, the universal spirit pervading all things. There are several schools that interpret the Vedanta, including the non-dual or Advaita school that regards Brahman as an impersonal or non-theistic all-pervading principle, as well as theistic schools that are dualistic in the sense that they regard God as personal and somewhat distinct from the human soul. Vivekananda is identified with the perspective of Advaita, a viewpoint that shaped his specific response to pluralism both within Hinduism and other religions.

Vivekananda's affirmation that all religions are true is nuanced and contains a number of considerations:

- First, he teaches that every religion has a soul, its unique feature, a difference that is not contradictory but supplementary—"Each religion, as it were, takes up one part of the great universal truth and spends its whole force embodying and typifying that part of the great truth. It is therefore addition and not exclusion."[12] The special feature, or soul, of Hinduism is spirituality—Hindus think religion begins when you have realized something about the nature of reality through direct experience.

- Second, Vivekananda expresses the Hindu view that human beings do not travel from untruth to truth, but from lesser truth to higher truth.[13]

- Third, he stresses that there are different temperaments and types of mind. One person may be a rationalist; another, artistic; a third, devotional; while another is philosophic and perhaps critical of the other types. Each has a place in the world; all these types are necessary. Consequently, it would be impossible for any one of the world religions to convert the followers of the others. For this reason, Vivekananda affirms, "Our watchword, then, will be acceptance and not exclusion."[14] In soaring language, he declares, "I accept all religions that were in the past and worship with them all; I worship God with every one of them, in whatever form they worship Him."[15] He proclaims that he will go to the mosque, enter the Christians' church or Buddhists' temple, go into the forest, and sit in meditation with the Hindu who seeks to see the light that enlightens the heart of everyone. Also, he affirms, he will keep his heart open to religions that may come in the future.[16]

Vivekananda believes there are innumerable types of human beings, which he classifies into four groups according to their nature: active, devotional, philosophic, and mystic. The paths of spiritual endeavor for each of these are called *karma yoga*, *bhakti yoga*, *jnana yoga*, and *raja yoga*. Here he reiterates the paths extolled in the *Bhagavad Gita*, where Krishna validates each one in his dialogue with Arjuna, though thus far in human history, many people consider these paths to be either opposites or exclusive.

Vivekananda's aim is to propagate a religion that is equally philosophical, emotional, mystical, and conducive to action, and thus equally acceptable to all minds, a combination approaching a universal religion.[17] He considers anyone having only one or two of these elements of character "one-sided" and feels the world is filled with such one-sided persons. "To become harmoniously balanced in all four directions is my ideal of religion," he writes. "And this religion is attained by what we, in India, call Yoga or communion. To the worker, it is union between men and the whole of humanity; to the mystic, between his lower and Higher Self; to the lover, between himself and the God of love; and to the philosopher it is union with *all* existence."[18] All these yogas, Vivekananda stresses, are meant not merely for intellectual assent. Religion, he insists, is *realization*—not talk, not doctrine, not theories. "It is the whole soul becoming changed into what it believes."[19]

The preceding discussion makes clear the sense in which Vivekananda affirms that all religions are true—each has its own distinctive emphasis; each moves toward greater truth; each is suitable for a certain type of person. His response to religious pluralism is evolutionary because it is characterized not only by *types* of people, but also by *stages* of development. He believes that religions, particularly with regard to ideas of God and the soul, have evolved throughout history. Among the ancient Jews, for example, each tribe fought for the truth and supremacy of its own god until the fighting gods disappeared and were replaced by a monotheistic God, omnipotent and omniscient—the one Lord of the universe. This God is an extra-cosmic Being, dwelling in heaven and grossly anthropomorphic, an idea that gradually develops into an immanent conception of God, no longer far away in heaven but within the soul of humans. Vivekananda observes that these two stages of monotheism are expressed in Jesus' teachings. When Jesus uses the phrase "Our Father, who art in Heaven" or "the Kingdom of Heaven," God and humanity seem to exist in separation—God in heaven, humanity on earth. But Jesus also teaches that "the Kingdom of Heaven is within you," stressing immanence. Vivekananda notes that these two stages, within the same religion, are not contradictory when they are understood to refer to two stages of spiritual development. In their spiritual infancy, humans can understand a thing as real only when it is outside of them, as something concrete; God essentially can be real only as an external power. In the second view, humanity has learned to look at God as immanent.

Vivekananda explains that religion also undergoes a third stage of development when immanence is understood more deeply. Instead of observing a covenant or obeying certain laws and rituals, religion becomes a matter of Self-realization, thereby evolving into practical steps for realizing God in the soul. The steps to which he refers are the yogas, the means of realization; Self-realization refers to the unity of the soul with God. He believes these stages of development are present in all religions; yet, while they are clearly recognized in some, as in Vedanta, in others they are not elucidated because orthodoxy stifles everything that is not congenial to it.[20]

Monotheism, for Vivekananda, is the highest development found in other religions, but it does not satisfy Vedanta. A monotheistic God is the final result of a quest for finding the cause of the world outside. The Vedantins turn the quest inward and discover the Atman, the Self, the universal soul, teaching that humans are not going from error to truth, but from lower truth to higher truth. The highest truth for Vedanta is the discovery of the unity of all existence. Vedanta extols all religions as different approaches to discovering this ultimate truth.[21]

While this inclusivist view implies that Vedanta presents the highest truth while other religions are still moving toward this goal, Vivekananda acknowledges that Vedanta was never practiced on a large scale since its conception of God is difficult for many persons to accept. Most people, in his view, want a monarchal God sitting on a throne, entirely apart, to be feared and propitiated. Here another aspect of Vivekananda's inclusivist response to pluralism emerges. He believes that if Vedanta—the conscious knowledge that all is one Spirit—were to spread, all of humanity would become spiritual. But he recognizes that this development is not likely to come for a long time because people are still attached to the old superstitions from their national and communal religions. Also, people must be led to it gradually through worship, prayer, and other prevalent religious practices that serve as valued "Kindergartens of religion."[22]

Vivekananda's speeches and writings show that he genuinely values the world's religions. As he affirms, "It is my belief that religious thought is in man's very constitution, so much so that it is impossible for him to give up religion until he can give up his body and mind, until he can give up thought and life."[23]

He passionately believes that religion provides the discovery of the unity of existence and accords humanity eternal life, that is, awareness of the birthless and deathless nature of the Self. Furthermore, he believes, it has enabled humanity to mature to its present condition and, in due course, will transform the human animal into a god. Religion does not bring happiness based on the gratification of the senses; it brings wisdom (*jnana*), the ultimate goal of life, and with such knowledge comes bliss that far outshines the ordinary pleasures of the world.[24]

Sarvepalli Radhakrishnan

Sarvepalli Radhakrishnan, a scholar of comparative religion and one of India's most influential twentieth-century philosophers and exponents of modern Hinduism, built a bridge between the East and the West by showing that the philosophical systems of each tradition were comprehensible within the terms of the other. Like Vivekananda, he identifies with the perspective of Advaita Vedanta and expresses a response to religious pluralism based on the tolerance he believes is inherent in the Hindu view of life. Like other modern Hindu religious thinkers, he believes in the essential unity of Hinduism. "Hinduism is not to be dismissed as a mere flow and strife of opinions, for it represents a steady growth of insight, since every form of Hinduism and every stage of its growth is related to the common background of the Vedanta."[25]

Radhakrishnan insists that religious experience is the core or essence of all religions and, while fixed intellectual beliefs split one religion off from another, Hinduism sets no such limits. Radhakrishnan believes that religion confers insight into the nature of reality, grounded in the direct experience of reality; creeds and doctrines have only instrumental value and must not be accorded finality; and a transcendental unity lies behind the world's diverse traditions.[26] The purpose of philosophy, in his view, is to articulate this vision for the practical purpose of solving the problems that spring from the conflict of cultures. Like other Vedantins, Radhakrishnan affirms that human beings differ and require a variety of paths to reach the same goal, and that the genius of Hinduism is its affirmation of unity through diversity.[27]

Deeply concerned with the relationships between religions, Radhakrishnan believes that religions change, reform themselves, and evolve through the ongoing reinterpretation of tradition. Accordingly, Hinduism may be described as a constant striving after truth. The Hindu contribution to the modern challenge of religious pluralism is to encourage an inquiring spirit and a devotion to truth that is larger than any individual tradition.[28] Religious life needs to be a cooperative enterprise that binds different traditions and perspectives together with the aim of obtaining a clearer vision of reality, the religion of the spirit—a "universal religion of which the historical faiths are but branches."[29] He insists we must recognize the partial and defective character of our isolated traditions and seek their source in the generic tradition from which they have all sprung. He points to the mystics as the models we should emulate:

> Whatever religions they may profess, the mystics are spiritual kinsmen. While the different religions in their historical forms bind us to limited groups and militate against the development of loyalty to the world community, the mystics have always stood for the fellowship of humanity. They transcend the tyranny of names and rivalry of creeds as well as the conflict of races and the strife of nations.[30]

Radhakrishnan believes that Hinduism is the most tolerant of religions and that it provides the best approach to religious pluralism, a claim that needs some qualification. Sometimes he describes tolerance in a manner that suggests an unqualified acceptance of other religious positions. Radhakrishnan writes:

> Hinduism does not distinguish ideas of God as true and false, adopting one particular idea as the standard for the whole human race. It accepts the obvious fact that mankind seeks its goal of God at various levels and in various directions, and feels sympathy with every stage of the search. The same God expresses itself at one stage as power, at another as personality, at a third as all-comprehensive spirit, just as the same forces which put forth the green leaves also cause the crimson flowers to grow. We do not say that the crimson flowers are all the truth and the green leaves are false.[31]

This implies a positive attitude toward accepting what is true, best, or valuable in other religions: "The positive side is sensitiveness to truth wherever it is found, an appreciation of the values found in other religions, a creative assimilation of the elements of truth and a consequent enrichment of our own beliefs."[32]

Radhakrishnan qualifies his concept of tolerance by indicating that some religious views are more adequate than others. As an Advaita Vedantin, he regards the highest understanding to be the non-dual realization of the identity of the Self with the formless and impersonal Brahman. Within Hinduism he accepts all religious positions, but he arranges them in a hierarchy indicating various degrees of significance: "Hinduism insists on working steadily upwards and improving our knowledge of God . . . The worshippers of the Absolute are the highest in rank; second to them are the worshippers of the personal God; then come the worshippers of the incarnations like Rama, Krishna, Buddha; below them are those who worship ancestors, deities and sages, and lowest of all are the worshippers of petty forces and spirits."[33] The same ranking or hierarchy applies to other religions, thus theistic religions such as Judaism, Christianity, and Islam are less adequate apprehensions of ultimate reality than Advaita Vedanta.

Sri Aurobindo

Sri Aurobindo, a twentieth-century Indian yogi, guru, and poet, developed an original vision of Vedantic philosophy and forms of yoga based on his yogic experiences. As a youth, he was sent by his father to Britain to receive an English education and upbringing free of any Indian influences. He learned Greek and Latin; won a scholarship to attend King's College at Cambridge University where he studied Western classical literature; and subsequently returned to India to join the Indian movement for freedom from British rule, becoming one of its most important leaders before being jailed for his activities. While in prison, he had the first of several mystical experiences that changed the course of his life. After his release, he moved to Pondicherry in South India and established an ashram where he lived for the remainder of his life. His writings synthesize Eastern and Western philosophy, religion, literature, and psychology. He was the first Indian to create a major literary corpus in English. The thirty volumes of his collected works include philosophy, poetry, and plays; translations and commentaries on the Vedas, Upanishads, and *Bhagavad Gita*; and political and social commentary.

Through his practice of yoga, he had four major realizations that serve as the basis for his philosophy and the practices he describes as Integral Yoga.

- First, after consulting a yogi, Aurobindo meditated with him for three days and was instructed to make a supreme effort to empty his mind completely in order that the divine could enter and take possession. A supreme calm descended upon him, the state of awareness called *nirvikalpa samadhi*, the formless experience of the divine generally regarded as the completion of the spiritual quest. The powerful experience made him see the world as a cinematographic play of vacant forms in the impersonal universality of the Absolute Brahman. This vision of reality accords with Advaita Vedanta, but was contrary to his own ideas. Aurobindo viewed this experience, also called nirvana, as the negative side of the realization of God. In nirvana, the ordinary sensory and rational experience of the world is blown out like a candle; on that level of consciousness, there is a void. Aurobindo regards this to be a valid experience, but sees it as only the beginning of the discovery of the spiritual world and the complete truth about Being. The stilling of the lower level of consciousness is but the prerequisite for the activation of higher levels.[34]

- His second realization occurred during the year he was imprisoned for his alleged role in revolutionary activities in India's independence movement. While in prison, he spent most of his time in meditation, read the Upanishads and the *Bhagavad Gita*, and practiced yoga per the instructions he found in the texts. He comments on the impact of this practice:

  > I had many doubts before. I was brought up in England amongst foreign ideas and an atmosphere entirely foreign. About many things in Hinduism I had once been inclined to believe that they were imaginations, that there was much of dream in it, much that was delusion and Maya. But now, day after day, I realised in the mind, I realised in the heart, I realised in the body the truth of the Hindu religion. They became living experiences to me, and things were opened to me which no material science could explain.[35]

The most profound experience during this year was his vision of Sri Krishna as the all-pervading Lord of creation, which he describes in a speech after his release:

> I looked at the jail that secluded me from men and it was no longer by its high walls that I was imprisoned; no, it was Vasudeva who surrounded me. I walked under the branches of the tree in front of my cell, but it was not the tree, I knew it was Vasudeva, it was Sri Krishna whom I saw standing there and holding over me His shade. I looked at the bars of my cell, the very grating that did duty for a door, and again I saw Vasudeva. It was Narayana who was guarding and standing sentry over me. [Vasudeva and Narayana are other names for Krishna.] As I lay on the coarse blankets that were given me for a couch, I felt the arms of Sri Krishna around me, the arms of my Friend and Lover. This was the first use of the deeper vision He gave me. I looked at the prisoners in jail, the thieves, the murderers, the swindlers, and as I looked at them, I saw Vasudeva, it was Narayana whom I found in those darkened souls and misused bodies.[36]

This second realization, a vision of the personal God, is no longer the unutterable void of nirvana or the formless Brahman, but the living Lord of creation. While in jail, Aurobindo had intimations of higher planes beyond the conscious mind, above even the highest level attained by traditional yoga. Seeking to realize those "overhead planes" and eventually bring down the power of a superior consciousness to transform the lower levels of ordinary mind, life, and matter into fit instruments of divine action, he withdrew from the active political life of Bengal and moved to the French territory of Pondicherry in South India. He dedicated himself entirely to the spiritual quest, conscious of his mission not to India alone but the whole world, and of his work's significance for the future of humanity.[37]

• The third great realization is a synthesis of the two preceding, that of the formless absolute and the vision of the all-pervading Lord—simultaneously static and dynamic, characterized by silence and expression, emptiness and creativity. It is the foundation for Aurobindo's unique distinction between the "higher, or divine Maya" and the "Lower, or undivine, Maya," which is one of his major contributions to the history of Indian philosophy and spirituality.[38] In practical terms, this realization enabled him to behold the dark levels of the unconscious as well as the planes transcending ordinary consciousness. There are several layers below rational consciousness: body consciousness, by which the organs, tissues, and cells are organized, each knowing what to choose, receive, or reject; physical subconsciousness, a vestige from our long evolutionary past; and further below is the vast inorganic realm in which life itself is embedded, but which appears as its opposite, as that which life and the values of life cannot penetrate. At the lowest layer, there is no meaning, only inexorable law, a realm the Vedic rishis speak of as "the infinite rock." Aurobindo calls it the *Inconscient*, and experiences it as a blind rejection of life's upward thrust. The aim of Aurobindo's yoga in this context is to transmute the negativities of every level of our being, down to the very bottom of existence. Moral evils, mental afflictions, physical diseases, obstacles inherent in matter—all must receive the transforming light descending from above and be brought into harmony. In this non-dual vision, supreme, divine consciousness inheres in the very heart of matter. Spirit is not literally "above"; it is here in all things.[39]

• Aurobindo's fourth realization is the crowning experience of his sadhana. Mirra Alfassa, a French woman later known simply as The Mother, became the spiritual collaborator to whom he turned over the administration of his ashram. He then withdrew into seclusion to focus on the effort of transforming the lower levels of being by the descent of the higher planes of consciousness. He became aware of planes of consciousness above the ordinary mind, which he names Higher Mind, Illumined Mind, Intuitive Mind, and Overmind. To him these are not ways of knowing, but realms of being. When a person ascends to one of them, its power descends into him.[40] Important extensions of consciousness take place in all the levels above the ordinary mind, but the ascent to the Overmind is particularly transformative, as the centralizing, individual ego-sense expands to a cosmic perspective. Beatrice Bruteau summarizes the implications: "In the Overmind one can know through any 'point of view' as readily as through any other, and one's concern likewise is as much for any other being as one's own self. The sense of selfhood is itself expanded; one 'identifies' with every other being."[41]

Each ascending stage of consciousness brings about an integrating transformation in the yogi and a closer feeling of unity with the human community. As one's spiritual practice unfolds, one experiences an increasing sense of peace, light, and unity within oneself, of being in harmony with others; one feels more awake, clear, and in touch with reality and in communion with the divine. Nevertheless, the lower levels of our nature resist the transformation and cling to their fixed habits. Aurobindo's Integral Yoga is designed to gradually transform these fixations so that evolution may advance. The key to the transformation entails bringing down into the lower planes of being the power of the original creative consciousness, which is unitive by nature. A truly integral transformation must come from the original unity itself, a unity that precedes and grounds all possible diversity. Aurobindo calls this highest level of reality the Supermind or supramental consciousness. On all levels of the mind, up to and including the Overmind, whatever unity is present presupposes diversity, whereas on the level of the supramental, diversity presupposes unity. This is why the realization of the Supermind is effective through all the layers of being, down to the least particle of matter, and can bring to pass the transformation of the whole mental, vital, and material world into a medium of expression of the divine spirit. This transformation is the unique feature of his Integral Yoga and the heart of his philosophy.[42] It is a grand and innovative vision within the context of yoga spirituality. It has become a primary source for integral philosophy in the West and has deeply informed my own spirituality.

Like other modern Indian religious thinkers, Aurobindo asserts that the essence of religion is experience, not doctrines, creeds, or practices. While he regards most religions as systems of belief, Hinduism, in his view, though having a variety of doctrinal traditions, reflects a unity that is more experiential. As we have seen, the essential religious experience for many Hindu teachers is of the Absolute or Brahman. In Aurobindo's rendering of Vedanta, Brahman is not only Being, but also Being manifesting as Becoming. With regard to Being, he argues that religions must recognize that ultimate reality is the true Self. In the language of the Upanishads, this is the recognition that the Self, or atman, is Brahman. Aurobindo believes that ignorance causes religions to suppose that an extracosmic deity has created a world outside and apart from its own existence.[43] With regard to Becoming, he believes that religions must recognize that ultimate reality has become, through involution, the phenomenal world, thereby conferring upon it ultimate significance. He criticizes traditional religions, including Buddhism and Advaita Vedanta, for their world-denying other-worldliness. The Upanishads, in his view, affirm the One and the Many, God and the world. Buddhism and Advaita Vedanta, by contrast, view the world as a place from which to escape rather than as a manifestation of the divine.

Aurobindo criticizes Mayavada, or Illusionism, espoused by the great Indian philosopher Shankara of the Advaita or non-dual school of Vedantic philosophy. This view teaches that Brahman alone is real and the world is *maya*, an appearance or illusion. Aurobindo's philosophy, *Purnadvaita* or Integral Non-dualism (from *purna*, meaning "full" or "complete," and *advaita*, meaning "non-dual"), an alternative to the Advaita Vedanta of Shankara, affirms the reality and value of the world. Aurobindo argues that the concept of cosmic illusion is a product of the ordinary level of the mind, concluding that Shankara and the Illusionists grasp only a partial truth by affirming only the reality of the One. His mystical or supramental experiences disclose the integral truth that apprehends both the One and the many (the phenomenal world) as Real. Contained within this philosophy is his theory of the three poises, or modes of Brahman. If the supreme Reality is both "One without a second," and yet "all this" (the world of form), then Brahman must be both transcendent and immanent, a view expressed in the Upanishads. But Aurobindo holds that the immanence has two aspects—Brahman is immanent not only in a cosmic sense, but in an individual sense, too.[44] The affirmation that Brahman is an individual accords great importance to the principle of individuation, the process by which each person becomes a unique expression of the divine through their personality and embodied existence.

Aurobindo's view of the Absolute as Becoming not only affirms the reality of the world, but also provides the basis for its transformation. The task of the integral yogi is to elevate the world's consciousness by bringing down higher levels of consciousness to the lower levels. Put differently, the purpose of spiritual practice is to embody or incarnate Spirit into matter. All of life is yoga, in Aurobindo's vision; nature itself expresses yoga, albeit unconsciously. Human beings, by contrast, undertake yoga consciously through sadhana, or spiritual practice, that engages all levels of our being (physical, vital, mental). Confident that his yoga can perfect the world in this way, Aurobindo criticizes religions for their failures. In his view, all religious and secular attempts to transform the world have failed. Moreover, he believes that religions have often interfered with the natural, evolutionary movement of the Spirit.

Aurobindo sees that religions do not recognize the relative and partial nature of their beliefs and practices. As a consequence, they take their partial truths and non-essential elements to be universal. This, then, leads to endless confrontations between religion and science, religion and ethics, and the disagreements between one religion and another. In his book, *The Human Cycle*, he calls the emphasis upon partial truths "religionism" and distinguishes this from true religion. True religion seeks what is beyond the intellect and is illumined by the higher light and law of Spirit, whereas religionism entrenches itself in the narrow and pietistic exaltation of exclusive dogmas, rigid moral codes, and rigid social systems.[45]

Religions tend to impose their non-essential or partial truths upon others. In so doing, they fail to recognize a variety of movements vital to the process of the spiritual evolution of humanity. He writes, "The ambition of a particular religious belief and form to universalize and impose itself is contrary to the variety of human nature and to at least one essential character of the Spirit,"[46] which is the Spirit's principle of unity in diversity that allows individuals to grow and develop according to their natures.

An even more critical assessment of religion is expressed by The Mother, Aurobindo's spiritual collaborator. In her view, religions are invariably distinguished by their exclusivism, an attitude natural to the religious mind and fundamental to its very existence. She regards religions as hindrances from which spiritual practitioners must be freed. Though she might have encouraged those outside the Ashram who held a religion to continue in it, to those inside the Ashram she expressed her judgment directly—religions are based on ignorance and imposed on people through fear.[47] From the standpoint of his evolutionary worldview, Aurobindo does not believe that various religions continue to hold much significance. He envisions the emergence of "a religion of humanity" grounded in spiritual experience, rather than a universal religious system based on conceptual doctrines:

> A religion of humanity means the growing realization that there is a secret Spirit, a divine Reality, in which we are all one, that humanity is its highest present vehicle on earth, that the human race and the human being are the means by which it will progressively reveal itself here. It implies a growing attempt to live out this knowledge and bring about a kingdom of this divine Spirit upon earth. By its growth within us oneness with our fellow-men will become the leading principle of all our life, not merely a principle of

co-operation but a deeper brotherhood, a real and an inner sense of unity and equality and a common life. There must be a realization by the individual that only in the life of his fellow-men is his own life complete. There must be the realization by the race that only on the free and full life of the individual can its own perfection and permanent happiness be founded. There must be too a discipline and a way of salvation in accordance with this religion, that is to say, a means by which it can be developed by each man within himself, so that it may be developed in the life of the race.[48]

Although Aurobindo believed there would be no need to actively promote this religion, his movement may be understood as a means for doing just that. His writings and those of The Mother have been published in a variety of popular and library editions. Ashrams, established throughout India and around the world, promote their transformative vision of the world. To support this goal, The Mother founded an international city called Auroville as "a center of accelerated evolution," designed to raise the consciousness of all the earth in accordance with Aurobindo's vision. "Auroville is for those who live a life essentially divine but who renounce all religions whether they be ancient, modern, new or future."[49]

This vision for the evolution of the Spirit is the basis for the ashram's attitude toward other religious traditions. Religions are seen as stages in the evolution of human experience that have become problematic by egoistically over-emphasizing partial truths and non-essential elements. The process of upholding integral truth, however, involves the integration of the essentials of other religious worldviews into Integral Yoga, thereby affirming all true insights. Beyond this, one need not worry about the ultimate fate of these separate religions. Religion has evolved through stages in the past and will continue to evolve in the future. The Mother describes this indifference toward other religions as follows: "A benevolent goodwill towards all worshippers. An enlightened indifference towards all religions. All religions are approximations of the one sole Truth that is far above them."[50]

Integral Yoga's response to pluralism is a form of inclusivism in which the partial truths of religions are integrated into a broader and deeper vision of the spiritual evolution unfolding within them. In this sense, Integral Yoga absorbs what it considers to be valid in religions while transcending their partiality and limitations. The task of the integral yogi is to promote the progress of the divine evolution as envisioned in the spiritual realizations of Aurobindo and The Mother.[51] In this great evolutionary process of Spirit's Becoming, religions are temporary or provisional agencies that contribute to that work.

Hindu inclusivism bears some similarity to Karl Rahner's doctrine of anonymous Christians as described in Chapter 3. Just as Rahner makes Hindus, Buddhists, and others into anonymous Christians, Vivekananda and Radhakrishnan incorporate or assimilate the adherents of other religions into their soteriological scheme. All religions are affirmed to be true and good and lead to the same goal; they are a means for eventually attaining the realization of the non-dual experience of the Absolute, the realization that ultimate reality (Brahman) is identical with one's true self (atman). Thus, other religions are true and good because they contain, at least implicitly, the truth of Advaita Vedanta.

Vivekananda and Radhakrishnan express an essentialist interpretation of religion by presupposing that a transcendental unity underlies the different forms of Hinduism as well as all other religions. That essence is the truth contained in the core teachings of Vedanta. On this basis, Advaita Vedantins posit a hierarchy of religions: all religions lead to the same goal, but some religious paths are truer and more efficacious than others. Other experiences of the divine, such as theistic experiences of a personal God, are less true or less complete. Tolerance consists of accepting or affirming other religious paths by reinterpreting them within the larger perspective of Advaita Vedanta.

Aurobindo and The Mother valued religions' importance during prior phases of human history, but viewed them as hindrances to the future evolution of humanity, suggesting that religions are, in effect, precursors to a yogic spirituality that goes beyond religion. While there are, in fact, forms of spirituality that are not identified with or contained by religious traditions, they dismiss the abiding value of religions as the efficacious sources of faith, ethics, and spiritual practice.

I believe there may well be forms of spirituality that are more effective than traditional religions, and these forms may someday proliferate, but in the foreseeable future religions will continue to play an important role in supporting our development from egocentric and ethnocentric to more inclusive and expansive modes of being in the world. These limitations notwithstanding, Hindu inclusivism has been an exemplary model for promoting more positive relationships between religions in the contemporary world.

Hindu pluralism

An unequivocally pluralist response to religions accepts all traditions as valid and complete on their own terms. Sri Ramakrishna and Mohandas Gandhi are, for me, the most influential and inspiring exemplars of Hindu pluralism.

Sri Ramakrishna

Sri Ramakrishna Paramahansa, a great nineteenth-century mystic born in rural Bengal, shared his life experiences and teachings, including his ecstatic meditations and visions of Hindu gods and goddesses, in *The Gospel of Sri Ramakrishna*. His life was an extraordinary, unparalleled embodiment of inter-spirituality—the capacity to directly engage in the spirituality of multiple traditions. He undertook spiritual practices that allowed him to experience the divine within the contexts of Christian and Muslim worship and Buddhist meditation. I regard Ramakrishna to be the figure who best exemplifies the Hindu response to religious pluralism, as expressed in the slogan "many paths, one goal."

As a young priest at the Kali Temple in Dakshineswar, Ramakrishna yearned for a living vision of the Mother of the Universe. As his love for God deepened, he spent hours singing devotional songs to Her and felt the pangs of childhood separation. His deep longing is described in his first vision of the Mother:

> I felt as if my heart were being squeezed like a wet towel. I was overpowered with a great restlessness and a fear that it might not be my lot to realize Her in this life. I could not bear the separation from Her any longer. Life seemed not to be worth living. Suddenly my glance fell upon the sword that was kept in the Mother's temple. I determined to put an end to my life. When I jumped up like a madman and seized it, suddenly the blessed Mother revealed Herself. The buildings with their different parts, the temple, and everything else vanished from my sight, leaving no trace whatsoever, and in their stead I saw a limitless, infinite, effulgent Ocean of Consciousness. As far as the eye could see, the shining billows were madly rushing at me from all sides with a terrific noise, to swallow me up! I was panting for breath. I was caught in the rush and collapsed, unconscious. What was happening in the outside world I did not know; but within me there was a steady flow of uninterrupted bliss, altogether new, and I felt the presence of the Divine Mother.[52]

The vision foretold many experiences to come and served as a profound encounter with the numinous, characterized by Rudolf Otto as the *mysterium tremendum*—a tremendous mystery that evokes fascination and terror.[53] The experience was reminiscent of Arjuna's vision of Krishna's universal form in the *Bhagavad Gita*, though in Ramakrishna's case, the Absolute revealed itself as the divine feminine in the form of Kali.

As his spiritual mood deepened, Ramakrishna felt himself to be a child of the Divine Mother, learned to surrender himself completely to Her will, and let Her direct his actions. His visions became more intense and more intimate until he no longer had to meditate to behold Her. Even while maintaining consciousness of the outer world, he saw Her tangibly as the temple, trees, river, and people around him. He also began to feel an unquenchable desire to enjoy God in various ways, worshipping Him like a servant toward his master. He imitated the attitude of Hanuman, the monkey chieftain of the *Ramayana*, the ideal servant of Rama and the traditional model for this form of selfless devotion known as *seva* in Hindu tradition. Soon he was blessed with a vision of Sita, the divine consort of Rama, who entered his body and then disappeared with the words, "I bequeath to you my smile."[54]

Ramakrishna experienced other Hindu paths to God through the guidance of gurus, including a Brahmin woman from East Bengal who was adept in Tantric and Vaishnava methods of worship. Hindu tradition characterizes ultimate reality as *Chit* or Consciousness, *Sat* or Being, and *Ananda* or Bliss. A human being is identical with this Reality but, under the influence of *maya* or illusion, forgets one's true nature. The apparent world of subject and object is taken as real, an error that causes humans existential bondage and suffering. The goal of spiritual practice is the rediscovery of one's true identity with the divine reality. To achieve this goal, Vedanta prescribes an austere method of discrimination and renunciation. Tantra, by contrast, takes human desires and the material objects of the world into consideration and makes use of them in spiritual practice, combining philosophy with ritual, meditation with ceremony, and renunciation with enjoyment. Through prescribed mystical rites, the sense objects become spiritualized and sense attraction is transformed into a love of God. In this approach, outward renunciation is not necessary. Instead, the aim of Tantra is to sublimate *bhoga* or enjoyment into *yoga* or union with Consciousness. Accordingly, the world with all its manifestations is nothing but the *lila* or play of Shiva and Shakti.[55]

In the philosophy of Tantra, Shakti is the active creative energy in the universe whereas Shiva is the consciousness aspect of the Absolute. Shakti is as inseparable from Shiva as fire's power to burn is from fire itself. As the Creative Power, Shakti contains the universe in its womb and is therefore described as the Divine Mother. All women are Her symbols and the goddess Kali is one of Her forms. Meditation on Kali is a central spiritual practice of Tantra. Ramakrishna undertook the disciplines of Tantra and accepted the female tantrika as his guru. He practiced all disciplines of the sixty-four principle Tantra texts and quickly achieved the promised results. Soon the whole world and everything in it appeared to him as *lila*, the creative play of Shiva and Shakti, and everything, animate and inanimate, was pervaded with *Chit* (Consciousness) and with *Ananda* (Bliss). The most extraordinary experience during this period was the awakening of the *kundalini shakti*, the "Serpent Power," the dormant spiritual energy residing in the subtle body of a human being. He saw this power first sleeping at the base of the spinal column, then waking up and ascending through the six chakras, until it reached the *sahasrara*, the thousand-petaled lotus at the top of the head.[56] The union of kundalini shakti with Shiva in this location is the consummation of Tantric spiritual practice.

Another of Ramakrishna's experiences illustrates the attitude of Tantra towards Shakti, the divine feminine, and towards women. Ramakrishna and his wife, Sarada Devi, lived together at Dakshineswar, though their minds were said to soar above the worldly plane. A few months after Sarada Devi's arrival, Ramakrishna arranged for a special worship of Kali. *The Gospel of Sri Ramakrishna* describes the occasion in this way: "Instead of an image of the Deity, he placed on the seat of the living image, Sarada Devi herself. The worshipper and the worshipped went into deep *samadhi* and in the transcendental plane their souls were united. After several hours, Sri Ramakrishna came down again to the relative plane, sang a hymn to the Great Goddess, and surrendered at the feet of the living image himself, his rosary, and the fruit of his life-long *sadhana*. This is known in Tantra as the Shorashi Puja, the 'Adoration of Women.' "[57]

After completing the Tantric sadhana, Ramakrishna engaged in the practices of Vaishnavas, the worshippers of Vishnu, the "All-Pervading One," the supreme God in a personal form, like the avatars Rama and Krishna. Vaishnavism is a religion of *bhakti* or devotional love. According to this tradition, one cannot realize God by self-exertion alone, for the vision of God's grace is absolutely necessary; this grace is felt by the pure of heart. During these practices, Ramakrishna had a vision of

Ramlala, Rama in the form of the Divine Child.[58] He then sought union with Sri Krishna as the Beloved of the heart. The Vaishnava scriptures advise one to propitiate Radha and obtain her grace for this purpose. Within a short time he enjoyed a vision of her in which she appeared within his own body and then vanished. This experience was a precursor to his vision of the resplendent Krishna who appeared and merged with him. Ramakrishna completely forgot his own individuality and the world; he saw Krishna in himself and in the universe, attaining the goal of worship for those who seek to experience God as the Supreme Person.[59]

Despite the extent and grandeur of these experiences, Ramakrishna's practice of different Hindu disciplines was not yet complete. His next guru was Totapuri, a wandering monk whom he addressed as the Naked One. Totapuri embraced the path of total renunciation of earthly objects and attachments. He taught Ramakrishna the non-dualistic Vedanta philosophy that regards the formless Brahman to be Absolute and the final or highest goal of spiritual practice. The path of Vedantic discipline is the path of negation; all that is unreal is negated and renounced. It is the path of *jnana*, knowledge, the direct method of realizing the Absolute. Even the vision of a personal God is, from this perspective, as illusory as any other object. After the negation of everything relative, the aspirant merges in the One-without-a-Second, in the bliss of *nirvikalpa samadhi*, where the distinction between subject and object is dissolved. Duality is transcended; *maya* is left behind with all its changes and modifications. Totapuri practiced this austere discipline for forty years on the bank of the sacred Narmada River before realizing his identity with the Absolute. Seeing that Ramakrishna was prepared to be a student of Vedanta, Totapuri offered to initiate him into its mysteries. Ramakrishna agreed to the proposal, submitted to Totapuri's guidance, performed the rituals of renunciation, and received the teachings. Although it was difficult for him to go beyond the vision of the Divine Mother, Ramakrishna used his powerful concentration and discrimination to enter the formless depths of *samadhi*. He astonished Totapuri by remaining in this exalted state for three days and then finally came back to the relative plane.[60]

Ramakrishna later helped Totapuri experience the power of Kali. One night when Totapuri was suffering a severe attack of dysentery and could no longer concentrate on Brahman because he felt his body to be a great obstacle, he decided to drown himself in the Ganges. As he entered the river, he suddenly had a vision of the Divine Mother, beholding her presence everywhere and in everything. He understood that She was the body and the mind; She was pain and comfort; She was knowledge and ignorance; She was life and death. Without Her grace, he realized, no embodied being could go beyond Her realm, the relative world of form; one is not even free to die. In the morning, he went to the Kali temple with Ramakrishna and prostrated himself before the image of the Mother. Ramakrishna describes the significance of Totapuri's lessons:

> When I think of Him as active—creating, preserving, and destroying—I call Him Shakti or Maya or Prakriti, the Personal God. But the distinction

between them does not mean a difference. The Personal and the Impersonal are the same thing, like milk and its whiteness, the diamond and its luster, the snake and its wriggling motion. It is impossible to conceive of one without the other. The Divine Mother and Brahman are one.[61]

Through these experiences, Ramakrishna validated most of the paths and yogas practiced by Hindus, but he did not stop there. *The Gospel of Sri Ramakrishna* also describes his experiments with other religions. Under the guidance of a Muslim guru, he dressed and prayed like a Muslim, repeating the name of Allah. The gospel tells us that he forgot the Hindu gods and goddesses, even his beloved Kali, and stopped visiting temples. After three days, he had a vision of a radiant figure, possibly Mohammad, who approached him and "lost himself in Sri Ramakrishna." In this way, Ramakrishna discovered that "the river of Islam also led back to the Ocean of the Absolute."[62]

Eight years later, Sri Ramakrishna was seized by an irresistible desire to learn the truth of the Christian religion. He had become fascinated with the life and teachings of Jesus. One day while intently gazing at a painting of the Madonna and Child, he was overwhelmed with emotion. The figures in the picture were enlivened and rays of light emanating from them entered his soul. The effect, was stronger than the vision of Mohammad and initially distressed him. He cried out, "O Mother! What are You doing to me?"[63] But, then, we are told, he broke through the barriers of creed and religion as Christ possessed his soul. For three days he did not enter the Kali temple. On the fourth, he saw a person coming towards him with beautiful large eyes and a serene expression. As he faced this figure a voice arose from the depths of his soul: "Behold the Christ, who shed His heart's blood for the redemption of the world, who suffered a sea of anguish for love of men. It is He, the Master Yogi, who is in eternal union with God. It is Jesus, Love Incarnate."[64] As the Gospel tells it, "The Son of Man embraced the Son of the Divine Mother and merged into him. Sri Ramakrishna realized his identity with Christ, as he had already realized his identity with Kali, Rama, Hanuman, Radha, Krishna, Brahman, and Mohammad. Thus he experienced the truth that Christianity, too, was a path leading to God-Consciousness. Till the last moment of his life he believed that Christ was an Incarnation of God. But Christ, for him, was not the only Incarnation; there were others—Buddha, for instance, and Krishna."[65]

The Gospel of Sri Ramakrishna depicts him as popularizing the idea of "many paths, one goal," through metaphors drawn from everyday lives of Indian people. In one passage, he says, "God can be realized through all paths. It is like coming to Dakshineswar by carriage, by boat, by steamer or on foot. You have chosen the way according to your convenience and taste; but the destination is the same. Some of you have arrived earlier than others, but all have arrived."[66] The attitude this text expresses seems to be that one path is as good as another. "Opinions are but paths. Each religion is only a path leading to God, as rivers come from different directions and ultimately become one in the same ocean."[67] Ramakrishna explicitly opposes an exclusivist attitude and criticizes quarrelling between adherents of different religions. As he says, "They haven't the intelligence to understand that He who is called Krishna is also Shiva and the Primal Shakti, and is He, again, who is called Jesus and Allah. There is only one Rama and He has a thousand names. . . . Truth is one; only It is called by different names. All people are seeking the same Truth; the variance is due to climate, temperament, and name . . . Everyone is going towards God. They will all realize Him if they have sincerity and longing of heart."[68] Ramakrishna's words make clear the sense in which all religions are true. The essential ingredient, what matters most, is devotion or *bhakti*. The efficacy of a religious path depends on the heart of the person taking it—it is the inner attitude or feeling of the seeker that counts.

Mahatma Gandhi

Exerting nonviolent civil disobedience, Mahatma Gandhi led India to independence from British rule and inspired nonviolent civil rights and freedom movements across the world. His true greatness, however, rests in his inner conquests rather than his outer political victories. In his autobiography, he describes his "experiments with Truth" and the aim of his existence: "What I want to achieve—what I have been striving and pining to achieve these thirty years—is self-realization, to see God face to face, to attain *Moksha*. I live and move and have my being in pursuit of this goal. All that I do by way of speaking and writing, and all my ventures in the political field, are dedicated to this same end."[69] Regarding himself as a humble seeker of Truth and servant of humanity, he was essentially a man of religion; his eventful life was a spiritual pilgrimage.

Born into a Vaishnava family, Gandhi did not formulate religious views until adulthood. Searching for insights from many religious traditions, he gradually integrated influences from diverse sources. His mother was deeply religious, and her saintliness created a lasting impression on him. In their home, his father had frequent discussions with Jain monks, Muslims, and members of the Parsee faith to whom he always listened with interest and respect.

Although he learned to become tolerant of all religions, initially Gandhi leaned toward atheism.[70] After moving to London to study law, he became more acquainted with religion. There, British Theosophists introduced him to the *Bhagavad Gita* which he agreed to read with them, though he felt ashamed that he had never read it before. The text, he reported, "struck me as one of priceless worth," and he came to regard it "as the book *par excellence* for the knowledge of Truth."[71] At about the same time, he became friends with a Christian who gave him a copy of the New Testament which also left a deep and lasting impression, especially the Sermon on the Mount, going straight to his heart.[72]

Challenges from Christians and Muslims

During his years in South Africa, the challenge of religious pluralism became a pressing issue for Gandhi. Some of his closest friends who were fervent Christians applied great pressure on him to convert to Christianity; their arguments for the superiority of Christianity posed challenges he could not ignore. One Protestant friend invited him to a convention designed to inspire religious revival among all the devout Christian attendees, hoping the atmosphere would lead Gandhi to embrace Christianity. Gandhi reported listening with unbiased attention and informed his friend that he would embrace Christianity if he felt the call, since he had taught himself to follow the promptings of his inner voice.[73] Gandhi appreciated the devoutness of those who attended the convention, including the many who prayed for him, but did not find a compelling reason to change his religion.

Gandhi's thinking aligns with my own reasons for adopting a religion different from my inherited tradition. It was impossible for him to believe that he could go to heaven or attain salvation *only* if he became a Christian. Nor could he believe that Jesus was the only incarnate son of God. "If God could have sons, says Gandhi, all of us are his sons."[74] Likewise, if Jesus was like God, then all of us are like God and can experience God-realization. He could not accept the belief that only humans have souls. Nor could he accept the literal belief that Jesus redeemed the sins of the world by his death and by his blood, though he acknowledged there may be some metaphorical truth in this idea. As he explains, "His death on the Cross was a great example to the world, but that there was anything like a mysterious or miraculous virtue in it my heart could not accept."[75] He could accept Jesus as a divine teacher, but not as the most perfect man ever born; the lives of pious Christians did not offer him anything that the lives of individuals from other faith traditions had failed to provide. Thus, he could not regard Christianity as a perfect religion or the greatest of all religions.[76]

While Gandhi was unable to accept either Christianity or Hinduism as a perfect—or even as the greatest—religion, Hinduism's defects were clear to him and he strongly opposed many traditional aspects of the Hindu culture, such as animal sacrifices in the temple, child marriages, and untouchability. "Untouchability," he states, "is a soul-destroying sin" and castes "a social evil."[77] Within his ashram, people of all castes, colors, nationalities, and religions ate and worked together with his family and with him, all joining in equally to accomplish the manual labor traditionally assigned to the *sudras* (the lowest caste).

Muslim friends attempted to convert Gandhi, inducing him to study Islam during a period of his life that he describes in his autobiography as one of religious ferment. Seeking help regarding his questions about religion, he corresponded with Raychandbhai, a Jain mentor in India, whose in-depth answers struck a chord, as they clearly articulated ideas that had been vague in his own mind and were consistent with his own religious aspirations. Gandhi adopted the Jain view that religion, or *dharma*, is the process by which individual souls gradually free themselves from the bonds of matter, forged by attachment and ignorance, and eventually attain liberation (*moksha*) from karma and the cycle of rebirth called *samsara*.[78]

While seeking Raychandbhai's help to better understand Hinduism and religion in general, Gandhi contacted others to help him understand Christianity. The

Christian friends to whom he turned were largely evangelicals who interpreted the Bible in a fundamentalist manner, believing that humanity had fallen into sin and could only be saved by the atonement of Christ. According to their beliefs, faith in Christ was the only hope for salvation, and proof for these beliefs could be found in the Bible which constituted the unique and final revelation of God.

Gandhi also came to know Christians who interpreted the Bible differently, such as Edward Maitland, founder of the Esoteric Christian Union. Maitland believed that the sacred scriptures of the various religions were but the recurring historical revelations of a basic universal revelation. Consequently, he categorically rejected a fundamentalist and historical interpretation of the Bible. In his view, the Christian scriptures do not deal primarily with historic events and persons; their purpose is to exhibit and illustrate processes and principles that are purely spiritual, a view that led him to an interpretation of Christ unlike that of the evangelicals. For Maitland, Christ is the hidden and true man of the Spirit, the ideal of perfect humanity, an ideal that is equally attainable by all human beings.[79]

Deeply influenced by Maitland's views, many of which are similar to those of Raychandbhai, Gandhi came to believe that religion is the process by which individuals attain spiritualization. All people could attain the final perfection, he found, and he advised them to turn to the scriptures not for a literal understanding, but for imperfect attempts to clarify that process. Gandhi's understanding of Christianity was also influenced by Russian novelist Leo Tolstoy's writings, especially *The Kingdom of God is Within You*, a work that overwhelmed him and left a lifelong impression.[80] The influence Gandhi received from these sources gave him a firm foundation for his views on Hinduism and other religions and put to rest his anxiety about the claims of Christianity's alleged superiority.

Jain ideas in Gandhi's worldview

Gandhi integrated into his worldview and way of life many Jain ideas (shared by many Hindus and Buddhists): asceticism; compassion for all forms of life; the importance of vows for self-discipline; vegetarianism and fasting for self-purification; and *ahimsa*, or non-violence. He also embraced two other Jain doctrines that he considered to be consistent with Hindu tradition.

- The first is that of "the many-ness of reality" (*anekantavada*): the view that reality is so complex that propositions about it may be very different, even contradictory, depending on the observer's viewpoint.

- The second closely related idea is that all propositions present only partial views. Thus, all views should be qualified or prefaced by the phrase "from one point of view" (*syadvada*). This doctrine allows for the possibility of different or divergent statements being equally true since they depend on the viewpoint that serves as a context for the statement.[81]

As Gandhi observes:

> It has been my experience that I am always right from my point of view and often wrong from the point of view of honest critics. I know that we are both right from our respective points of view. And this knowledge saves me from attributing motives to my opponents or critics . . . It is this doctrine that has taught me to judge a Mussalman from his own standpoint and a Christian from his.[82]

Gandhi's pluralist views on religious pluralism

Although Gandhi did not create a theory regarding religious pluralism, he does express strong pluralist convictions that are scattered throughout many of his speeches and writings. Gathered here are five of his essential views in response to this challenging issue:

- First, Gandhi does not believe in the exclusive divinity of the Vedas and regards other scriptures, such as the Bible and Qur'an, as divinely inspired. Moreover, his belief in the Hindu scriptures does not require him to accept each verse as inspired; nor does he feel bound to any interpretation of the texts that is repugnant to his reason or moral sensibility.[83]

- Second, Gandhi believes that all religions are God-given and necessary for the people to whom they are revealed. He never anticipates a time when there is only one religion or no religion at all. No two persons, he observes, have the identical conception of God, therefore he feels it is likely that there will always be different religions to answer to different temperaments.[84] His favorite metaphor for religion affirms both its diversity and underlying unity—"Even as a tree has a single trunk, but many branches and leaves, so there is one true and perfect Religion, but it becomes many, as it passes through the human medium."[85] Imperfect people express the truth of religion as well as they can; then, other people equally imperfect interpret their words. Tolerance for others' views is thus a necessity; it does not mean indifference to one's own faith, but rather a more intelligent and purer love for it.

  Like other Hindus discussed in this chapter, Gandhi believes Hinduism is the most tolerant of religions. However, he came to feel that this claim implied the superiority of the Hindu religion. At his ashram he used the slogan "equality of religions," rather than "tolerance," which went beyond a mere respect for religions. Gandhi believes that true knowledge of religion breaks down barriers.[86] He also feels that the reverent study of other religions does not weaken one's own faith; rather, reading the scriptures of other faiths from the viewpoint of the faiths' followers reveals that, at the core, they are all one and need to help one another.[87]

- Third, Gandhi can be seen as a seeker of Truth, not one who claims to possess it. If we had attained the full vision of Truth, he observes, we would no longer be mere seekers but would become one with God. Religion, as we conceive it, is imperfect and always subject to a process of evolution. Reverence for other faiths need not blind us to their faults, though we need to be keenly aware of the defects of our own religion and strive to overcome them. Gandhi strongly believes that if we look at all religions with an equal eye, we will not hesitate to think it our duty to blend into our faith every acceptable feature of other faiths.[88] Religion, for Gandhi, is not the Hinduism that he personally prizes above other religions, but the religion that changes one's nature, which binds one to the truth within. God, he feels, must rule and transform the heart.[89]

• Fourth, Gandhi longs to see God face to face, but understands this in a very human way: "The immediate service of all human beings becomes a necessary part of the endeavor because the only way to find God is to see Him in His creation and be one with it. This can only be done by service to all."[90] In other words, Gandhi exemplifies the path of *karma yoga*, the path of selfless service. Gandhi was not given to ecstasies; he was too busy for that. Yet he is able to affirm, "I am surer of His existence than of the fact that you and I are sitting in this room."[91] Here he comes close to the perspective of *jnana yoga*, the path of wisdom that apprehends the non-dual experience of the Absolute. In another passage, he states: "Often in my progress I have had a faint glimpse of the Absolute Truth, God, and daily the conviction is growing upon me that He alone is real and all else is unreal. Let those, who wish, realize how the conviction has grown upon me; let them share my experiments and share also my conviction."[92] Furthermore, Gandhi's spirituality also includes the path of love, since, for him, truth is inseparable from love. As he explains, "When you find Truth as God, the only inevitable means is love, that is, non-violence, and since I believe that ultimately the means and the ends are convertible terms, I should not hesitate to say God is love."[93]

• Fifth, Gandhi repeatedly admits he has not yet attained the Truth or self-realization, but he claims to be making a ceaseless effort to find it; he knows the path of *sadhana*, or spiritual practice, and devotes his life to walking it. If all religions are but branches of one tree, what is the fundamental essence of all religions? Gandhi's answer distills the essence of his life experiences, including his encounters with various religious views: "After a study of those religions to the extent that was possible for me, I have come to the conclusion that, if it is proper and necessary to discover an underlying unity among all religions, a master-key is needed. That master-key is that of Truth and non-violence. When I unlock the chest of religion with this master-key, I do not find it difficult to discover its likeness with other religions."[94] Therein lies the essence of Gandhi's response to religious pluralism, the two principles that hold the promise for creating peace among the religions, and, thereby, peace in the world.

Truth and non-violence epitomize Gandhi's core Hindu beliefs. Each of us in our deepest nature is identical with the universal atman; all life (not only human beings, but all sentient beings) come from the One universal source, variously called God, or Allah, or Brahman. All life in its essence is one, and persons are striving consciously or unconsciously towards the realization of that identity. The political implication is that no one can be an irredeemable enemy. If all life is ultimately one and there is a divine element in every person, it follows that in injuring others we are injuring the whole of which we ourselves are a part.[95] These beliefs are the basis for Gandhi's unconquerable faith in the possibility of a better human future—if only we will trust the power of nonviolent openness to others and the deeper humanity and underlying divinity within us all. While such a future may seem impossible to many, Gandhi's great legacy is that his own life demonstrates how we, too, may embody the peace we long to experience in the world.[96]

Insights for integrative spirituality

Vivekananda's articulation of his views at the first Parliament of the World's Religions in 1893 is, I believe, the paradigmatic event that initiates a sea change in how people come to view the beliefs and practices of those from other faith traditions. The views of Vivekananda and other Hindus discussed in this chapter inspire countless people who have felt confined by Christian beliefs that seem constraining or untenable. My own faith journey is a case in point. In the preceding chapter, I disclosed that I left Christianity, my inherited tradition, for several reasons. I find myself unable to accept a worldview that presupposes the concept of sin, a fundamental separation from God or the Ground of Being, and the related notions of human guilt, divine judgment, and the need for redemption. I also find myself dissatisfied with the traditional Christology that asserts that Jesus is the only incarnation of God who thus performs a unique salvific role in human history. Christian pluralists express innovative perspectives that not only address many of my misgivings, but also help others grapple with the challenge of religious pluralism. I have incorporated many of their ideas into my thinking, but my own views and my spiritual identity are more deeply informed by the teachings and spiritual practices of Hindu traditions.

Exemplary Hindus offer many useful perspectives on religion that help us think more pluralistically about our global religious heritage:

- All religions are true in the sense that they lead to the same goal. Hindus describe that goal as Self-realization or as *moksha*. Self-realization means that a person recognizes her true nature to be the Atman or Self, which is identical to Brahman, the all-pervading Ground of Being, and which is expressed in the great saying of the Upanishads as "That thou art" (*tat tvam asi*). There is no separation or estrangement between humanity and divinity. *Moksha* refers to the experience of liberation or freedom from *maya*, the spell of the ego-personality. This can be articulated in more generic language, consistent with John Hick's philosophy described in the preceding chapter: All religions are authentic responses to the divine and fulfill a common transformative function, and each enables people to move from self-centeredness or egocentricity to a Reality-centeredness, a life centered in the Transcendent, the Real, or ultimate reality.

Hindu teachings maintain that religion confers insight into the nature of reality (*darshana*). Primacy is given to mystical or spiritual experience rather than to doctrine and ritual. The divine can be experienced as personal and immanent (*Saguna Brahman*) or as impersonal and beyond form (*Nirguna Brahman*). The personal aspect of the divine can take myriad forms, personified as gods and goddesses. Aurobindo's mystical experiences demonstrate that we need not rank the realization of the impersonal Brahman higher than the apprehension of the divine as personal. Being both personal and impersonal, Brahman may be experienced in three ways—as the transcendent, the immanent, and the individual.

Ramakrishna's ability to experience the divine is deeply inspiring in many ways. As the preeminent pioneer of inter-spirituality, he is a model for those who yearn to be nourished by multiple religious traditions. His vision of Christ is a striking example of this attitude. Like many other Hindus, he reveres Christ as one of the world's greatest illumined spiritual teachers. He sees Jesus as a master yogi, as love incarnate, a guru of the highest order, and a great liberator of humankind.

I have been deeply moved by Hindus like Ramakrishna who have written about Jesus, expressing profound insights into his teachings. In a way, I have returned to Christianity—finding myself able to embrace Christ's sublime teachings on love—by learning to see Jesus through Hindu eyes. My daily *puja*, or devotional practice, includes salutations to him as well as an invocation of his spirit of love to inspire my actions. In this way, I have come to regard Jesus as a spiritual ancestor and have integrated him into the pantheon of God-images that inspire my spiritual practice.

- Ramakrishna's veneration of Kali as the Divine Mother is a God-image that contrasts with the Christian image of God as Father. Although Roman Catholicism venerates Mary as the Blessed Virgin, the religious traditions of the West lack comprehensive appreciation of the divine feminine. Hinduism provides a rich alternative. No other living religious tradition displays such an ancient, continuous, and diverse history of goddess worship. Aurobindo's Integral Yoga, for example, emphasizes Shakti, the feminine creative aspect of Brahman, which is embodied in matter, in the evolutionary process, and as the energy that animates spiritual practice. Shakti is also central to other Hindu yogic traditions that have taken root in the West. The teachings and practices of each of these traditions have enabled many Westerners, including myself, to engage in a spirituality that is deeply inspired by the feminine aspects of divinity.

- Hinduism respects the fact that people have different natures and that the paths of spiritual aspirants must match the typology of the individual. The tradition acknowledges four temperaments: active, devotional, philosophical, and mystical; the corresponding paths are *karma yoga, bhakti yoga, jnana yoga,* and *raja yoga.* These paths can be combined as they are not exclusive. The *Bhagavad Gita,* one of the most influential of the Hindu scriptures, fully endorses each path. Vivekananda and Aurobindo encourage us to overcome one-sidedness and harmoniously integrate various aspects of our humanity, providing us with non-dualistic models of embodied spirituality that connect rather than dissociate spirit from matter. These inclusive and integral attitudes toward God-images and pathways to the divine exemplify Hinduism's extraordinary capacity to apprehend unity-in-diversity, an encompassing yet differentiated perspective that is often extended beyond its internal plurality and applied to other religions.

- Hinduism has a complex and nuanced theory of truth—our apprehensions of reality are partial in nature; each is a perspective, a point of view. For this reason, Hindu tradition affirms that different propositions about the nature of reality—even contradictory ones—may be true or partially true. This attitude engenders tolerance and the possibility of integrating other perspectives into our own. Consequently, Hindus do not tend to think of themselves as possessing the truth while others are in error. As Vivekananda says, human beings do not travel from untruth to truth but from lesser truth to higher truth. Gandhi, likewise, claims not to possess the truth but rather to have found the path to it through ceaseless striving.

- The Hindu attitude towards truth has relevance for how we may regard scriptures and the traditional forms of religion. The exemplars I have discussed do not insist that the Vedas are the only revealed scriptures or that there is only one way to interpret sacred texts. Vivekananda and Gandhi criticize many traditional aspects of Hindu culture and implement reforms that mitigate the defects they perceive. In so doing, they re-enact once more the vast recombinant powers of Hinduism to change and reinterpret tradition. Hinduism, however, like other religions, remains far from perfect, and its capacity to transform itself has limitations.

Vivekananda, Aurobindo, and Gandhi all agree on one point, though in differing ways and degrees—all believe that religion evolves and thus exhibits developmental stages. Vivekananda expresses the view that religion helps people develop morally; the lower stages of spirituality are preparation for more advanced stages that culminate in realization. Aurobindo and his collaborator, the Mother, look beyond traditional religion with a vision of where humankind and the earth are headed in the evolutionary process; they absorb and integrate what is valuable in religion into their form of yoga. Gandhi, by contrast, values religions as the essential means for transforming the human heart and ways of acting in the world. Religion can be embodied in our lives in the form of service to fellow human beings; it can also be the nonviolent means by which we overcome injustice in human society.

Advaita Vedanta has been criticized for differentiating between lower and higher forms of religion. I believe that while the critique is valid with regard to privileging the formless Brahman as the highest form of spiritual realization, most Vedantins genuinely respect and value the various forms of religion that all people, Hindus and non-Hindus alike, practice. I agree with Aurobindo, and with John Hick among Christian pluralists, that the Real or transcendent can assume a variety of personal and non-personal forms, and that we need not concern ourselves with which form is ultimate. In another respect, I believe that viewing religion in evolutionary or developmental terms is not only valuable but imperative. The point is not to rank one religion higher than another, but rather to differentiate the ways that individuals within any particular religion configure their faith.

The main criterion for differentiation pertains to the perspective one takes toward others. Religious persons who identify with and care only about other members of their group or community are insular and tribal. As faith matures and develops, it becomes less egocentric and ethnocentric until one's concern or care extends to everyone—even to all of life. This more expansive perspective or field of regard may be described as a cosmocentric vision of life, a worldview that embodies conjunctive and universalizing faith.

Notes

1 William T. DeBary, ed., *Sources of the Indian Tradition*, New York: Columbia University Press, 1958, 2:76.
2 Ibid., 40.
3 Ibid., 44–45.
4 Ibid., 47–50.
5 Robert D. Baird, "The Response of Swami Bhaktivedanta", in *Modern Responses to Religious Pluralism*, ed. Harold G. Coward. Albany: State University of New York Press, 1987, 106–07.
6 Quoted in Baird, 109.
7 Baird, 111–12.
8 Ibid., 122.
9 Ibid.
10 Swami Vivekananda, *The Complete Works of Swami Vivekananda*, 17th ed. Kolkata: Advaita Ashrama, 1986, 1:43.
11 Romain Rolland, *The Life of Vivekananda and the Universal Gospel*, trans. E. F. Malcolm-Smith. Kolkata: Advaita Ashram, 2009, 32.
12 Swami Tapasyananda, *The Philosophical and Religious Lectures of Swami Vivekananda*. Madras: Sri Ramakrishna Math, 1984, 28.
13 Ibid., 28–30.
14 Ibid., 32.
15 Ibid.
16 Ibid.
17 Ibid., 37–38.
18 Ibid., 38.
19 Ibid., 42.
20 Ibid., 48–49.
21 Ibid., 69–70.
22 Ibid., 182–83.
23 Ibid., 117.

24 Ibid., 118.
25 Sarvepalli Radhakrishnan, *The Hindu View of Life*. New York: Macmillan, 1973, 18.
26 Ibid., 13.
27 Ibid., 42–43.
28 Sarvepalli Radhakrishnan, *Eastern Religions and Western Thought*. London: Oxford University Press, 1969, 338.
29 Ibid., 347.
30 Ibid., viii–ix.
31 Radhakrishnan, *The Hindu View of Life*, 24.
32 Robert N. Minor, "Sarvepalli Radhakrishnan on the Nature of 'Hindu' Tolerance," *Journal of the American Academy of Religion* 50 (1982): 276.
33 Radhakrishnan, *The Hindu View of Life*, 24.
34 Beatrice Bruteau, *Worthy is the World: The Hindu Philosophy of Sri Aurobindo*. Rutherford, NJ: Fairleigh Dickinson University Press, 1971, 26–28.
35 Quoted in Bruteau, 29.
36 Quoted in Bruteau, 30.
37 Bruteau, 29–31.
38 Ibid., 30–31.
39 Ibid., 33.
40 Ibid., 36.
41 Ibid., 36–37.
42 Ibid., 36–37.
43 Sri Aurobindo, *Sri Aurobindo Birth Centenary Library*, vol. 18. Pondicherry: Sri Aurobindo Ashram Trust, 1970, 397.
44 Quoted in Bruteau, 47.
45 Sri Aurobindo, *Sri Aurobindo Birth Centenary Library*, vol. 15. Pondicherry: Sri Aurobindo Ashram Trust, 1971, 166–67.
46 Ibid., 249.
47 Robert N. Minor, "The Response of Sri Aurobindo and the Mother," in *Modern Indian Responses to Religious Pluralism*, ed. Harold G. Coward. Albany: State University of New York Press, 1987, 98–99.
48 Sri Aurobindo, "Sri Aurobindo Birth Centenary Library" 15:554.
49 Quoted in Minor, "The Religious Response of Sri Aurobindo and the Mother," 100.
50 Quoted in Minor, "The Religious Response of Sri Aurobindo and the Mother," 101.
51 Minor, "The Response of Sri Aurobindo and the Mother," 100–01.
52 Swami Nikhilananda, trans., *The Gospel of Sri Ramakrishna*. New York: Ramakrisna-Vivekananda Center, 1942, 13–14.
53 Otto, *The Idea of the Holy: An Inquiry into the Non-Rational Factor in the Idea of the Divine and its Relation to the Rational*, 12–24.
54 Nikhilananda, 15–16.
55 Ibid., 20–21.
56 Ibid., 21–22.
57 Ibid., 37.
58 Ibid., 24.
59 Ibid., 25.
60 Ibid., 29.
61 Ibid., 32.
62 Ibid., 33–34.
63 Ibid., 34.
64 Ibid.
65 Ibid.
66 Ibid., 1010.
67 Ibid., 264–65.
68 Ibid., 423; 115 see also 191.

69 Mohandas K. Gandhi, *An Autobiography: The Story of My Experiments with Truth*, trans. Mahadev Desai. Boston: Beacon Press, 1993, xxvi.
70 Ibid., 33–34.
71 Ibid., 67.
72 Ibid., 68.
73 Ibid., 135.
74 Ibid., 136.
75 Ibid.
76 Ibid., 136–37.
77 Quoted in Hick, *The Fifth Dimension*, 193.
78 J. F. T. Jordens, "Gandhi and Religious Pluralism," in *Modern Indian Responses to Religious Pluralism*, ed. Harold G. Coward. Albany: State University of New York Press, 1987, 4.
79 Ibid., 9.
80 Gandhi, *An Autobiography*, 137.
81 Jordens, 8.
82 Quoted in Jordens, 9.
83 Mohandas Gandhi, *All Men Are Brothers: Life and Thoughts of Mahatma Gandhi as Told in His Own Words*, ed. Krishna Kripalani. Ahmedabad: Navajivan Publishing House, 1960, 80.
84 Ibid., 79.
85 Ibid., 87–88.
86 Jordens, 10–11.
87 Gandhi, *All Men Are Brothers*, 79.
88 Ibid., 87.
89 Ibid., 73–75.
90 Ibid., 82.
91 Ibid., 89.
92 Ibid., 87.
93 Ibid., 92.
94 Quoted in Jordens, 12. Mohandas Gandhi, *The Collected Works of Mahatma Gandhi, 89 vols.* Ahmedabad: Navajivan Trust, 1958–1983, 72:254.
95 Hick, *The Fifth Dimension*, 194–95.
96 Ibid., 204.

5

BUDDHISM

In its true state, consciousness is naked, immaculate, clear, vacuous, transparent, timeless, beyond all condition. O Nobly Born, remember the pure open sky of your own true nature.
—*Tibetan Book of the Great Liberation*

The process of becoming a Western Hindu and embracing its contemplative spirituality has shaped the religious aspect of my individuation, though not entirely. I have also been deeply influenced by the Buddhist teachings and practices I have incorporated into my worldview and spiritual practice. For instance, I received an empowerment conferred at the Vajra Crown Ceremony, transmitted by the Sixteenth Karmapa, and teachings on the *Precious Garland Sutra* given by His Holiness the Fourteenth Dalai Lama; I have participated in Tibetan Buddhist and Theravada Vipassana meditation retreats; I have taught academic courses on Buddhist traditions for two decades; and I regularly read contemplative Buddhist literature. In my daily sadhana, I offer salutations to Shakyamuni Buddha, while invoking the blessings of other enlightened beings, gurus, and teachers. For me, Hinduism and Buddhism are sister religions; the latter complements and enriches my practice of the former.

In my view Buddhism is as profound and beautiful as any of the world's great religions. I find several qualities of the tradition exemplary. First, the Buddha's First Noble Truth strongly counters the pervasive human tendency to disavow or repress the existential suffering inherent in our lives; instead, the focus is on transforming suffering by looking deeply into its causes and conditions. Second, I am inspired by Buddhism's emphasis on compassion, and the kindred intentional attitudes of lovingkindness, empathetic joy, and equanimity. Buddhism regards these virtues as capacities that can be expanded limitlessly. The cultivation of these qualities helps to ameliorate self-centeredness, including the spiritual narcissism that arises in people who become obsessed with their own quest for enlightenment. This *relational* element of Buddhist spirituality is epitomized in *the bodhisattva ideal*, taken up by some practitioners who vow to work tirelessly for the liberation of all sentient beings. Third, Buddhism emphasizes the non-clinging and non-grasping of objects and experiences, including attachment to pleasurable meditative stages and to religious doctrines. As I show in this chapter, Buddhism also mitigates the exclusivist, literalizing, and dogmatic tendencies that often arise within religious traditions.

Buddhism is an ancient tradition that takes many forms, including Theravada, Mahayana, and Vajrayana, in the Asian countries in which it has flourished for centuries. Theravada Buddhism (the Way of the Elders, sometimes described as the Hinayana or smaller vehicle), the oldest and most conservative form, emphasizes purification, morality, renunciation, and monastic life. The aim of this spiritual practice is to become an *arhat*, one who is liberated from mental and emotional afflictions. Lay practitioners of this tradition gain merit and improve their karmic condition by receiving the support of monks. Mahayana Buddhism, the greater or larger vehicle, focuses on lay practitioners and emphasizes the cultivation of compassion. The Vajrayana, or Diamond Vehicle, adds teachings and practices that accelerate the process of becoming enlightened, thereby enhancing a Buddhist's capacity to fulfill the aim of the bodhisattva. Each of these forms of Buddhism has been transmitted to the West.

Historically, the Buddhist attitude toward other religions has blended critical tolerance with a missionary goal. During its long history, Buddhism has spread from India across the globe—south to Sri Lanka and Southeast Asia; north to Tibet; east to China and Japan; and, most recently, west to Europe and North America. Although coming into contact with established religions at every turn, Buddhism has demonstrated a remarkable degree of tolerance and flexibility throughout its expansion, with little evidence of war or persecution associated with these encounters. In this respect, Buddhism is similar to Hinduism. Arnold Toynbee, a historian of civilizations, regarded Hindu-Buddhist tolerance as a prototype of the religious attitude necessary for peace in the pluralistic world in which we now live.[1]

The historical Buddha, Siddhartha Gautama, was born into Hindu society and lived during a period marked by considerable pluralism of philosophy and practices, when a large number of conflicting philosophical theories were proposed regarding the nature of the universe and the destiny of humanity. At this time, a variety of ascetic self-disciplines were being pursued as paths to liberation, or the release from the cycle of rebirth (*samsara*) and the suffering it engenders. The Buddha followed the teachings of two of the greatest sages of his time, but was not satisfied with the results he experienced from performing the practices they taught. He continued his quest on his own, ultimately discovering the path to awakening that subsequently became known as Buddhadharma, or Buddhism. He summarized many of the theories and practices of his day in the *Brahmajala Sutta*, a text describing a "net" of theories that ensnare seekers in search of liberation. The method he developed for getting disentangled from the net was based on a critical outlook and the empirical criterion of personal experience. The Buddha did not expect followers to adopt his teachings on the basis of blind faith, nor did he appeal to scriptural and institutional authority. Instead, he taught a provisional faith that must be tested by a practitioner's personal experience. Thus, in Buddhism, religion is what one finds to be reasonable and true after taking it provisionally on faith and testing it out for oneself; when such faith results in knowledge or has a liberating effect, Buddhism regards it as rational faith.

The process of rational faith parallels modern science—a scientist conveys a new discovery to colleagues so that it can be tested and verified by other researchers.[2] In the case of religion, the researchers are individuals who engage in spiritual practices that awaken the mind and alleviate existential suffering. The Buddha's critical outlook is also based upon a causal conception of nature. His meditations reveal that physical, psychological, and moral laws govern the universe; like the law of gravity, they simply exist. The Buddha discovers and teaches these laws to aid others in attaining the goals of spiritual practice. He describes his most important and unique discovery as dependent origination, or the law of inter-dependent arising (*pratitya samutpada*), the central doctrine upon which his teachings are based.

According to this doctrine, all psychological and physical phenomena constituting individual existence are interdependent and mutually condition one another. Dependent origination is comprised of twelve links that perpetuate the wheel of causation. The links that are due to one's past life are ignorance and predisposition. Those due to one's present life are: consciousness; name and form; the six fields or five sense organs; the mind along with its objects; sense-object contact; feeling; craving; and attachment. And those due to one's future life are: coming to be; rebirth; old age; and death. From each antecedent factor comes the succeeding one and thus, together, they form the individual's chain of bondage to the wheel of birth and death. Attainment of enlightenment and realization of one's Buddha nature depend upon comprehending these interdependencies. Additionally, The Four Noble Truths contain the means for understanding and practicing the teachings that lead to spiritual awakening—the truth of suffering; the truth of the cause of suffering; the truth of the cessation of suffering; and the path that leads to the cessation of suffering.

Buddhist exclusivism

Since Buddhists do not regard their sacred texts to be revealed scriptures in the same way that Christians regard their Bible, or Hindus their Vedas, their responses to religious pluralism differ somewhat from Christian and Hindu exclusivist views. The traditional Buddhist attitude of critical tolerance allows for spiritual salvation or liberation outside of Buddhism, but it does not consider all religions to be equally efficacious guides to the truth. Buddhism exhibits softer and subtler forms of critique than other religious worldviews.

The way Buddhism evaluates religions is outlined in the *Sandaka Sutta*, an early text from the Theravada tradition. In reporting on the Buddha's teachings, one of the Buddha's main disciples states that there are four false religions: (1) materialism, characterized here as asserting the reality of the material world alone and the denial of life after death; (2) any religious philosophy that supports an immoral ethic; (3) any religion that denies free will and moral responsibility and asserts that people are either miraculously saved or doomed; and (4) any religion that asserts the inevitability of eventual salvation or release for all people. The text also states there are four religions that are unsatisfactory, but not necessarily false, based on: (1) the omniscience of the founder; (2) revelation or tradition; (3) logical and metaphysical speculation; and (4) pragmatic skepticism or agnosticism.[3]

Buddhism judges the satisfactoriness of these religions based on the degree to which they approach the core requirements of the Buddhist religion itself: moral values, freedom, and responsibility for achieving liberation. This stance toward other religions is similar to that of some Christian theologians discussed in Chapter 3, especially the Catholic theology of Karl Rahner who maintains that other religions are a means of salvation to the extent that they conform to the criterion of Jesus Christ. For Buddhism, the criterion is the Buddha's experience of truth. Based on this, religions dependent upon the founder's omniscience, revelation or tradition, metaphysical speculation, or pragmatic skepticism, are deemed helpful but unsatisfactory since they are grounded in uncertain foundations. The point being made in the Buddhist argument is that while these foundations may be either true or false, they cannot be verified. Buddhism, by contrast, is a religion that can be verified by reason and experience.[4]

Buddhism appeals to direct experience and is less dogmatic than forms of Christian and Hindu exclusivism that also claim to rely on reason and experience as part of the basis for validating religious belief. The Hindu mystics discussed in Chapter 4 are a clear case in point. Similarly, there are many forms of Christian theology and mysticism that accord authority to experience as a reliable basis for religious belief. Although Buddhists often make the claim, Buddhism is not the only "verifiable religion."

Buddhist inclusivism

A different Buddhist response to other religions, emerging in the Mahayana tradition early in the Common Era, is the approach developed by the Madhyamika school of Buddhist philosophy that uses a method of negation as a means of supporting meditative practice. Its critical analysis of religious doctrines is not aimed at rejecting a religion or demonstrating its inferiority. Here critical analysis functions as a medicine to cure the disease of ego attachment to religious concepts and doctrines, so that spirituality can be directly experienced and lived. To use a famous Zen metaphor, the purpose is to keep the religious practitioner's attention on the moon rather than on the finger pointing at the moon. Concepts often prove to be a substitute for experience. For instance, Mahayana Buddhism teaches that the goal of religion is compassion; attachment to one's own religious beliefs can be a major obstacle to cultivating it. When religious views are made absolute or held too rigidly, they undermine tolerance, objective criticism, and compassionate action.[5]

In this context, the Madhyamika attitude toward other religions—including various viewpoints within Buddhism—entails openness and a desire to enter into a special form of dialogue. Following the method developed by Nagarjuna, the great second-century Madhyamika philosopher, one first attempts to clearly understand the position of the other and then ruthlessly subjects that view to dialectical criticism until it collapses from its own internal inconsistencies. For centuries the Madhyamika critique of other religions has had a significant impact. It influenced Hindu Vedantic philosophers such as Shankara, for example, who borrowed the critical method as he refined and systematized Advaita Vedanta. Within Buddhism itself, the Madhyamika stance has had a purifying effect—it reminds Buddhists that they should neither take the Buddha's works nor the formulations of any Buddhist school as absolute truth. However, the effect of Madhyamika's critical method is complex and controversial. As Harold Coward observes, "In one sense Madhyamika would seem to be the most intolerant of approaches in that it negates, without exception, all possible views. In another sense it can accommodate and give place to all religious views so long as they don't claim to be absolute."[6] Thus, the Madhyamika method contains within itself the danger that it can lead its practitioners to attach their egos to the critical outlook itself and, in so doing, lose touch with the Buddha's spirit of tolerance and compassion. This would be to absolutize the dialectical method, a temptation as real as absolutizing the philosophy or worldview of a particular religion. In my view, this method is not among the most constructive vehicles for inter-religious dialogue in the contemporary world. We need more empathetic approaches for finding common ground between religions, as exemplified by the Buddhists presented in this chapter.

As is the case in Hinduism, the distinction between Buddhist inclusivism and pluralism is subtle. Both viewpoints are useful for engendering inter-religious understanding and harmonious relationships between religions. I present Thich Nhat Hanh's writings to exemplify the inclusive approach of an influential Buddhist, followed by the views of several pluralists who more fully affirm the validity of other traditions on their own terms.

Thich Nhat Hanh

Thich Nhat Hanh, poet, peace advocate, and one of the best known and most respected Zen masters in the world today, embodies the principles of inclusivity and interconnectedness. Born in central Vietnam in 1926, he became a Buddhist monk at the age of sixteen. When the Vietnam War confronted monks and nuns with the question of whether to adhere to the contemplative life and remain meditating in monasteries or help the villagers who were suffering the bombings and devastations of war, Nhat Hanh was among those who chose to do both.

He helped found the Engaged Buddhism movement and dedicated his life to the work of inner transformation for the benefit of individuals and society.

After visiting the United States and Europe on a peace mission in 1966, he was banned from returning to Vietnam until 2005. He persuaded Martin Luther King, Jr. to oppose the Vietnam War, which helped galvanize the peace movement in the United States. Subsequently, he led the Buddhist delegation at the Paris Peace Talks. After the war, he was exiled to France and founded Plum Village, a Buddhist community where he continues working to alleviate the suffering of refugees, political prisoners, and hungry families in Vietnam and throughout the Third World. He has received recognition for his work with Vietnam veterans and for his prolific writings on mindfulness, meditation, and cultivating peace in a world fraught with conflict.

Nhat Hanh's practical form of Buddhist inclusivism is grounded in his encounters with Christianity:

- His understanding of Christianity did not emerge in the ivory tower, but from the crucible of war. The Vietnam War enacted a clash between capitalist and communist ideology, two conflicting worldviews that prevailed during the second half of the twentieth century.

- His inclusivist approach is a practice-oriented way of engaging Buddhist and Christian teachings, emphasizing the importance of direct experience.

- He seeks to renew Buddhist and Christian teachings, not for the sake of the religions, but for the sake of humanity, other species, and the earth, our shared habitat.

In addition, he offers psychological insight into complexities concerning faith, negative emotions, and religious identity.

The Buddha's teachings on the interdependent nature of reality

Buddhism teaches that the Buddha's legendary awakening under the Bodhi tree involved a profound understanding of the interdependent nature of reality as expressed in the doctrine known as dependent origination. According to this doctrine, no being or thing has inherent or self-sufficient existence; all phenomena arise in a matrix of causes and conditions. This insight is the basis of the Buddha's teaching of "no-self," an idea that I suggest is better understood as "no separate self." The Buddha taught that a human being is an assembly of five aggregates (*skandhas*): body, feelings, perceptions, mental states, and the consciousness that arises from contact between an object and the corresponding sense organ. In his re-telling of the story of the Buddha's enlightenment, Nhat Hanh uses the metaphor of rivers to describe how each aggregate requires the others:

> Beneath the pippala tree, the hermit Gautama focused all of his formidable powers of concentration to look deeply at his body. He saw that every cell

of his body was like a drop of water in an endlessly flowing river of birth, existence, and death, and he could not find anything in the body that remained unchanged or that could be said to contain a separate self. Intermingled with the river of his body was the river of feelings in which every feeling was a drop of water.[7]

Among these feelings, he noted, were some pleasant, others unpleasant or even neutral, but they arose and disappeared, ever-changing, like the changing body. Likewise, he saw that perceptions and mental states also flowed in this way, and that erroneous perceptions veiled reality. His penetrating insight revealed that the mental states of fear, anger, hatred, arrogance, jealously, and greed were the cause of suffering and that each of these arose from ignorance. When one is liberated from ignorance, these mental obstructions vanish on their own, "like shadows fleeing before the rising sun."[8]

Through these cascading insights, Gautama clearly saw the interdependent nature of all phenomena—that all things are empty of a separate, isolated self. Nhat Hanh poetically expresses this sublime, liberating moment:

He smiled, and looked up at a pippala leaf imprinted against the blue sky, its tail blowing back and forth as if calling him. Looking deeply at the leaf, he saw clearly the presence of the sun and stars—without the sun, without light and warmth, the leaf could not exist. This was like this, because that was like that. With this insight, ideas of birth and death, appearance and disappearance dissolved, and the true face of the leaf and his own true face revealed themselves. He could see that the presence of any one phenomenon made possible the existence of all other phenomena. One included all, and all were included in one. [. . .] The leaf and his body were one.[9]

Nhat Hanh skillfully applies this principle to the contemporary global issues of war, environmental crises, and religious pluralism. He coins the term "interbeing" to convey the teaching of interdependence, an idea that helps us understand the individual in a relational context. "You need people in order to be. You need other beings in order to be. It is impossible to be yourself alone. Therefore, to be is to inter-be."[10] As it relates to environmental issues, he observes, "Human beings are made of non-human elements. Therefore, to protect non-human elements is to protect human beings. Interbeing is an ecological principle."[11]

The concept of interbeing also helps us understand relationships between religions such as Christianity and Buddhism. Nhat Hanh acknowledges that the philosophical foundations for each tradition are quite different. For example, Buddhism teaches the doctrine of rebirth, while Christianity teaches that a person has one life and thus one chance for salvation.[12] However, Nhat Hanh believes that if we take the time to practice our own traditions deeply enough, we will see that these differences are not significant. We need to appreciate that there are many forms of Buddhism and many ways of understanding it. The same is true of

Christianity. People from many different religious backgrounds come to Plum Village, Nhat Hanh's practice center in France. There, at times, a Buddhist recognizes a Christian as being more Buddhist than another Buddhist, and a Christian may feel that a practicing Buddhist is more akin than a fellow Christian.[13]

Jesus and Buddha as great teachers and ancestors

Nhat Hanh identifies common ground between the two traditions in *Coming Home: Jesus and Buddha as Brothers*, based on his annual talks on Christmas Eve and Christmas day at Plum Village. In these teachings, Nhat Hanh describes both Jesus and Buddha as great teachers and ancestors, and he advises that just as we have blood ancestors, we also have spiritual ancestors. A person born in the West is likely to be a child of Jesus and have him as an ancestor even if she does not think of herself as a Christian. She may have had a grandfather who transmitted the love and insight of Jesus to her. Put another way, religious attitudes and values are transmitted to us through our family and culture whether or not we embrace them; they become part of our psyche and exert an influence, though not always consciously. Nhat Hanh further observes that there are some who hate Christianity and want nothing to do with it; they wish to leave it behind. But in the body and spirit of these people, Jesus may be very present and real; his energy, insight, and love may be hiding in them.[14] Therefore, whether or not one identifies with one's inherited tradition, it is important to understand the ways in which spiritual ancestors shape and influence our worldviews.

Nhat Hanh affirms that the Buddha is his ancestor and lives within him—"I can touch him at any time I want, I can profit from his energy and insight any time I want. It is very real. He is in every cell of my body. Every time I need him I have ways to call to him and to make his energy manifest."[15] This connection to Buddha seems quite natural for a Buddhist, but Nhat Hanh also regards Jesus as one of his spiritual ancestors. While in Europe and North America, he met with many Christians who embodied Jesus' spirit of love, understanding, and peace. During the Vietnam War, he worked hard to stop the killing. Thanks to these experiences, he was touched by Jesus as a teacher and spiritual ancestor.[16] A statue of Jesus sits next to the Buddha figures on his altar, symbolizing Nhat Hanh's inclusive attitude toward Christianity.

Nhat Hanh helps us understand other affinities between Christianity and Buddhism. While Christians traditionally describe the religious ultimate as God, Nhat Hanh notes that theologians such as Paul Tillich also describe it as "the ground of being," the noumenal aspect of reality, rather than a being in the phenomenal world.[17] Having studied Christian thought, he is familiar with its discussion of "horizontal" theology, the perspective of immanence, which helps us understand ourselves in relation to history and nature. But Christianity also holds that God is transcendent and timeless. It is also essential, says Nhat Hanh, to be in touch with this "vertical" dimension of reality. He embraces both these dimensions that help Christians understand life and sees the relationship between them as the interbeing between the two—if one cannot succeed in getting in touch with the horizontal dimension, it will be difficult to get in touch with the vertical. In other words, if you cannot love human beings, animals, and plants, he doubts that you can love God. Likewise, one's capacity for loving God depends on one's capacity for loving humankind and other species.[18]

The ocean and the waves metaphor helps to further explain this teaching. He asks us to visualize an ocean and a multitude of waves: Imagine we are a wave on the ocean, surrounded by many other waves. If the wave looks deeply within itself, it will realize that its being depends upon the presence of all the other waves. By looking into yourself, you touch the whole, or everything, and realize that you are conditioned by what is around you.[19] One thing contains the whole cosmos— this is the Buddha's teaching on dependent co-arising, described above. But how can we experience this for ourselves and come to know that it is so? Buddhists discover this truth about phenomena through mindfulness, which Nhat Hanh describes as "deep looking." Mindfulness entails careful attention to what is arising in the present moment, whatever is arising, pleasant or not. He teaches that with the energy of mindfulness—which is the energy of the Buddha, or wakefulness— we can see deeply. Moreover, for Nhat Hanh, the Holy Spirit is the energy of God; it grants the capacity to be present, fully alive, deeply understanding, and loving. We need this energy and the understanding it engenders. If we do not live each moment deeply, we cannot touch the ultimate dimension, the noumenal reality that Christians call God.[20]

Buddhism speaks of nirvana in its teachings about the noumenal or vertical dimension of reality. Yet Buddhists usually refrain from speaking about nirvana because all notions, concepts, and words are inadequate to describe it. Nhat Hanh presents the ineffable—that which is beyond language—as immediately present to us. It is something we can touch and express in our lives.[21] Nirvana is our true substance, just as water is the true substance of the wave. We practice, he says, to realize that nirvana is our substance. God is an equivalent expression—nirvana, like God for Christians, is the ground of being.[22] We can touch nirvana and express it in our lives.

The Buddha's teaching is called the Dharma. Here, too, is another affinity with Christianity. The Dharma, Nhat Hanh explains, is not a set of laws and practices, a stack of sutras, or audio-visual recordings of talks by Buddhist teachers. The Dharma is understanding—it is the practice of lovingkindness expressed in life. As a Christian, when you love God you have to love your neighbor. Then, he notes, you have to go further—you have to love your enemy, too.[23] But why must we love our enemies and how can this be done? His response connects the Christian and Buddhist teachings on love. Buddhism teaches that understanding is the very foundation of love; if understanding is not there, no matter how hard you try, you cannot love. When you are mindful, you become aware of the suffering of another person. As you begin to see that person's suffering, compassion is born, and you no longer consider them your enemy. The moment you realize that your so-called enemy suffers, you naturally want to help ease their suffering. Loving your enemy, then, is only possible when you no longer see them as your enemy, and the way to see clearly is to practice mindfulness or deep looking.[24]

While Nhat Hanh embraces Jesus as a brother of the Buddha and a kindred soul, he finds it troubling that the image typically portrayed is that of the crucified Jesus on the cross. He feels, as I do, that this image does not do justice to Jesus because it so overshadows the spirit of joy and peace also associated with the man. In the New Testament, St. Paul describes the cross as a stumbling block for the Greeks. I believe this remains so for many contemporary people, Christians and non-Christians alike. Nhat Hanh suggests that Christians portray Jesus in ways that would allow a feeling of peace and joy to penetrate our hearts, such as sitting in the lotus position or in walking meditation.[25] He connects this more affirmative idea of the *living* Christ, albeit non-traditional, to his rendering of baptism and resurrection, Christian teachings that can be understood as parallel to Buddhist mindfulness. The ritual of baptism is undertaken for Christians who desire to be born into spiritual life. Jesus is also born every time Christians touch the Holy Spirit within themselves. The Christ child is born every day, not just on Christmas; this, too, is the practice of resurrection. Redemption and resurrection are not just words or objects of belief—they are the essence of daily practice.[26]

Taking refuge and faith

Confessions of faith or belief clearly distinguish religions, often giving the impression that a person must choose one or the other. Nhat Hanh's inclusivism presents another way to think about whether allegiance to Christianity or Buddhism precludes embracing teachings from both traditions. Buddhists take refuge in the Buddha, or teacher, the Dharma, or the teaching, and in the Sangha, or the community, of those who practice the teaching. But what is meant by refuge and faith? Nhat Hanh's perspective is instructive and stresses the importance of direct experience. Taking refuge, in his view, is not so much a question of belief as it is of practice. He distinguishes "popular Buddhism" from "deep Buddhism" on the basis of the depth of a Buddhist's insight and understanding. For example, there are people who think of Buddha as a god, while others regard the Buddha as a human being like us, but one who has practiced and reached a very high level of enlightenment, understanding, and compassion. As he explains, if you practice well, the day will come when you understand that the Buddha is not really another person, but is within you, because the substance that makes up a Buddha is the energy of mindfulness, understanding, and compassion. You will see that you have Buddha nature within you. The Buddha ceases to be the other; the Buddha can be touched everywhere and especially within yourself. As Nhat Hanh further explains, in the beginning of practice we say, "I take refuge in the Buddha." Later on we say, "I take refuge in the Buddha within myself."[27] Faith or taking refuge becomes a matter of direct experience. The object of faith is no longer an idea about a person named Gautama, about Buddhahood, or Buddha nature. Now you touch Buddha nature not as an idea, but as a reality.

The Buddhist practice of taking refuge has a parallel in Christianity. Christians have faith or take refuge in Jesus Christ, the Gospel, and the Church, and are nourished by each. When we consider the Nicene Creed, Nhat Hanh believes we find teachings in Christianity equivalent to Buddhism. Here his inclusivity provides us with a way to overcome the exclusive status traditionally ascribed to Jesus Christ, that is, *I believe in one God, the Father, the Almighty, maker of heaven and earth.* Nhat Hanh feels that this credal statement—*I believe in Jesus Christ, his only Son, our Lord*—is the equivalent of the ultimate dimension of reality that Buddhists describe as nirvana. For Buddhists, the Buddha is not unique, because there are many Buddhas—Buddhas of the past, the present, and the future. All Buddhas embody the supreme enlightenment and supreme compassion. We, too, are future Buddhas and embody the Buddha nature. Nhat Hanh contends this is why the notion is not *only* applied in Buddhism. While this does indicate a difference between Christianity and Buddhism, Buddhists need not regard this Christian teaching as foreign. As Nhat Hanh observes, "Many of our Catholic, Protestant, and Orthodox friends live and know that God the Father is not out there in space but is in our hearts. The question is how to touch him or how to touch that ultimate dimension."[28] In his view, the sacraments of Baptism, Confirmation, and the Eucharist are just ways of allowing us to touch that ultimate dimension. So he invites us to reflect on the word "only," as in "his only Son," and proclaims, "*You* are also a daughter or son of God. You are Jesus. All of us are Jesus."[29] Every wave is born from water and each wave has water as its substance. For Nhat Hanh, the metaphor includes Christians and Buddhists alike—all human beings live in the historical dimension while also containing the ultimate dimension.

Cultural and religious identities

Wars often displace people and cause them to lose their cultural and religious identities. Nhat Hanh is acutely aware of this problem since many Vietnamese suffered a great deal in their native country due to the division and conflict caused by the war in Vietnam. Some of them who emigrated to Europe or America wanted to become purely European or American, leaving their heritage behind; they hated anything Vietnamese. However, he believes it is impossible for these people to become something completely different; he encourages them instead to go back to their roots. Likewise, after teaching the Dharma in the West for over thirty years, Nhat Hanh has met many Europeans and Americans who bear similar wounds and desires, people who no longer want anything to do with their family, church, society, and culture. They want to become Indian, Vietnamese, or something else; some want to become Buddhists. When these people come to Plum Village, he recognizes them right away as wandering or hungry souls, longing for something beautiful and good to believe in.[30] What they need, in his view, is to embrace their spiritual ancestors and include them in their new hybrid identities.

Working with negative emotions

Nhat Hanh relates the acknowledgment of our ancestors to our ability to work with negative energies in the psyche. Put another way, this enables us to do what Jungians refer to as shadow work—engaging and owning aspects of ourselves that we disavow and that fall into our unconscious. Sometimes we are overwhelmed by hate, anger, or despair; we forget there are other kinds of energy that can also be manifested. He teaches that if we know how to practice mindfulness, we can summon the energies of insight, love, and hope to accept the negative emotions when they arise. Our spiritual ancestors, he says, are capable of negating the unwholesome energies, what Christians might call the evil spirits within us, by engaging the Holy Spirit to help us heal and be healthy and joyful again.[31]

Buddhism also talks about these energies as both the negative and positive forces, though a little differently. In Buddhism, Nhat Hanh explains, we do not have to chase the evil spirit away. Instead, we can honor the energy of anger, despair, and hate. When embraced by the energy of mindfulness, these negative forces are transformed. For example, when feeling angry, the practice is to note the anger with your breath—*Breathing in, I know the energy of anger is in me. Breathing out, I embrace my anger.*[32] While breathing in and out in this way, you acknowledge your anger. By owning or including it, the energy transforms; it is incorporated into your being rather than projected onto others. You can do this, says Nhat Hanh, because the Buddha is in you; the Buddha is an ancestor protecting you; the Buddha is true energy—the energy of mindfulness, peace, concentration, and wisdom. If you are a Christian, the practice can be similar. You ask Jesus to manifest within you in order to recognize and come to terms with the negative within yourself. From this perspective, the Holy Spirit is the energy you must utilize to take care of the negative emotions within; it is the kind of energy that is capable of fostering acceptance, understanding, love, and healing.[33]

Double belonging

Nhat Hanh's views raise the question of "double belonging" advocated by Paul Knitter, the Buddhist Christian discussed in Chapter 3. Can one be truly rooted in more than one tradition? Though Nhat Hanh does not use the term double belonging, he affirms this option and declares it is possible to know the Buddha and Jesus at the same time. There are people who have roots within both traditions, and he includes himself among them. The religious pluralism of the contemporary world provides an opportunity for Christians and Buddhists to relate to each other in new ways. If Jesus and Buddha met today, what would they tell each other? Nhat Hanh says, "Not only have they met today, but they met yesterday, they met last night, and they will meet tomorrow. They are always in me and they are very peaceful and united with each other. There is no conflict at all between the Buddha and Christ in me. They are real brothers, they are real sisters within me."[34] He believes this is also so for others. A Christian is a continuation of Jesus

Christ and a Buddhist is a continuation of the Buddha. These continuations are another expression of the concept of interbeing; in this case, the current generation is a continuation of past ones. You are a continuation of your mother and your father. Your son or daughter is a continuation of you. In an analogous way, when the Buddhist meets the Christian, the Buddha is meeting Jesus; they do this every day, in Europe, in America, and in Asia.[35] But what do Jesus and Buddha tell each other that helps us understand the change in our historical and cultural circumstances? What do they say to one another to address the challenge or opportunity of religious pluralism?

Nhat Hanh uses his imagination to answer this question along the following lines: *Imagine three hundred years ago when Jesus came to Vietnam via Christian missionaries. Would the Buddha have said, "Who are you? What are you doing here? The Vietnamese people already have a spiritual tradition. Do you want them to reject Buddhism to embrace Christianity?" How would Jesus reply? Would he say to Buddha, "Well, you Vietnamese people are following a false religious path. You need to reject it and learn the new path that I am going to offer to you. It is the only path that brings salvation."*[36] A conversation of this kind reflects the exclusivist attitude of Christians who seek to convert Vietnamese and other Asians to Christianity, though other responses are now possible.

Nhat Hanh, again in an imaginary dialogue, asks us to envision Jesus and Buddha meeting today in Europe and in America: *Now the Buddha is saying to Jesus, "I am new to this land. Do you think I should stay here or go back to Asia?"* There are so many refugees who come to the West from Indochina, Thailand, Burma, and Tibet who bring their religious beliefs with them. Do they have the right to continue their Buddhist practice in these lands? Do they have the right to share their beliefs and practices with non-Buddhists? Do we think that Jesus would say, "No, since we already have Christianity here you should not try and propagate a new faith in this land"?[37]

Nhat Hanh imagines yet another conversation in which he sees the Buddha and Jesus having tea together: *Buddha says to Jesus, "My dear brother, is it too difficult to continue in this time of ours? Is it more difficult now to be fearless, to help and love people, than it was in the old time?"* For Nhat Hanh, Jesus is a fearless teacher with a great capacity for loving, healing, and forgiving. *Buddha might continue, "What can I do to help you, my brother? How should we design spiritual practice so that it will be understood, accepted, and effective, so that we can restore what has been lost: faith, courage, and love?"*[38] The Buddha also finds it difficult to do the things he did twenty-five hundred years ago in India. *People talk a little too much about teaching and have gone astray, inventing too many things and organizing too much. They lose the true essence of Dharma; they teach and practice archaic forms that no longer transmit the true teaching to new generations.* Thus, while Buddha asks Jesus a question about how to teach, he is asking himself the same question—How do we renew Buddhism as a spiritual tradition? How can the practice generate the true energy of love, compassion, and understanding?[39]

Nhat Hanh's proposition is that in today's world, Buddha and Jesus are brothers who have to help each other. Buddhism needs help and so does Christianity, not for the sake of the religions, but for the sake of humankind and the other species on earth. We live at a time when many people, feeling helpless in the face of destruction from war and environmental distress, are in despair. Instead of discriminating against each other, the Buddha and Jesus need to come together every day. Their meeting, in his view, is the hope for the world.[40] How do they meet? They must meet every moment within us. Each of us in our daily practice needs to touch the spirit of Buddha or Jesus so that it manifests in our lives. We need these energies—both mindfulness *and* the Holy Spirit—in order to ameliorate our fear, despair, and anxiety. We must include, own, and transform destructive emotions into energies that engender understanding, compassion, and love. This psycho-spiritual process is a basis for hope in our future and a path to peace.

Buddhist pluralism

As I have previously said, the distinction between Buddhist inclusivism and pluralism is subtle. I turn now to several exemplary Buddhists who more fully acknowledge the validity of other traditions.

His Holiness the Fourteenth Dalai Lama

While Thich Nhat Hanh's inclusivism relativizes Buddhism and Christianity, His Holiness the Fourteenth Dalai Lama offers a fully Buddhist pluralist approach, pointing out affinities and showing us how intimately these traditions are related. Indeed, I believe the Dalai Lama's stance, in which he *relativizes religion itself* by including secular worldviews within his scope of concern, is the supreme exemplification of pluralism from an influential leader of a major world religion. The Dalai Lama's well-considered, deeply informed, and pragmatic response to pluralism emerges from his own journey out of an isolated life in Tibet into one with extensive contact with other faith traditions.

In 1959, at the age of twenty-four, the Dalai Lama was forced to escape from Tibet and began a journey to freedom in India. He lived for more than fifty years in India, a land that has given birth to four of the world's great religions—Hinduism, Buddhism, Jainism, and Sikhism—and provides a home for many others.[41] The great lesson of India's history, he writes, is that genuine religious pluralism and tolerance are achievable. He regards India as a beacon for the rest of the world, seeing his own work as that of a humble messenger of India's ancient teachings on nonviolence and religious tolerance.[42]

The Dalai Lama's life is an extraordinary example of how a person may come to embrace religious pluralism. He tells us that when he arrived in India as a refugee, he knew very little about religions other than Buddhism, the religion of his country. For more than fifty years he has devoted much of his time and attention to learning and thinking about the world's great religions.[43] He acknowledges that from the age of fifteen forward, based on his extensive studies of classical and Buddhist thought and practice, he thought Buddhism was the best religion. No other faith tradition, he felt then, could rival the depth, sophistication, and inspirational power of Buddhism, and by comparison, all other religions were "so-so." In retrospect, he feels embarrassed by his naiveté and an attitude that could only have been sustained as long as he was isolated from any real contact with other religions.[44]

His attitude changed radically during his first visit to India, where he encountered Jains, Hindus, and members of the Theosophical Society in Madras. Within three months he described himself as "a changed man." In his words, "I could no longer live in the comfort of an exclusivist standpoint that takes Buddhism to be the only true religion."[45] This process deepened when he returned to India two years later as a refugee. As he explains, "Ironically, exposure to the grandeur of India's great religions brought me to let go of the mental comfort zone, a space where my own Buddhism was the one true religion and other faith traditions were at best mere similitude."[46] Although most of us do not face the dire political circumstances of the Dalai Lama, his life is a testament to how we, too, may move out of the comfort zone of our inherited faith traditions (or lack thereof) in order to understand the millions of our fellow human beings who live in accordance with worldviews that may seem so different from our own.

Thomas Merton, a Catholic Trappist monk, was among the first Christians the Dalai Lama encountered. Merton, who visited the Dalai Lama in Dharmasala just three months before Merton's tragic accidental death, opened his eyes to the richness and depth of the Christian faith, an appreciation of Christianity that continues to deepen as the Dalai Lama, committed to inter-religious dialogue, engages with other Christians. The Dalai Lama describes Merton's attitude as exemplary and feels that he showed great courage in exploring traditions beyond his own, penetrating into them so deeply that he was able to "taste the actual flavor of the teachings that other traditions represent."[47]

Why, we may ask, do the Dalai Lama and Thomas Merton give such great importance to the cultivation of inter-religious understanding? The answer is that the future of humanity and the planet depend upon it. We live in a world that is truly global and interdependent. "The challenge of peaceful co-existence," he believes, "will define the task of humanity in the twenty-first century."[48] The line between exclusivism that regards one's own religion to be the only legitimate one, and fundamentalism is a dangerously narrow one. The line between fundamentalism and extremism is even narrower. After 9/11, he observed, the upholding of exclusivist religious bigotry in the world could no longer be the private matter of an individual's personal outlook, because it has the potential to affect the lives of all. The lesson he drew is clear—understanding and harmony between members of the world's religions are among the essential preconditions for genuine world peace.[49]

Respecting the other's reality

Accepting the legitimacy of other faith traditions poses a threat to many religious people. To accept that other religions are legitimate may seem to compromise a commitment to one's own faith.[50] Can a single-pointed commitment to one's faith be reconciled with the acceptance of other religions being equally legitimate? Many people feel an affirmative answer to this question requires the acceptance of some kind of ultimate unity of religions. As revealed in Chapter 4, Hindus often employ the metaphor of multiple rivers converging into the great ocean. Others suggest the world's religions, though exhibiting distinct beliefs and practices, all ultimately lead to the same place. That place may be union with the Godhead, regardless of the differing names or descriptions being used for this Godhead (Yahweh, God, Ishvara, Allah, or others).

The Dalai Lama offers an alternative view that is not contingent upon proving the ultimate oneness of all religions. The problem with such an approach, he argues, is that it demands a precondition that remains impossible for the majority of the world's great religions—that all religions be regarded as the same when in fact they are not. Consequently, recognizing the diversity among the world's faiths is not only essential, it is the necessary first step toward creating a deeper understanding of each. As he explains, "True understanding of the 'other' must proceed from a genuine recognition and respect for the other's reality."[51] This requires a state of mind that resists the strong tendency to subsume the other in one's own framework. He adds that whether we like it or not, the existence of other religions is an undeniable fact, and the myriad teachings of the great religions provide great benefits to their adherents. His position is realistic and clearly recognizes the impossibility of our planet's six billion human inhabitants following the same religion.[52]

The reasoning behind the Dalai Lama's pluralistic stance entails two other important observations:

- The first is psychological, recognizing that the diversity of mental dispositions, spiritual inclinations, and different kinds of conditioning have always been a feature of human society; therefore, no single set of spiritual teachings can serve everyone.

- The second observation is historical. During the long history of the world's religions—in some cases extending over thousands of years—complex and specific cultural sensibilities engendering different habits of mind have evolved. These cultural traditions cannot be changed overnight, nor would this be desirable.

Creating a single world religion, whether it is new or formed from the old, is not feasible. We need to focus, instead, on accepting the value of other religions.[53]

Promoting inter-religious harmony and understanding

Throughout history, the world's religions have been a source of conflict. Examples abound, from the Crusades in medieval times to jihad and the recent phenomenon of religion-inspired terrorism. While acknowledging this historical legacy of violence, the Dalai Lama believes we must now move on. The critical question is not, he says, "Are religions only a source of trouble?" but rather "What can we do to ensure that the differences between religions no longer continue to give birth to divisions and conflicts in society?"[54]

As a deep believer in the positive nature of human potential, he is committed to the view that harmony among religions is achievable, but only by promoting genuine understanding between them. His program for promoting inter-religious harmony and understanding entails four elements:

- The first is dialogue among scholars of religion on convergences and divergences in traditions, including the purpose of different approaches religions have taken.

- The second is the deep sharing of religious experience between genuine practitioners. He believes that understanding at this level is deeply moving. It quickly breaks down barriers that separate faith traditions, and it reveals affinities at the religious feeling level that lie just below the surface of foreign and unfamiliar cultural differences. The increasingly common interfaith religious services hosted by churches, temples, or mosques in large cities are a powerful means for creating harmonious relationships between religions.

- High-profile meetings of religious leaders who speak and pray from one platform is a third element the Dalai Lama recommends. He has participated in gatherings with such figures as Pope John Paul II and Desmond Tutu to promote world peace.

- The fourth element for promoting inter-religious harmony and understanding takes the form of joint pilgrimages to holy places.[55]

Three aspects of religion

To facilitate inter-religious understanding, the Dalai Lama, like many scholars of religion, distinguishes between three key aspects—doctrines and metaphysics; ethical teachings; and cultural characteristics, ranging from attitudes to images.

- The first aspect pertains to a religion's understanding of ultimate truth.

- The second aspect involves practitioners' daily lives, the way in which they live in accordance with the ethical principles espoused by the religion.

- The third aspect, which is often closely tied to cultural and historical circumstances, determines how believers may behave at a given place or time.

With these distinctions, devout believers can see in a different light how to deal with the challenges posed by pluralism. On the metaphysical and cultural levels, it is easy to discern differences between religions, some of which are quite fundamental. However, at the level of ethical teachings, the Dalai Lama asserts there is an undeniably great convergence among the world's great religions. "The central message of all religions," he believes, "is love, compassion, and universal brotherhood and sisterhood."[56]

The purpose of all religions, he maintains, remains the same—to contribute to the betterment of humanity by creating more compassionate and responsible human beings. Furthermore, not only are the ethical teachings of the religions essentially the same, the fruits of love and compassion are also the same. For example, just as Mother Teresa of Calcutta is a product of Christian teachings on compassion, so too, another great soul such as Mahatma Gandhi is primarily a product of Hinduism.[57]

A model for understanding doctrinal differences

Before taking a more detailed look at the ethical teachings religions share in common, it is important to acknowledge that the different religions' doctrines are often divergent, and to consider how this may be understood from a Buddhist perspective. Divergent doctrinal and philosophical standpoints have always been an important part of Buddhism's self-understanding. Soon after the Buddha passed away, his followers formed distinct schools, each espousing different views. Each of these teachings was based on the words ascribed to the Buddha which, the Dalai Lama notes, may have given the impression that one and the same teacher professed divergent—and in some cases even contradictory—views of reality to his followers.[58] Was the Buddha himself confused when it came to defining the ultimate nature of reality? A devout Buddhist cannot accept such a possibility. This, the Dalai Lama asserts, is where the role of Buddhist hermeneutics comes into play, a principle that may serve as a model for dealing with the doctrinal divergences among religions. Buddhists invoke the principle as a means of interpreting the Buddha's conflicting teachings and explain that what the Buddha teaches is contingent upon the needs within a given context and its potential for efficacy. For example, the Buddha teaches the Dharma as a cure for the ailments of the spirit; it is a medicine and its effectiveness can only be judged in relation to the treatment of a particular person's illness. As the Dalai Lama points out, "Since there are so many diverse mental dispositions, or spiritual and philosophical inclinations, among human beings, there should be equally corresponding numbers of teachings. The idea that there should be only one teaching—a kind of panacea that is valid for all beings—from this point of view is untenable."[59] The Buddhist concept of *upaya*, or "skillful means," conveys a similar idea. The Dharma must be taught in a manner that can be heard and understood by particular individuals.

The Dalai Lama provides an example of how Buddhist hermeneutics applies to the doctrinal differences between Buddhism and the Abrahamic religions. For some, he observes, the idea that this very life has been created by God is deeply inspiring and provides a powerful spiritual anchor; for others, the notion of an all-powerful creator is troubling, even untenable. Likewise, the idea that what we are today is the result of our past karma, and what we will become is determined by how we live today, appeals to some, while others find the idea of future lives and previous births incomprehensible. Within a Buddhist context, if the Buddha were to teach the doctrine of no-self to someone whose mental disposition would lead him to understand this in nihilistic terms—as if denying the very existence of a person who is responsible for his actions—not only would this be most unskillful on the Buddha's part but, more importantly, the teaching would be harmful for that person.[60]

A skilled physician, when prescribing medicine, takes into account the specific physical condition of a patient—age, fitness, proneness to negative reactions to certain substances—and, depending on these factors, prescribes the remedy that is needed. Likewise, with deep sensitivity, a skillful spiritual teacher adapts her teachings to the specific needs of a given situation. Therefore, when commenting on the Buddha's teachings, the Dalai Lama observes that a Buddhist cannot say, "This [a particular doctrine] is the best teaching," since such evaluations cannot be made independent of specific contexts.[61] Similarly, for the therapeutic relationship to be efficacious, skillful psychotherapists must consider each particular client's age, gender, cultural background, level of education, temperament, and values when recommending suitable interventions that help them work through their emotional suffering.

The Dalai Lama often describes the religious pluralism of the contemporary world as a "supermarket of religions." A supermarket features an abundant and nourishing array of foods. Similarly, the world of religions can take pride in its rich diversity of teachings and practices, even though, as noted in Chapter 2, individuals are increasingly faced with the heretical imperative—the need to choose among them. Buddhist hermeneutics offers an insight into why some people find certain religious teachings more effective than others, while others react negatively to the very same teachings. The Dalai Lama explains this from the Buddhist and classical Indian religious and philosophical viewpoints, saying that preferences are largely due to a person's own conditioning, including his or her karma, whereas from a theistic perspective, they are a matter of God's mysterious workings.[62] The Dalai Lama typically advises people to stay within their own traditional faith unless they have a strong affinity for a different tradition.

Each religion, the Dalai Lama affirms, has its own beauty, logic, and uniqueness. This diversity enables the world's religions to serve a vast number of human beings. With only one historical religion, the world would be impoverished, especially in relation to its spiritual resources. Seen in this way, religious pluralism is not an awkward problem but rather an adornment of the human spirit, something to be celebrated rather than bemoaned. The urge to convert others to one's faith is diminished when diversity is understood in this way; in its place arises a genuine acceptance of the viability of other religions. Then, the Dalai Lama observes, one can relate to the other faith traditions with a sense of appreciation for their profound contributions to the world.[63]

The need for a secular ethics

Although the Dalai Lama is a strong advocate of religion, he nevertheless insists that we need a secular ethics. In *Beyond Religion: Ethics for a Whole World*, he clearly and forcefully states his conviction on this matter:

> Certainly religion has helped millions of people in the past, helps millions today, and will continue to help millions in the future. But for all of its benefits in offering moral guidance and meaning in life, in today's world religion alone is no longer adequate as a basis for ethics. One reason for this is that many people in the world no longer follow any particular religion. Another reason is that, as the peoples of the world become ever more closely interconnected in an age of globalization and in multicultural societies, ethics based on any one religion would only appeal to some of us; it would not be meaningful for all. [. . .] Today [. . .] any religion-based answer to our neglect of inner values can never be universal, and so will be inadequate. What we need today is an approach to ethics which makes no recourse to religion and can be equally acceptable to those with faith and those without: a secular ethics.[64]

He notes that this statement may seem strange coming from someone who has lived most of his life as a monk, but sees no contradiction in his assertion. As he explains, "My faith enjoins me to strive for the welfare and benefit of all sentient beings, and reaching out beyond my own tradition, to those of other religions and those of none, is entirely in keeping with this."[65] Moreover, he is convinced that we have within our grasp a way and a means to ground inner values without contradicting religion, and yet, crucially, without depending on religion. Here the Dalai Lama models a truly integral approach, a perspective that transcends the dualistic tendency to view religious and secular thinking as oppositional.

Difference and commonality

As a pluralist, the Dalai Lama fully acknowledges the differences between religions, which are particularly evident at the doctrinal level, while discerning a convergence of ethical principles and practices that all religions share in common. All religions agree upon the necessity to control the undisciplined mind that harbors selfishness and destructive emotions. Each, in its own way, helps its adherents avoid misery and gain happiness. Most importantly, each teaches some version of the Golden Rule, thereby expressing an ethics of constraint, the idea that a person's behavior should be guided by the ways in which he wishes others to behave toward him. In addition, beyond this limited principle of reciprocity, each religion exhorts its adherents to cultivate compassion, a generous and empathic regard for the well-being of others. Here ethics moves beyond a *self*-referential framework—"*I* do not do to others what I wish them not to do to *me*"—to a larger frame that extends beyond self-reference.[66] In the ethics of compassion, one moves toward genuine selflessness or non-egocentricity. Compassion, for the Dalai Lama, entails fostering the qualities of "a good heart," a phrase that summarizes what he regards to be the best aspect of human nature.[67] Indeed, it is his fundamental conviction that compassion is our basic nature, and that all ethical teachings, whether religious or not, aim to develop and perfect this human capacity.[68]

While celebrating cultural diversity and the temperamental differences among individuals, the Dalai Lama insists that we are all equal physically, emotionally, and mentally. All of us have the same basic needs for food, shelter, safety, and love. All aspire to happiness and seek to avoid suffering. On this basic level, religion, ethnicity, culture, and language do not make any difference. The great challenge of promoting peaceful co-existence is that we remain in touch with this basic part of our nature. One way to meet this challenge is to situate specific problems within a wider context. When we are caught up in a disagreement with someone, we cannot allow the matter to cause conflict. We have the option of understanding the contrasting views in relation to the differing mental dispositions and aspirations that characterize the diversity of the human family. What is required of us, insists the Dalai Lama, is the ability to recognize the truth of the interconnectedness of all things, even in our disagreements.[69] This shift in perspective alone, he believes, can open our hearts. He summarizes his urgent commitment to inter-religious understanding and harmony in the form of an appeal to his fellow religious believers of all faiths, to realize and embody the essence of their traditions and to promote peace in the world:

> Obey the injunctions of your own faith. Travel to the essence of your religious teaching, the fundamental goodness of the human heart. Here is the space where, despite doctrinal differences, we are all simply human. Make the vow today that you shall never allow your faith to be used as an instrument of violence. Make the vow today that you may become an instrument of peace, living according to the teachings of compassion in our own religion. Open your heart so the blessing of your faith may reach into its deepest recesses.[70]

Likewise, his appeal to all people, religious or not, is to always embrace the common humanity that lies at the heart of us all. We must, he implores, find a way to transcend our differences and live in peace. The stakes are higher than ever before for the survival not only of humanity, but of the planet itself and the myriad creatures who share our home.[71]

The Dalai Lama, like Thich Nhat Hanh, articulates a vision of life that radically challenges the egocentricity of human beings. The teachings on emptiness and "no self" affirm the fundamental interconnectedness of life and the need to shift toward an understanding of our personal identity in relation to the whole of which we are a part. This vision, I believe, is Buddhism's most distinctive contribution to the collective wisdom gathered from the world's greatest religions. Consistent with this, recent modes of thought in the West, such as integral philosophy, provide us with developmental perspectives on how to shift our identities from egocentric to more inclusive frames of reference. These developmental perspectives also help us understand how religious persons from all traditions move from exclusivist to genuinely pluralist attitudes.

Rita Gross

An American religious studies scholar and feminist theologian, Rita Gross was a pioneering figure in several respects. Her dissertation about women's roles in Aboriginal Australian religions was the first application of a women's studies perspective in the academic study of religion. An essay she published on female God-language in Judaism was probably the first article to deal theoretically with the issue of God-language within a Jewish context; later, her feminist analysis and reconstruction of Buddhism in *Buddhism After Patriarchy* was groundbreaking. She was a proponent of the scholar-practitioner in the study of religions, a methodological approach integrating rigorous scholarship in the comparative study of religions with active engagement in the practices of particular religious traditions. Early in her career as a university professor, Gross took refuge with Chögyam Trungpa Rinpoche, becoming a Tibetan Buddhist. In 2005 she was made a *lopön* (senior teacher) by Jetsün Khandro Rinpoche, and began teaching at her Lotus Garden Center located in the United States.

Concern for how different religions can relate more harmoniously became Gross's lifelong, heartfelt project, first emerging during her youth in rural Wisconsin. As a teenager in the conservative Lutheran denomination, the pastor of her church rebuked her for playing the piano in the high-school baccalaureate service and failing to heed a scriptural verse often quoted in her church, "Be ye not unequally yoked together with unbelievers" (2 Cor. 6.14). She challenged this view by asking, "Weren't people of other faiths trying to do the same thing, in their own terms and their own way, as we are trying to do? Didn't all prayers go to the same place anyway?" "Definitely not," she was told.[72]

A few years later, while home from college for her mother's funeral, she faced an inquisition from her pastor to determine her eternal salvation. "Do you," he asked, "hold completely to the doctrines to which you swore lifelong loyalty when you were confirmed?"[73] If she said yes to whatever theological proposition was put before her, her eternal salvation would remain intact, but if she asked questions or nuanced her answers, it would not. Much to his consternation, she raised her questions. She subsequently received a letter stating that she had "sold her soul for a mess of academic pottage," and that she would spend eternity in hell unless she repented and apologized.[74] She did not repent; instead, she enrolled in graduate school to study the history of religions.

Gross's attitude toward religious diversity became the antidote to the exclusivism she experienced in her youth. Commenting on her stance as a teacher and her own individuation, she writes: "I never forgot or relinquished my original motivation to provide students with better tools with which to think about religious diversity than those that had been given to me or have been given to many of my students. My own spiritual questing landed me in Buddhism, after a happy ten-year sojourn in Judaism. For reasons I do not fully understand, Buddhism was and is my true home. I am not wishy-washy about how Buddhism has brought me peace and joy."[75]

An exemplary figure for me in many respects, Gross's writings validate my stance as a scholar-practitioner, inspire my passion for contemplative practices, strengthen my advocacy for religious pluralism and feminist concerns, and resonate with my self-understanding as a Western Hindu. Like Gross, I do not understand why Hinduism has become my true home, but I know it brings me the peace and joy that she derives from Buddhism. In addition, her reflections on hyphenated identity (discussed below) have enabled me to integrate insights and practices from Christian and Buddhist traditions, comparative philosophy of religion, and Jungian depth psychology. I, too, am a religious hybrid—a Hindu-Buddhist-Jungian—whose values derive from the Christian tradition in which I was raised.

Gross offers extensive reflections on the challenge of religious pluralism. Her approach is pragmatic and psychological rather than theological or metaphysical. She argues that religious diversity is to be expected and thus should not be spiritually or intellectually troubling; it is an inevitable, universal aspect of human experience. In actuality, however, religious diversity is often troubling, even more so for those who consider themselves to be especially religious. Why, she asks, are people uncomfortable with diversity, whether religious or otherwise? The answer, in her view, is that others who are different from us are threatening to our identity. We do not respond to people we perceive as being different from us in the same way we respond to those we perceive to be like us.[76] In her view, most of our problems in accepting religious diversity have to do with our issues about ourselves, not about the others with whom we interact.[77] For this reason, she focuses on how people become the kind of self that is uncomfortable with diversity, and how this discomfort may be overcome. Accordingly, her Buddhist approach identifies the root problem and a practical approach for transforming one's experience of diversity, a developmental model that moves from religious narrow-mindedness to a flourishing of religious diversity.

Dualistic perception and the means to overcome it

According to Gross, dualistic thinking is common in the usual processes of education and maturation. Duality is, in fact, the default mode of human consciousness. Most people define the world and others as being completely separate from themselves. The duality between self and other is simply taken to be the way things really are. People do not notice that self and other co-arise; there can be no self without other. The basic impression of seeming duality is not in itself very problematic. However, it is a short step away from developing hostility toward others when they trouble us, or fear of others who are different from ourselves.[78]

While this human characteristic may seem to be a tragic flaw, Buddhism teaches that this default position of dualistic consciousness is only a temporary obscuration (to use common Buddhist terminology), not something to which we are forever condemned. Much more basic and fundamental to our being is our potential to clear away temporary obscurations. This potential, traditionally called Buddha-nature or, in more contemporary language, basic goodness, is present as our bedrock nature, even when we are unaware of it and acting contrary to its inclinations. The Buddhist view is that as we come into closer contact with the basic goodness inherent in our true nature, obscurations diminish. The tradition often uses the analogy of sun and clouds to explain this dynamic of consciousness—the sun is there, even on cloudy days, and the clouds eventually dissipate.[79]

How do we remove the obscuration of default dualism? How does the sun come out? Using this analogy, Gross regards the sun as flourishing with religious diversity and the clouds as our discomfort with diversity. The clouds are our assessment that there is something wrong with religious diversity based on the presumption that, in an ideal world, everyone would belong to the same religion.[80] Gross proposes two basic tools that address our tendency towards oppositional duality and enable us to utilize our basic goodness—real contact with religious others, and spiritual disciplines. The latter give us the ability to become more introspective and help us detach from fixed views. Basic mindfulness practices, for example, typically involve focusing on one's breathing as a means of quieting the wandering, distracted mind in the immediate present. The breath is usually chosen because it is always with us and is religiously and culturally neutral. Mindfulness does not inculcate specific intellectual, theological, or religious content; instead, it engenders mental health by allowing a relaxed, stable, and flexible state of mind to emerge. Spiritual practices that develop such states of mind are contemplative, not just discursive; they ground a person in a non-conceptual intuitive mode of being, and can free one from fixed beliefs and theories, especially about right and wrong.[81]

Gross points out that practices which focus on inner states are often insufficient for developing the capacity to flourish with religious diversity. Contact with people from other religious traditions may also be necessary. The Dalai Lama's first trip to India, described earlier in this chapter, serves as a powerful example of the efficacy of contact with religious others, an experience that left him forever changed and engendered his deep commitment to inter-religious harmony. As Gross observes, if such a well-educated and deeply spiritual person as the Dalai Lama needs such contact, how much more so do the rest of us. There are many ways to establish contact with religious others. One can take a course on world religions, read informative books on the topic, visit the religious sanctuary of another faith, or become friends with members of other religions.[82]

Hyphenated identity

Dualistic perception conditions our sense of identity. Gross observes that the simple *experiential* duality of self and other becomes a *metaphysical* belief in the real and enduring existence of both self and other. From a Buddhist perspective, this is only how things seem conventionally. For this reason, Gross urges us to question our deep-seated assumptions about identity—Is identity a singular thing? Is identity not already differentiated? Her reply to these questions is that we are a composite of many different experiences, which inevitably leads to a hyphenated identity. When this is acknowledged, we are much less likely to fixate on any one element of identity and, as a result, we can be much less uncomfortable with others. The implications of this view for how we experience religious diversity are far-reaching:

> One may be a member of any given religion, and that identity may be very strong, but it is never one's sole identity. It would be self-deceptive to claim otherwise. One may have a religious identity, but one also has family roles, an occupation, political views, a sexual orientation, a cultural identity, a racial identity, national citizenship, an educational level, membership in an age cohort, sexual identity, gender identity, membership in a denomination within one's larger religion, a relationship with the arts and/or sports . . . and other identities depending on the specifics of one's experience. Even for people for whom their religion is very important, these other identities— especially family roles and occupational identities, as well as political identities—are also important and may well absorb more time, money, and energy than religious activities. For some people, it is hard to believe that their religious identity is more important to them than their identity as a fan of their favorite sports team. Furthermore, one's identity is never confined to a single element in this list of possible identities; who one is is always a combination of various possible identities. One is never only a Christian or a Buddhist and nothing else, a father or a child and nothing else, a political conservative or liberal and nothing else. It is an illusion to imagine that one identity ever trumps all others. Even if one is not biracial, bicultural, or a multiple religious belonger, one always has a hyphenated identity.[83]

Moreover, throughout one's life, these various identities shift and change; some become more dominant, others decline in importance or drop away completely. Many people, she points out, discover a whole new self relatively late in life.[84] Viewed in such a context, discomfort with religious diversity seems quite unnecessary.

Just as our personal identity changes over time, so do religions. No matter how much they may claim they are unchanging—that they proclaim only eternal verities—every living religion has changed significantly throughout its history. That is why, as Gross observes, it is still a living religion. Under current conditions, no change, she argues, is more vital than those changes that lead to accommodating religious diversity.[85] Gross's views differ from many theologies of religious pluralism. *Diversity*, she points out, refers to the fact that there are many religions, whereas *pluralism* refers to an evaluation of that fact. She argues that the need to accept, accommodate, and live well with that diversity overrides any theological evaluation of that diversity, including her own evaluation that religious diversity is a blessing.[86] Here she exemplifies the Buddha's admonition not to get caught in the net of theories and the pragmatic nature of Buddhadharma. In her view, the various religions are a skillful means for coping with diverse human needs in diverse situations, rather than monolithic prescriptions for all human beings everywhere.[87]

Insights for integrative spirituality

Exemplary Buddhists offer many useful ways to think about religious pluralism that complement the perspectives of Christians and Hindus:

- Although Buddhism has spread to many cultures during its long history, it has been remarkably tolerant of the established religions it has encountered. It serves as a prototype for the religious attitude necessary for cultivating peace in the global world of the twenty-first century. Buddhists such as Thich Nhat Hanh and the Dalai Lama have made peaceful co-existence the centerpiece of their work as influential writers and religious leaders.

- The Buddha teaches in a manner that helps seekers avoid getting caught in the net of competing theories. His pragmatic teachings emphasize the empirical criterion of personal experience; he teaches a provisional faith that is to be tested by each individual. This attitude makes Buddhism particularly attractive to many people in the modern West who seek a non-dogmatic approach to spirituality. The emphasis on verification appeals to scientifically minded people. The Buddhist teachings about the causes of suffering and how it can be ameliorated attract those looking for a psychological approach to spiritual life. In these ways, Buddhism serves as a model for how religion can be grounded in experience and non-dogmatic, and capable of addressing the existential issues of modern people living in secular societies.

- Thich Nhat Hanh, the Dalai Lama, and many contemporary Buddhist teachers model how to regard religious others with reverence and respect. Jesus and Buddha, as well as the sages and prophets of other religions, may be seen as spiritual ancestors who belong to all of us regardless of what our native tradition may be.

- The Buddhist teaching regarding the interdependent nature of reality is a strong antidote to feelings of alienation and separation so endemic in Western modernity. Thich Nhat Hanh's rendering of this idea as interbeing, for example, helps us recognize the interconnectedness that pervades our existence and our relationship to our environment.

- Exemplary Buddhists help us overcome our dualistic perceptions regarding self, others, and personal identity. They help us understand that people different from ourselves need not threaten our identity. Dualistic perception is shown to be a natural aspect of human development (the default mode of human consciousness, as Rita Gross puts it), but is not something to which we are condemned forever. The dichotomy between self and other is conventional rather than ontological; it is an inaccurate or distorted apprehension of reality rather than the way things actually are. The obscurations are temporary like clouds that occlude the sun. The Buddhist view, in fact, affirms that our basic goodness or Buddha-nature is more basic and fundamental than our tendency to perceive in a dualistic manner. As we come into closer contact with this potential, or our true nature, our obscurations diminish, and we may expand our circle of concern, enabling us to move from egocentric and ethnocentric frames of reference to an identity that is worldcentric, or even cosmocentric, in scope.

Buddhists also point out that a narrow sense of identity, particularly religious identity, does not accurately describe human existence. We are composite beings with hyphenated identities, most of which change over the course of a lifetime. When this fact is appreciated, discomfort with religious diversity can be attenuated.

Buddhist pluralists, such as the Dalai Lama, acknowledge that there are significant differences between religions at the doctrinal level. However, at the level of ethical teachings, there is a great convergence. The central message of all religions, he persuasively maintains, is love, compassion, and universal brotherhood and sisterhood. His appeal to all people, whether religious or not, is to focus on the basic needs that all human beings have in common. All of us aspire to happiness and seek to avoid suffering. Accordingly, we need an ethics for a global society that is viable both for people who belong to a faith tradition and those who do not. Buddhism, in this way, offers a model for how religions can look beyond themselves in the service of the entire human community.

- Buddhist contemplative practices, such as mindfulness meditation, have proven to be useful for physical and emotional well-being for persons belonging to other faith traditions and to others in secular contexts. It is noteworthy that Christians, including Paul Knitter and John Hick, incorporate Buddhist forms of meditation into their Christian spirituality. As Rita Gross points out, these practices typically focus on the breath and are neutral with regard to theological content. These Buddhist practices are helpful for cultivating non-judgmental, flexible states of mind that can free persons from fixed beliefs and theories, thereby making it more possible for them to accommodate religious diversity and different worldviews.

- Buddhism, as a non-theistic religion, is helpful for those who struggle with or have rejected traditional God-images. The Buddhist concept of emptiness frees the mind from conceptions that are problematic for some individuals, for instance God conceived of as an anthropomorphic being or a male deity. Doctrines, as Buddhists have traditionally explained, are best understood as fingers pointing to the moon, or rafts taking us to the other shore. This perspective aligns well with John Hick's pluralist hypothesis (described in Chapter 3)—religions are different culturally-formed human responses, utilizing different conceptual systems, to an ultimate, ineffable transcendent Real.

Notes

1 Harold Coward, *Pluralism: Challenge to World Religions*. Maryknoll, NY: Orbis Books, 1985, 81.
2 Ibid., 82–86.
3 Ibid., 86.
4 Ibid., 86–87.
5 Ibid., 88–89.
6 Ibid., 89.
7 Thich Nhat Hanh, *Old Path White Clouds: Walking in the Footsteps of the Buddha*. Berkeley, CA: Parallax Press, 1991, 114.
8 Ibid., 115.
9 Ibid., 115.
10 *Peace is Every Step: Meditation in Life: The Life and Work of Thich Nhat Hanh*, directed by Gaetano Kazuo Maida, 1997; Oakland, CA: Media Festival, 2005, DVD.
11 Ibid.
12 Thich Nhat Hanh, *Coming Home: Jesus and Buddha as Brothers*. New York: Riverhead Books, 1999, 13–15.
13 Ibid., 15–16.
14 Ibid., 189–90.
15 Ibid., 190.
16 Ibid., 195.
17 Ibid., 7.
18 Ibid., 2–3.
19 Ibid., 3–4.
20 Ibid., 5.
21 Ibid., 9–10.
22 Ibid., 43.
23 Ibid., 31–33.
24 Ibid., 34–35.
25 Ibid., 46–47.
26 Ibid., 92.
27 Ibid., 110–11.
28 Ibid., 138.
29 Ibid.
30 Ibid., 181–83.
31 Ibid., 191–92.
32 Ibid., 192.
33 Ibid., 193–94.
34 Ibid., 195–96.
35 Ibid., 196.
36 Ibid., 197.
37 Ibid., 197–98.
38 Ibid., 198.
39 Ibid., 199.
40 Ibid., 200.
41 Dalai Lama XIV, *Toward a True Kinship of Faiths: How the World's Religions Can Come Together*. New York: Three Rivers Press, 2010, 19–20.
42 Ibid., 38.
43 Ibid., ix–xiv.
44 Ibid., 1–2.
45 Ibid., 6.
46 Ibid., 6–7.
47 Ibid., 9.
48 Ibid., x.

49 Ibid., xi–xii.
50 Ibid., 145.
51 Ibid., 148.
52 Ibid.
53 Ibid., 148–49.
54 Ibid., 131.
55 Ibid., 132–33.
56 Ibid., 150–51.
57 Ibid., 151.
58 Ibid., 159.
59 Ibid., 154.
60 Ibid.
61 Ibid., 155.
62 Ibid.
63 Ibid., 156.
64 Dalai Lama XIV, *Beyond Religion: Ethics for a Whole World*. Boston: Houghton Mifflin Harcourt, 2011, xiii–xiv. The ideas proposed in this book are a further development of the views he presented in his *Ethics for a New Millennium*. New York: Riverhead Books, 1999.
65 Ibid, xiv.
66 Dalai Lama XIV, *Toward a True Kinship of Faiths*, 114.
67 Ibid., 115.
68 Ibid., 109.
69 Ibid., 180–81.
70 Ibid., 181.
71 Ibid., 182.
72 Rita M. Gross, *Religious Diversity: What's the Problem?* Eugene, OR: Cascade Books, 2014, x.
73 Ibid.
74 Ibid.
75 Ibid., ix–xii.
76 Ibid., 4–5.
77 Ibid., 15.
78 Ibid., 327–28.
79 Ibid., 328–29.
80 Ibid., 330.
81 Ibid., 177–78; 332.
82 Ibid., 332–33.
83 Ibid., 158.
84 Ibid., 158–59.
85 Ibid., 326.
86 Ibid., 8.
87 Ibid., 14.

6

JUNGIAN DEPTH PSYCHOLOGY AND INDIVIDUATION

> If you bring forth what is within you, what you bring forth will save
> you. If you do not bring forth what is within you, what you do not
> bring forth will destroy you.
> —*The Gospel of Thomas*

I was enthralled with Jung's memoir *Memories, Dreams, Reflections*, when I first read it as an undergraduate. Like Jung, I had an inkling that the myth I was living was significantly different from the one I had inherited. Here was a man who had burst through the constraints of his Christian heritage, mined the myths and symbols of various religions, and created a psychological form of spirituality that went beyond religious tradition.

Jung's project continued to animate me and, as I disclosed earlier, my Jungian analysis compelled me to heed the guidance of dreams, made sense of a life-changing *enantiodromia* that ensued from an extended meditation retreat in India, and has guided me in navigating the complexities of relational life at home and at work. While much of my study of religious traditions has been done in an academic context, important insights have emerged all along the path of my individuation, or what Jung has described as the journey toward wholeness, in which one aims to integrate disparate aspects of one's life into a meaningful narrative. Additionally, vital insights have come through my spiritual practice and in my teaching at an institute dedicated to the study of depth psychology.

Jung's work continues to inform my life both personally and professionally, but contrary to some Jungians, I have come to believe that a psychological approach to spirituality need not preclude or inhibit one from engaging in contemplative practices long valued by religious traditions. Jung himself discouraged Westerners from practicing contemplative yoga, an admonition, in my view, that is overstated and is not applicable to individuals who engage these practices in a mature manner.

Jungian psychology need not be considered a replacement or substitution for traditional spiritual practices; rather, it can be seen as a complementary endeavor that adds a dimension to spirituality that is often neglected or missing altogether.

In the introduction to this book, I articulated the principal concerns of my academic career and personal spiritual quest. The first of these—religious pluralism —pertains to how the study of exemplary religious thinkers and contemplatives can inspire and inform one's spirituality, which has been discussed in the chapters devoted to Christianity, Hinduism, and Buddhism, the traditions that have been most influential in my life. In this chapter, I consider the existential basis of Jung's ideas as well as perspectives of contemporary Jungians, with regard to individuation, religion, God-images, and the divine feminine. While Chapter 8 is devoted to the complementarity of psychological and spiritual forms of inner work, it is best to explore Jungian psychology first in its own context and focus on its specific aims. I also elucidate Jung's interest in Eastern yoga, particularly his commentary on the chakra symbolism of kundalini yoga, to highlight some similarities and differences between his depth psychology and Hindu yoga traditions.

Jungian psychology as a form of spirituality

Jung's depth psychology can be engaged as a form of spirituality, one that emerged from his own individuation process, and it provides an important alternative for those who do not feel confined to or identified with a single religious tradition. In *The Red Book*, a deeply personal account of his own spiritual crisis and recovery of soul, he refers to *the spirit of the times* and *the spirit of the depths*.[1] For Jung, the first of these phrases characterizes the materialistic culture of modernity and the eclipse of the sacred; it describes the loss of soul that characterizes modernity. The second refers to the call to interiority, in which a person discovers the deepest dimension of his being; it names the deeply personal journey within that leads to soul's recovery.

Jung's personal crisis

Jung's personal journey led him to develop depth psychology as a way of helping individuals discover and express the Self in their lives. Jung describes the Self as the totality of the psyche, which encompasses both conscious awareness and the unconscious. The Self is "the centre of this totality, just as the ego is the centre of consciousness."[2] While Jung's definition of the Self came from his empirical study of the unconscious, he acknowledged his debt to Indian thought. The Self to which he refers is a primordial image akin to the ideas found in the Upanishads regarding Brahman, the ground of all being, and the Atman, the innermost being of an individual.[3] Jung describes the developmental process of discovering the Self as individuation, a ceaseless endeavor that requires a vigilant engagement with one's interiority, by which a person becomes a separate, indivisible unity, or whole.[4] Individuation, Jung asserts, is the primary purpose of a well-lived human life; it is the opus of a lifetime.

The distinction between the ego and the Self is of central importance in Jung's depth psychology. As he articulates, the ego is the conditioned personality that develops primarily through interactions with other people, while the Self, or non-ego, is a larger psychological reality—the dynamic ground of the psyche and the matrix out of which the ego arises. Although the Self is the center and totality of the psyche that encompasses consciousness and the unconscious, most people are estranged from it. "Somewhere deep in the background," he says in his memoir, "I always knew that I was two persons."[5] One is his public persona; the other, a deeper more authentic being with roots that transcend the biographical facts of his time and place. Personality No. 1, he explains, is the respectable son of his parents, an intelligent, hard-working schoolboy; personality No. 2, however, is already grown up, a being "remote from the world of men, but close to nature" and "above all, close to the night, to dreams, and to whatever 'God' worked directly in him."[6] For Jung, however, the biblical notion that humans are made "in the image of God" is too anthropocentric. He tells us that high mountains, rivers, trees, flowers, and animals better exemplify divinity than the vanity, mendacity, and egotism of human beings, qualities which, he acknowledges, inhere within personality No. 1. What matters, for Jung, is his deep conviction that another realm exists beyond the conventional social reality. "Here," he writes, "lived the 'Other,' who knew God as a hidden, personal, and at the same time suprapersonal secret. Here nothing separated man from God; indeed, it was as though the human mind looked down upon Creation simultaneously with God."[7]

The importance he gives to the deeper level of his being is emblematic of the mode of analytical work he developed in his writings and work with patients:

> The play and counterplay between personalities No. 1 and No. 2, which has run through my whole life, has nothing to do with a "split" or dissociation in the ordinary medical sense. In my life, No. 2 has been of prime importance, and I have always tried to make room for anything that wanted to come to me from within. He is a typical figure, but he is perceived only by the few. Most people's conscious understanding is not sufficient to realize that he is also what they are.[8]

The profound tension Jung experienced between the two personalities precipitated a mid-life crisis. Early in his career, Jung became Sigmund Freud's close friend and associate. As a Freudian seeking to discover his authentic self, Jung felt compelled to break from Freud. In effect Jung committed "egocide," or symbolic death. As a Freudian, he had to kill his false self, or ego–identity, to allow his authentic being to emerge into the foreground.[9]

The period that followed was one of isolation and inner chaos in which Jung was assailed by material that made him doubt his own sanity. These were the years of his confrontation with the unconscious. His memoir tells us that one day while sitting at his desk, he let himself plunge into the depths of his psyche, submitting to the spontaneous images arising in his unconscious.[10] This was the beginning of an experiment that lasted for several years, producing a wealth of material that later became his most important work. Throughout this time, he carefully observed and documented his dreams, experiences, and fantasies and embellished them with his creative artwork. He felt utterly compelled to understand the meaning of this material, saying, "I had to draw concrete conclusions from the insight the unconscious had given me—and that task was to become a life's work."[11]

Drawing mandalas enabled Jung to emerge from his inner darkness. As an image that arises from the unconscious and takes shape in times of psychic disorganization, the mandala offers the psyche a way to restore balance and order. As his psychic state changed, so did his mandalas, as Jung explains:

> I was being compelled to go through this process of the unconscious. I had to let myself be carried along by the current, without a notion of where it would lead me. When I began drawing the mandalas, however, I saw that everything, all the paths I had been following, all the steps I had taken, were leading back to a single point—namely, the mid-point. It became increasingly plain to me that the mandala is the center. It is the exponent of all paths. It is the path to the center, to individuation.[12]

This insight gave Jung stability, gradually restored his inner peace, and served to hold great significance for both his life and his psychology. "I knew that in finding the mandala as an expression of the self I had attained what was for me the ultimate. Perhaps someone else knows more, but not I."[13] Thus, the mandala symbolizes for Jung the ultimate goal of the individuation process, the realization of the Self, and the attainment of wholeness. He also discovered that for his patients, dreams could symbolize this centralizing process and reveal a new center of the personality. Jung envisions the quest for wholeness as a process of transformation that begins with the psyche in a state of fragmentation and ends with its eventual unification.[14]

This period of Jung's life proved decisive for his work. He writes: "The years when I was pursuing my inner images were the most important in my life—in them everything essential was decided. It all began then; the later details are only supplements and clarifications of the material that burst forth from the unconscious, and at first swamped me. It was the *prima materia* for a lifetime's work."[15]

Jung's inner work, in my view, has affinities to contemplative yoga, especially tantric practices; his understanding of mandalas as symbols for the Self offers an important parallel between his depth psychology and yoga. The priority Jung gives to introspection parallels the interiorization of meditation, though with a notable difference. Jung was familiar with the yogic concept of *tapas*, the psychic force generated by spiritual practice. In Jung's view, the yogi concentrates his psyche by withdrawing libido from both external objects and interior thoughts. This practice is akin to the process of active imagination in Jung's psychology.[16] The difference in yoga traditions is that a practitioner focuses on an image or object to achieve one-pointed attention or concentration, a process that generates meditative absorption in the object. Jung's psychology, by contrast, does not prescribe a particular object, image, or set of exercises. His memoir reveals that Jung practiced yoga during the time of his confrontation with the unconscious, but only for a limited purpose. He tells us, "I would do these exercises only until I had calmed myself enough to resume my work with the unconscious. As soon as I had the feeling that I was myself again, I abandoned this restraint upon the emotions and allowed the images and inner voices to speak afresh. The Indian, on the other hand, does yoga exercises in order to obliterate completely the multitude of psychic contents and images."[17]

According to archetypal psychologist James Hillman, Jung's approach involves a dialogue with the contents of the unconscious. In active imagination, attention is given to the images, emotions, or body sensations that arise in the mind; it is concerned with the ego's relationship with and personal reactions to these phenomena. The emotional involvement with these images and their spontaneous reactions to the ego's attitude are as important as the images themselves.[18]

Jung's depth psychology centers upon the relationship between the ego and the unconscious. Typically during the first half of life, we are involved with ego development, which entails a progressive separation of the ego from the Self (ego–Self separation). The second half, however, requires the surrender or relativization of the ego as it experiences and relates to the Self (ego–Self reunion). The conscious work of individuation requires a religious attitude, which Jung characterizes as a careful and scrupulous observation of one's psychological life.[19] A person must make a steadfast effort to discover and attune to the Self so that it becomes an inner partner toward whom one's attention is continually turned.[20] In this way, Jung's psychology functions as a religious pathway, especially for an individual who is no longer able to find meaning in traditional religions. For such a person, neither sin and redemption nor ignorance and wisdom, but rather fragmentation and wholeness form the center of the religious quest.[21]

Jung and religious pluralism

Jung's depth psychology is grounded in an extensive study of religious symbols and myths. On this basis he proposes that all mythologies have a common source in the collective unconscious, and that we are heirs to all the world's religions. No god or goddess is utterly alien to anyone; all deities have a place in the psyche's pantheon. This idea embraces all the gods and is completely counter to the "no other gods" injunction of the biblical myth expressed in Exodus. As Murray Stein puts it, "There are no 'other' gods. Each image of God—whether male or female, animal or human or superhuman, concrete or abstract—sheds some additional light on the Wholeness of the God image embedded in the human psyche."[22] This understanding of the psyche is the antidote to exclusivism and accords well with the pluralist attitudes we have encountered in the work of influential Christians, Hindus, and Buddhists in preceding chapters.

Jung's writings affirm the religious function of the psyche, an impulse that arises in each person at all times and places. In his view, "The collective unconscious contains the whole spiritual heritage of mankind's evolution, born anew in the brain structure of every individual."[23] Elsewhere he observes, "One could almost say that if all the world's traditions were cut off at a single blow, the whole of mythology and the whole history of religion would start all over again with the next generation."[24] While archetypes—formative principles in the unconscious that animate and condition our life experience—are common to all religions, the symbols and myths differ among traditions depending on their cultural and historical contexts.

Jung found that he could not really distinguish, psychologically, between the realization of the Self and the *imago Dei*, the image of God. The Self bears all the characteristics that religious persons and theologians have given to the reality they call God. From his discoveries of the unconscious and the presence of the God-image within it, Jung drew conclusions concerning the nature of established religions. His psychological interpretation of the notion of revelation provides a common foundation from which all religions can speak to one another since all revelation, in his view, has at least a part of its origin in the personal and collective unconscious. In Jung's words, "Revelation is an unveiling of the depths of the human soul first and foremost, a 'laying bare,' hence it is an essentially psychological event, though this does not of course tell us what else it could be."[25] It is the experience of God speaking from within, which is essentially the same for all human beings. The differing dogmas and doctrines are attempts to give symbolic expression to this essentially ineffable experience.

An important implication of Jung's perspective is that no religion or symbol can claim to be absolute. "It is altogether inconceivable," affirms Jung, "that there could be any definite figure capable of expressing archetypal indefiniteness."[26] In other words, the God-image is an utter mystery, ever beyond our realization; it cannot be captured in any one form. Although these statements clearly show that Jung is a pluralist, he gives special emphasis to Christ and certain Christian theological concepts. For example, "The Christ symbol is of the greatest importance for psychology insofar as it is perhaps the most highly developed and differentiated symbol of the self, apart from the figure of the Buddha."[27] For Jung, the archetypal Christ represents the completion of the process of individuation, the realization of the Self. Jung also regards the theological concept of the incarnation to be a model of individuation and understands the passion of Christ as a further symbolic representation of the pain and trust involved in this transformative process—the experience of surrendering the ego to integrate it into the mystery of the Self.[28]

Jung acknowledges the efficacy of other symbols by saying, "In the West the archetype [of the self] is filled out with the dogmatic figure of Christ; in the East, with Purusha, the Atman, Hiranyagarbha, the Buddha, and so on."[29] Jung's attitude toward religious pluralism encourages us to learn from traditions however different they may be from our own. He believes that an understanding of Eastern religions helps the West in its quest for spiritual renewal. The East has long been aware of the reality of the unconscious and the necessity of penetrating its depths. Yet, he recognizes that just as the West has lost touch with the inner life and the God within, the East has tended to ignore the reality of the material world. He feels there is much to be learned on both sides. "The East," he observes, "is at the bottom of the spiritual change we are passing through today," one that "lies essentially within us."[30] Thus, in encountering Eastern meditation traditions, we are challenged to discover the divine—which for Jung means the unconscious— within ourselves. While Jung himself learned from the East, he discouraged Westerners from practicing contemplative yoga. Instead, he felt that we needed to mine Gnosticism, Kabbalah, and alchemy, esoteric traditions indigenous to the West. Eventually, he believed, the West would produce its own yoga on a basis laid down by Christianity.[31] While I entirely agree that the contemplative and esoteric traditions of the West are valuable sources for contemporary spirituality, I believe Eastern traditions also present forms of contemplative yoga that have been successfully transmitted to the West.

Individuation and numinous experience

I regard individuation to be at the heart of Jung's psychology and an important aspect of an integrated spirituality. Just as I turn to exemplary Hindus, Christians, and Buddhists for guidance and inspiration for my spiritual quest, I seek assistance from Jungian writers who elucidate Jung's psychological path to wholeness. Murray Stein is one of my most reliable guides regarding Jung's views on the individuation process and its relationship to religion, numinous experience, and spirituality.

Individuation is a dynamic, innate tendency that impels individuals to become aware of who and what they are, conveys Stein. This self-realizing drive seeks to expand ego-consciousness beyond its personal traits, habits, and culturally conditioned attitudes into a much wider horizon of self-understanding and wholeness.[32] The process entails two movements, one analytical and the other synthetic. The analytical movement differentiates or separates a person from identities that have been forged through socialization and acculturation—perspectives and attitudes derived from parents, authority figures, and the internalized voices these figures engender. The synthetic movement conjoins rather than separates; it involves paying careful attention to the archetypal images in the unconscious as they appear in dreams, active imagination, or syncretistic events so they may be integrated into conscious awareness.[33] Jung's own process, described above, exemplifies the way in which he navigated his midlife crisis and found his way, through active imagination and the making of mandalas, to the center of his being.

Jung regards individuation as a lifelong process of making conscious a vast amount of unconscious material—all the introjections and identifications accumulated through a lifetime.[34] The ego's perspective, or ego attitude as Jungians often refer to it, is at best partial and one-sided. As Stein sees it, while the ego is the most intimate and individual thing that we know, it is also a dark mystery.

Shadow contents—aspects of ourselves that we disavow and typically project onto others—must be assimilated into awareness if our authentic individuality is to emerge. For this to happen we must engage in a process that seems irrational— we must intentionally open ourselves to images and feelings that emerge from the unconscious. Jung describes the integration of unconscious contents as *the transcendent function*[35] and the main method for activating this function is *active imagination*, the process Jung used during his personal crisis. Through active imagination one enters into dialogue between the conscious and unconscious aspects of the psyche until a "third thing" is formed that is a union of the two parts. When this conjunction occurs, one can become oneself in an expanded and more complex manner than before.[36]

While numinous experience is typically discussed in relation to religion and mysticism, it is also important in Jungian psychology as an ingredient of the individuation process. *Numen* refers to an experience of the sacred; more broadly, numinous experiences are encounters that transcend the ego in a manner that is powerful—even overwhelming—but generally uplifting. In secular language, these are "peak experiences" that expand a person's sense of self and perspective on life. Jung suggests that his psychology is less concerned with the treatment of neuroses than with experiences that give rise to wholeness in the psyche. "The approach to the numinous," he writes, "is the real therapy and inasmuch as you attain numinous experiences you are released from the curse of pathology."[37] Stein explains, however, that this statement must be understood psychologically— "While the psychological hero(ine) of the individuation journey is by no means identical to the spiritual hero(ine) of the journey to God (however this word may be defined), it is not always easy to tell where their paths diverge."[38] Yet they do diverge, he insists, and decisively so. An integrative spirituality, I would add, requires that seekers understand how to relate these two distinct, yet complementary journeys.

From a Jungian perspective, numinous or religious experiences of a mystical nature may make life feel more meaningful. Such experiences sometimes even lead us to feel that problems such as addiction or behavioral disorders are trivial when seen in the light of the vision of wholeness imparted by a mystical state. Stein argues, however, that for modern and psychologically astute people, spiritual awareness itself does not suffice, nor does it offer real solutions to problems caused by neurosis. Thus, while going on spiritual quests or having numinous experiences may be important, they do not constitute or complete an individuation process. At most, he believes, numinous experiences hint at larger, non-egoic powers in the psyche that must be analyzed through psychological inquiry and made conscious.[39]

Stein goes further in differentiating the psychological journey from a religious or spiritual one. Jungian analysis, he states, dissolves attachments to religious objects, traditional practices, and theologies. Identification with any religious figure or archetypal pattern blocks the further movement of individuation, by fixing the ego to objects that have been, in Stein's words, *unconsciously* acquired.

Consciousness, he maintains, must be freed from these fixations if a person is to realize individuality and uniqueness.[40] The psychological journey of individuation enters the realm of the numinous, but the path then leads out of it again; it is not tantamount to a mystical journey that regards a union with God as the goal of the process, nor is it the same as the *via negativa* of religious traditions such as Zen Buddhism. For Jungian psychology, the greater goal is the integration of conscious and unconscious aspects of the psyche, which goes on indefinitely. To remain attached or stuck in mystical experiences, Stein explains, "would amount to becoming assimilated to the unconscious," a condition evidenced by pathologies such as grandiose inflation, loss of ego boundaries, or even entrapment in a paranoid psychotic defense.[41]

While these pathologies are real enough, I challenge Stein's assumption regarding identification with religious figures or archetypal patterns. I suggest we take a look from another angle at what I regard to be his one-sided view. From my perspective, numinous or mystical experiences are just as likely to engender integration and wholeness in psychologically healthy people. To the extent that one engages a spiritual practice intentionally and *consciously*, I believe that one's engagement with aspects of a religious or spiritual tradition can enhance rather than inhibit one's individuation. Such engagement also curbs tendencies toward literalism or fundamentalism, especially when one embraces religious pluralism and acknowledges that there are multiple ways in which one can experience the Real or Ultimate. The Christian, Hindu, and Buddhist pluralists discussed in earlier chapters clearly attest to this possibility.

A new god-image and Jung's *Answer to Job*

Throughout his life Jung engaged in a conscious dialogue with religion, especially Christianity, his inherited tradition. In *Memories, Dreams, Reflections*, written near the end of his life, he recalls his childhood in a Protestant parsonage, the disappointing discussions with his Swiss Reformed pastor father, and his early and late life struggles with faith and belief. Jung does not fully identify with the Enlightenment and the supreme value of reason and science. Instead, his temperament reflects the influence of German Romanticism and its high regard for myth, symbols, and mystery. In his deepest registers, Stein observes, Jung responded to life as a person deeply attuned to spirituality even though he stood apart from religious organizations. When Jung uses the religious language of his ancestors, he uses the terminology in a symbolic and psychological sense. He does not speak of God as traditional religious people or theologians do, as a metaphysical and transcendent being; he speaks of God-images that are generated by the psyche.[42]

Stein notes that in his mature years, Jung took it upon himself to offer Christianity a type of psychotherapeutic treatment, concerned with Christianity's deeply ingrained tendency to split the polarities of the human psyche into irreconcilable opposites—good against evil, masculine against feminine, and spirit against body. The treatment failed, however, since the patient—institutional Christianity—was not interested in pursuing wholeness. Jung's psychology became an alternative approach to spirituality, neither premodern/traditional nor modern/secular. It is, shares Stein, a new vision of humanism based on the idea of integrating the divine into the human. The vision involves transposing the theological gods of traditional religions into psychological God-images that can be integrated into human consciousness.[43]

Jung's vision of a psychological spirituality is expressed in his late and highly controversial work, *Answer to Job*, in which he maintains that "God wanted to become man, and still wants to."[44] This assertion conveys the spiritual aspect of individuation that is characterized as continuing incarnation. In other words, the divine incarnates not only in Christ, but in all human beings who engage in the psychological process of becoming more conscious of disavowed aspects of their lives and who move toward wholeness. The radical message of *Answer to Job* shifts the location of the biblical drama from the metaphysical and mythical realm to the psychological. Through this shift, Stein explains, human beings become individually responsible for redemption, atonement, and the reconciliation of opposites. Salvation and atonement no longer come from above, but must instead come from within.[45]

Stein presents his cogent commentary on Jung's psychological perspective regarding the Book of Job and the rest of the Bible, a unique narrative of the biblical God-image's individuation, in a series of insights for reflection:

- God is the main character of the Bible and, in this sense, is a literary figure or God-image, not the Godhead as it might be in and of itself.

- The arc of the biblical narrative runs from the creation of the world to the end of time and tells the story of the biblical God-image's psychological development. Jung rewrites, in effect, the biblical myth. *Answer to Job* becomes a poem of the psyche that lays out a vision for a new kind of humanism, one that is neither traditionally religious nor atheistic or secular. By means of this creative approach, Jung advocates knowledge by experience, a type of modern gnosis.

- Jung places the Book of Job at the center of the biblical narrative, which is the pivotal point upon which the transformation of the Bible's main character, the God-image Yahweh, turns. In this book God is found guilty of unconsciousness and misconduct. He is wrong to treat the blameless and noble figure of Job as He does. Job holds his ground and shows supreme integrity; God, by contrast, displays sheer unconsciousness and an arrogant misuse of power. Human consciousness has surpassed that of the Divine in the sense that Job's pleas of innocence are right and God's treatment of him as his inferior is wrong. In the confrontation with Job, God has been found to be inept and cruel. He has violated his own sense of justice, broken his covenant, and lost his integrity. God realizes that power cannot prevail over righteousness— He must make amends; He must recognize His inferiority to humankind.

The critical issue is shadow awareness—God is not fully aware of what He is doing, and He has treated Job unjustly.

• The drama produces a crisis in God's conscience. As a psychological factor, the God-image can be influenced and affected by what is going on in consciousness. The God-image, even though it is collective and embedded deeply within the archetypal layers of the unconscious, can be affected by what transpires within the consciousness of the individual. In order to catch up with Job and regain His moral standing, God enters into a profound relationship with humanity and becomes incarnated as an individual person within His own creation. In this way an important aspect of the archetypal Self enters into the domain of ego consciousness. Now God's experience of suffering, in and through the life of a human figure, Jesus of Nazareth, becomes equal in quality and degree to that which He earlier inflicts upon Job. God's life as a human being culminates in an experience of betrayal and abandonment—the crucifixion. Like Job, Jesus becomes a scapegoat, first lifted up as an ideal and then violently rejected by the mob. When Jesus utters from the cross, "My God, my God, why hast thou forsaken me," God fully partakes in what Job has experienced. Jesus, who has placed his trust in his Father in Heaven, suffers the same betrayal Job suffers by trusting Yahweh. This is God's heartfelt "answer to Job"—the betrayer becomes the betrayed and thus experiences the full effect of His own shadow. The reversal is complete, and the result is greater consciousness. In effect God advances in consciousness and brings His own standard up to that set by Job. This represents an enormous increase in consciousness on the part of the archetypal Self; it is a historic advance of consciousness on a collective level.

• In addition, God surpasses Job because He recognizes his own fidelity, something Job never did nor had to do. A God-image is reborn from this ordeal as a figure of an unimaginably higher standing than He held before, a model of integrated consciousness. This represents a dramatic change, from God-image as an arbitrary power to a being conscious of and responsible for His own shadow. This is a new God-image and a psychologically advanced image of divinity. In this, the archetypal Self, which is the basis of all God-images worldwide and throughout all mythologies and theologies, has achieved a new level of individuation.[46]

Stein elucidates two important implications for contemporary spirituality. First, within the context of the postmodern world, human consciousness has advanced past the traditional/premodern mode of mythical and metaphysical consciousness. I would add that it has also moved beyond the rational/secular mode of consciousness that has eclipsed the sacred (the death of God or traditional God-images). With this development comes the psychological attitude, exemplified by Jungian psychology, which offers a new way of thinking about religious experience. In this new paradigm, the psyche takes the place once occupied by the divine.

The second implication pertains to Christian theology. Traditionally, the myth of the incarnation is regarded as a unique event in which God becomes human in the person of Jesus Christ. This happens only once and will not occur again. Jung, however, recasts the theological conception of incarnation in a psychological mode as a developmental process in which the unconscious becomes assimilated over the period of an individual's lifetime. This may be rendered not only as individuation, but as all continuing incarnation or incarnation for all.[47] "The human task," affirms Stein, "is to incarnate as much of the self, and therefore also of what stands behind the self, which is the Ground of Being, as possible in a single lifetime."[48] The same task for humanity, as a whole, is to incarnate the Ground of Being as fully as possible on a collective level. While this has been the project of religions in the past, for better or worse, since the onset of modernity, the more fully conscious individuals are the ones most able to fulfill this purpose.

The divine feminine and the sacred marriage

The recovery of the divine feminine is at the leading edge of contemporary spirituality, and Jungian psychology is among the most important modes of thought and practice contributing to this vital endeavor. Why is this so important? Jungian analyst Anne Baring and the contemporary mystic Andrew Harvey provide a fourfold explanation. First, the divine feminine is initiating a new phase in our evolution, urging us to discover a new ethic of responsibility toward the planet and bringing us a new vision of the sacredness and unity of life. Second, the divine feminine is the unseen dimension of soul to which we are connected through our instincts, our feelings, and the longings of the imaginative heart. Third, soul is not limited to the psychic life of individuals; it is also an aspect of the cosmos, the immense web of relationships concealed beneath the veil of matter. Fourth, the numinous power of the divine feminine is needed for arousing the will and energy to act on behalf of life in restoring balance to our image of God and so to us.[49]

Jungian thought also helps us integrate masculine/solar and feminine/lunar aspects of the psyche. As Marion Woodman argues, our culture has depended upon three thousand years of cultural process focused through masculine eyes. The myth of the biblical god has been won at a high cost. The masculine values of instrumental rationality have degenerated into a lust for control that has wounded both our femininity and masculinity. Feminine values, by contrast, pertain to feelings, emotional vibrancy, relatedness, and connection. These terms—masculinity and femininity—are not bound by gender; they refer to two different energies that comprise the human spirit. Just as health and growth depend on both dark and light, so maturity and wholeness depend on an inner balance of Yin and Yang, Shakti and Shiva, Doing and Being.[50]

Anne Baring and Jules Cashford have traced the stages of the diminishing influence of the goddess from the Paleolithic Age to the present, a trajectory that has left Western culture without a collective feminine image of the divine. While the myth of the goddess partially survives in the figure of the Virgin Mary, mother of Christ, she is ultimately excluded in the prevailing myth of the god. In their view, the long historical process of replacing the Great Mother Goddess with the myth of the masculine God of the Abrahamic traditions may be understood as the gradual withdrawal of humanity's participation with nature.[51] They seek to restore the divine feminine to the God-image in a manner that conjoins the masculine and feminine aspects of divinity. In the traditional language of the old myth, this union is the sacred marriage of the Goddess and God. In the symbolic language of Jungian psychology, it is the "sacred marriage" of "god" and "goddess" images that can be translated into the more prosaic, yet more negotiable, terms of the reunion of transcendence and immanence, spirit and nature, soul and body, in order to make possible a new mythic vision.[52]

In an autobiographical section of *The Dream of the Cosmos: A Quest for the Soul*, Baring recounted dreams that symbolize the return of the divine feminine. Here is an excerpt from the dream to which she refers as the most awesome dream of her life, the true awakener of her soul:

> I dream that I come round the side of a huge dolmen and enter another world, an utterly strange and barren landscape. It is lit by the brilliant radiance of the full moon. I am searching for someone I love and my longing for him is so great that I have embarked on a journey in search of him. The landscape is transformed from a desert into field after field of brilliant green corn. The moonlight is so bright that it is like daylight and the corn is the color of an emerald . . . Suddenly, I find that two enormous men have caught me in a gigantic net that stretches the whole width of the valley and are drawing me into something tremendously powerful and numinous. I am frightened, yet at the same time fascinated. I lie on my back on the ground, helplessly enmeshed in the net and look up, half in terror, half in awe. I see the figure of a woman towering above me, filling the entire space between heaven and earth. She is naked, with white skin and golden hair and is very beautiful, like Aphrodite. Yet she is not young, but ageless. In the center of the abdomen is an immense revolving wheel that is also a rose and a labyrinth, like the one I had seen inlaid in the floor of Chartres Cathedral. Awestruck, I gaze up at her, then down at my own body which is exactly like hers, only tiny in relation to it. I too have a revolving wheel but mine is not centered; it is too far to the left. She does not speak but indicates that I am to center my wheel, like hers.[53]

Baring's analysis of this visionary dream, replete with symbols, exemplifies how Jungian psychological work may be practiced as a form of contemporary spirituality. Dreams of this kind, as she explains, have to be held close to the heart and allowed to live so that gradually, over time, they act as "leaven in the soul." She notes that in a traditional culture she might have worshipped the image of the goddess and built a temple or shrine to her, but in today's world this kind of belief and worship would no longer satisfy her.

At the time she felt it best not to speak of the dream to anyone. She did, however, tell her analyst, thinking she would receive an interpretation, but she was told she would later come to understand it and integrate its meaning into her life on her own. For years Baring pondered who this goddess might be—Aphrodite, Demeter, Isis, an angelic being, a personification of Nature? Naked and beautiful, neither young nor old, she realized that the figure was too pagan to be the Christian Mary, but she was not like Aphrodite nor the other Greek goddesses she had come to know. Eventually she came to understand that the goddess in her dream might be a manifestation of the neo-Platonic image of *anima mundi*, the Soul of the World, first mentioned by Plato in the *Timaeus* and later by Plotinus in the *Enneads*. Baring was familiar with Indra's Net from Indian mythology, a vast net containing an infinite number of jewels. Each individual jewel reflects all the others, a metaphor that illustrates the interpenetration and interconnectedness of all phenomena. Within the context of her dream, it might also signify the net of material reality in which she is caught. The two immense male figures holding it might represent the power of the unconscious drawing her into the presence of the cosmic goddess.[54]

Other symbols of transformation are also clearly evident. The barren desert becomes a radiant landscape. The dream is animated by masculine and feminine energies. Baring searches longingly for a man she loves, a figure representing the soul or Beloved, and encounters powerful feminine symbols such as the radiant moon, rose, and labyrinth. The emotions of terror and awe, quintessential qualities of numinous experience, relativize her ego and open her to the archetypal power of the Self. Here the Self, personified by a goddess like Aphrodite, reveals that she has a body "exactly like hers." She also shares in common with the goddess a revolving wheel, like a chakra (a spiritual energy center in Hindu yoga traditions), and she will need to center it through inner work as she integrates the import of the dream into her life.

Kundalini yoga and individuation

While Jung wrestled with and revisioned his inherited Christian tradition, he also devoted significant time to the study of Eastern traditions such as yoga. For Jung, *yoga* is a general term that encompasses all of Eastern thought and psychological practice. He uses the term to designate traditions as diverse as Hinduism, Indian Buddhism, Tibetan Buddhism, Japanese Buddhism, and Chinese Taoism. His interest in the term concerns the spiritual development of the personality.[55] As Jung puts it, "Yoga was originally a natural process of introversion, with all manner of variations. Introversions of this sort lead to peculiar inner processes which change the personality."[56] His concern is not primarily with the methods and teachings of yoga, but rather with the natural processes of introversion that underlie them. Yoga represents a rich storehouse of symbolic depictions of inner experience and the individuation process; it provides invaluable comparative material for interpreting the collective unconscious.

Jung regards the tantric chakra symbolism of kundalini yoga as parallel evidence from another culture of the individuation process. In Jung's view, the aim of Indian philosophy is to bring about a connection between the non-ego and conscious ego. The non-ego is the dynamic ground or matrix out of which the ego emerges. While tantric yoga represents the developmental phases of the psyche's impersonal or transpersonal aspects,[57] kundalini, for Jung, is the divine urge that animates the individuation process.[58] The chakras, he observes, are of great value to us because they provide a symbolic theory of the psyche.[59] He also points out how the Indian theory differs from Western approaches to the psyche:

> The *chakras*, then, become a valuable guide for us in this obscure field because the East, and India especially, has always tried to understand the psyche as a whole. It has an intuition of the self, and therefore it sees the ego and consciousness as only more or less unessential parts of the self. All this seems very strange to us: it appears as though India were fascinated by the background of consciousness, because we ourselves are entirely identified with our foreground, with the conscious.[60]

Jung's primary interest is with the symbolic content that arises out of the unconscious rather than with consciousness or awareness itself.

Jung provides an insightful commentary on the chakras. In his view, if one succeeds in awakening kundalini, what unfolds must not be regarded in terms of personal development even though the process may have a favorable effect. He explains that what takes place is impersonal and must be observed from a stance of detachment. Jung regards *muladhara*, the lowest or root chakra located at the base of the spine, to be a symbol of the ordinary world of mundane transactions. Here the ego is conscious, but the Self is asleep. Nevertheless, it is essential that one be grounded in *muladhara*; otherwise, he suggests, one is never born and cannot realize the Self.[61] He considers the second chakra located in the genital region, *svadhishthana*, to be the mandala of baptism where one descends into the unconscious "sea" and encounters "the leviathan."[62] For Jung these terms signify the part of the analytic process that entails working through personal complexes and repressed material. Here one engages the shadow that belongs to the personal level of the unconscious. This process continues as a person engages the energies of the *manipura*, the third chakra, or the fiery center of emotions located in the region of the navel. A person's ability to experience and tolerate the strong affective content symbolized by this chakra is essential for psychological development; the fire or heat provides the fuel or libido necessary for transformation.[63]

Joseph Campbell observed that the biological drives connected to the first three chakras typically dominate the first thirty-five years of a person's life, a view that is compatible with Jung's perspective on human development. If these energies are unconstrained, they become destructive. To transcend this order of life requires an awakening of the heart. The awakening entails "the turning about of the energy, which is to say, simply, an application of all the available malice and aggression of *chakra* 3, not outward to the correction of the world, but inward, upon oneself."[64] For Jung this transformation correlates with the psychology of the fourth chakra, *anahata*, located in the region of the heart. He notes that in *anahata*, something new happens in the psyche—the possibility of rising above the emotional events and dramas of one's life. When one becomes capable of detaching from emotional entanglement, one becomes truly human. Prior to this an individual is in the womb of nature, living a life that is largely an automatic or unconscious process; it is in the experience of *anahata* that individuation begins.[65]

Jung warns that the impetus for individuation may lead to an inflation in which the ego identifies with the Self. He insists that individuation does not mean that a person becomes an egotist or individualist. An individualist, he maintains, is a person who does not succeed at individuating. Jung defines the problem this way: "Individuation is becoming that thing which is not the ego, and that is very strange. Therefore, nobody understands what the self is, because the self is just the thing you are not, which is not the ego."[66] If, however, one truly reaches *anahata*, the heart chakra, one glimpses a being within that is greater and more important than one's personality.[67] Jung notes that in analysis the transpersonal process can begin only when the personal life has been integrated. At this point psychology opens itself to a standpoint and to types of experience that are found beyond ego consciousness.[68]

Jung observes that Westerners do not trust the existence of the psyche, the level of development symbolized by *vishuddha*, the chakra located in the area of the throat; it is beyond our actual conception of the world.[69] The primary reality for Westerners is a world consisting of matter. Jung offers a brief commentary on the perspective associated with *vishuddha*. He suggests that one's understanding of the world becomes profoundly psychological: "You begin to consider the game of the world as your own game, the people that appear outside as exponents of your psychical condition. Whatever befalls you, whatever experience or adventure you have in the external world is your own experience. The world itself becomes a reflection of the psyche."[70] However, Jung does not consider existence at the level of *vishuddha* to be a desirable state. He advises that if one were to successfully reach this level of being, one would complain, for it is "ether, an airless space, where there is no earthly chance for the ordinary individual to breathe."[71]

Jung feels it does not help to speculate about *ajna*, the chakra located at the forehead, but comments on the mystical mode of experience it symbolizes. "There is another psyche," he asserts, "a counterpart to one's psychical reality, the non-ego reality, the thing that is not even to be called the self . . . The ego disappears completely; the psychical is no longer a content in us, but we become contents of it."[72] This condition, he believes, is almost unimaginable; it is a rare instance in which there is the possibility of experience devoid of ego.

The level of human development symbolized by *sahasrara*, located at the crown of the head, transcends the boundaries of Jung's psychology. In his view, it is beyond human experience and thus is an entirely speculative philosophical concept without practical value for us.[73] This judgment may, however, be qualified in several ways. First, "for us" refers to Western people who lack a system of contemplative practice as sophisticated as yoga. Second, in an appendix to the seminar, Jung clarifies that this is a parallel between meditation and psychological analysis. The typical course of an analysis, he explains, is when awareness expands through working through repressions and projections but the relation of the ego to its objects persists; the ego is intertwined in conflict with the objects. However, by continuing the analysis to a deeper level, there is an analogy with yoga *if* consciousness can be severed from its objects, a detachment that he links to the process of individuation. As he explains, "It is as if consciousness separated from the objects and from the ego and emigrated to the non-ego—to the other center. [. . .] This detachment of consciousness is the freeing from the *tamas* and *rajas*, a freeing from the passions and from the entanglement with the realm of objects."[74] Jung adds that this is not something he can prove philosophically; rather, it is a psychological phenomenon, which is experienced as a feeling of deliverance. "What has caused one to be previously seized with panic is not a panic anymore; one is capable of seeing the tension of the opposites of the world without agitation. One does not become apathetic but is freed from entanglement."[75] This experience has palpable effects in practical life and, he notes, is exemplified beautifully in the legend of Buddha being threatened by Mara when he was at the threshold of his enlightenment. "Mara and all his demons assail him," Jung writes, "but the throne of Buddha is empty—he is simply not sitting there anymore. Or as the *Rig Veda* I, 164 has it: 'Two closely united friends both embrace one and the same tree. One of them eats the sweet berry, the other looks down only composedly'."[76]

Thus, Jung correlates the emotional entanglements associated with *tamas* and *rajas* with the early phases of analytical work; that is, with the process of working through the shadow material associated with the first three chakras. Genuine individuation can then occur when one develops the capacity to detach from the sense objects, emotional complexes, and identification with the ego. Through such detachment, Jung observes, comes a profound experience of release from the ordinary travails of life; it is a mode of being that is grounded in the non-ego or Self that observes or witnesses the tensions and opposites of worldly existence. Here Jung provides the language that describes not only wholeness, the integration of the personality, but the liberation or freedom that is the aim of yoga.

Finally, Jung's views on kundalini yoga may be seen anew in relation to a dream he recounts in his memoir where he appears to himself as a yogi meditating in a temple:

> I was walking along a little road through a hilly landscape; the sun was shining and I had a wide view in all directions. Then I came to a small wayside chapel. The door was ajar, and I went in. To my surprise there was no image of the Virgin on the altar, and no crucifix either, but only a wonderful flower arrangement. But then I saw that on the floor in front of the altar, facing me, sat a yogi—in lotus posture, in deep meditation. When

> I looked at him more closely, I realized that he had my face. I stared in profound fright, and awoke with the thought: "Aha, so he is the one who is meditating me. He has a dream, and I am it."[77]

He interprets the dream as a parable concerning the return to life after his near death experience during a heart attack. Jung notes that the aim of the dream is to effect a reversal of the relationship between ego consciousness and the unconscious; he also states that it depicts the unconscious as the source of phenomenal reality. He tells us this reversal suggests that our unconscious existence is the real one and our conscious world is a kind of illusion, like a dream which seems a reality as long as we are in it. This perspective closely resembles the Hindu concept of *maya*.[78]

Jung's reflections convey a vision of life that is consistent with the aim of yoga. The decisive question, in Jung's view, is whether or not humankind is related to something infinite.

> Only if we know that the thing which truly matters is the infinite can we avoid fixing our interest upon futilities, and upon all kinds of goals which are not of real importance . . . If we understand and feel that here in this life we already have a link with the infinite, desires and attitudes change. In the final analysis, we count for something only because of the essential we embody, and if we do not embody that, life is wasted.[79]

This attitude evokes values and priorities associated with Indian philosophy and contemplative yoga. An experiential relationship with the infinite is more important than finite goals. For Hindus, freedom or liberation from conditional existence (*moksha*) is more essential and fulfilling than a life constrained by the limitations of ordinary desires and ambitions.

While Jung sees affinities between his psychology and kundalini yoga with regard to the first four chakras, I disagree with his assessment concerning the *vishuddha*, *ajna*, and *sahasrara* chakras. By focusing on the chakras as symbols for explicating his own psychology, he fails to acknowledge their significance for practitioners of Hindu yoga traditions. Jung focuses on the developmental process of individuation, but he does not—here or elsewhere—encourage people to actually practice yoga as a spiritual discipline. In my view, his admonitions unnecessarily deter mature individuals from undertaking time-tested practices for awakening to the inmost Self, or to unconditional awareness or consciousness itself, which the Hindu tradition describes as the Atman or witness.

Insights for integrative spirituality

C. G. Jung's depth psychology is a psychological form of spirituality grounded in his own spiritual crisis and the recovery of his soul. Many aspects of the Jungian approach to the inner life are important for integrative spirituality:

- Jung's account of how he navigates his own midlife crisis provides a model for how others may discover the Self and engage in the individuation process. The latter involves the analytical work of differentiating from external influences and the synthetic work of integrating archetypal images from the inner world into conscious awareness. Along the way, one attends to disavowed shadow material by taking back projections (positive as well as negative) on others, and comes into greater alignment with the Self. Jung's method of active imagination provides a means for entering into dialogue with images and symbols arising from the unconscious. This process activates the transcendent function, which arises from the union of conscious and unconscious content, engendering greater integration and wholeness in the psyche.

- Jung's notion that all mythologies and religions have a common source in the collective unconscious strongly affirms the value of religious pluralism. We are heirs to all the world's religions. No god or goddess is alien to anyone. The religious function of the psyche is an impulse that arises in each of us at all times and in all places. The archetypes are common to all religions, but the symbols and myths differ among traditions depending upon their cultural and historical contexts. There is much to learn from religions that differ from our own heritage. The Eastern traditions, for instance, are helping Westerners rediscover the inner world and contemplative practices.

- Jungian depth psychology provides an effective response to the death of God in the modern West. Unlike most of his contemporaries, Jung distrusts the philosophical materialism and deification of reason that develop in the wake of the European enlightenment. Likewise, many of us in the twenty-first century resist the contemporary spirit of the times and seek a way to respond to the spirit of the depths. Secularism and consumerism are insufficient bases for a fulfilling life. Jung's psychology offers an alternative approach to spirituality, neither premodern/traditional nor modern/secular, based on the idea of integrating the divine into the human. Jung's concept of the Self embodies the characteristics that religious people and theologians refer to as God. The Self, in effect, is the God within.

- Numinous experiences that transcend the ego attitude may catalyze the individuation process, provided they are integrated into the fabric of the person's conscious identity. From a Jungian perspective, these experiences are viewed through the symbolic lens of alchemy as prima materia that can be used for further refinement in the opus of individuation. Yet, the psychological journey of individuation is said to differ from the spiritual journey to the divine. Numinous experiences may make life more meaningful or expand one's perspective on one's difficulties, but spiritual awareness is insufficient and does not provide real solutions for problems caused by neurosis. Furthermore, analysis dissolves attachments to religious objects, practices, and theologies. The danger is that people can get stuck in numinous experiences, a condition that leads to various pathologies.

While acknowledging the dangers that may accompany numinous experiences, this view is one-sided. Numinous or mystical experiences, aswell as mindful engagement with aspects of a religious or spiritual tradition, can enhance rather than inhibit a person's individuation, especially when one embraces religious pluralism and acknowledges the multiple ways in which one can experience the Real or Ultimate. I consider the psychological work of individuation to be imperative, but not contrary to or lesser than the quest for spiritual awakening. The greater opus, in my view, is to integrate the psychological and spiritual modes of inner work in a way that fully acknowledges the essential and distinctive aspects of each approach to human flourishing.

• Jung's conscious dialogue with Christianity, his inherited tradition, addresses many issues with which Christians and others struggle in the contemporary world. Most significant is the tendency to split the psyche into irreconcilable opposites—good against evil, masculine against feminine, spirit against body. Jung counters this in his *Answer to Job*, a creative narrative concerning the biblical God-image's individuation. God's image in the Book of Job is shown to be deficient. The incarnation—the integration of the Divine into the human figure of Jesus—symbolizes the archetypal Self's entrance into the domain of ego consciousness and represents a dramatic change in the God-image, from an arbitrary power to a being conscious of and assuming responsibility for his own shadow. Through this shift, human beings become individually responsible for redemption, atonement, and the reconciliation of opposites.

This new God-image also revisions the Christian myth of the incarnation. Instead of viewing the incarnation as a unique event in which God becomes human in the person of Jesus Christ, we can understand it in a psychological way as a process by which the unconscious becomes assimilated during the course of an individual's lifetime. This process may be rendered not only as individuation, but also as continuing incarnation or incarnation for all. In this respect, Jung's psychology aligns with the Christian pluralist theology of John Hick and the comparative mythologist Joseph Campbell.

• Jungian psychology further revisions the prevailing God-image of the West by recovering the divine feminine that has been eclipsed by the Abrahamic traditions. This endeavor helps us to engender a new ethic of responsibility for the planet, restoring a vision of the sacredness and unity of life. The divine feminine is understood to be the unseen dimension of soul to which we are connected through our instincts, feelings, and longings. Furthermore, in this view soul is not limited to the psychic life of individuals, but rather is also the *anima mundi* or the Soul of the World, the immense web of relationships that connects us to each other and the earth. This mode of thought also restores balance to Western culture by integrating the masculine/solar and feminine/lunar energies of the psyche. Through the symbolic language of Jungian psychology, the traditional myths of the sacred marriage of God and Goddess are translated into contemporary terms expressing the connection between transcendence and immanence, spirit and nature, soul and body.

The commentary on Anne Baring's visionary dream of a goddess figure exemplifies how Jungian psychology may be practiced as a form of contemporary spirituality. Dreams and visions need to be tended mindfully; to be amplified by knowledge of myths and religious symbols; allowed to gradually reveal their meaning from within; and ultimately, integrated into one's life.

- Jung's pioneering interest in the East has led many in the West to explore Eastern teachings such as yoga, though he cautions Westerners from actually undertaking the practices. His commentary on the chakra symbolism of kundalini yoga elucidates aspects of the analytical process, but does not help us understand contemplative yoga on its own terms. Jung's psychology emphasizes individuation, a journey of becoming that leads to the integration of the personality and wholeness. Yoga's emphasis is in cultivating states of consciousness that confer a profound experience of being. Individuation confers meaning and purpose in life; yoga bestows awakening and freedom from all limiting identifications.

Individuation and yoga, in my view, both express and emphasize two distinct yet complementary modes of human development. Both are essential. Psychological inquiry is especially important for healing emotional wounds, engaging shadow material, working through relationship issues, grappling with moral dilemmas, and navigating major life transitions. Any of these issues may be obstacles to effectively practicing contemplative yoga. Meditation and yogic Self-inquiry, by contrast, are the principal means for developing capacities for witnessing the contents of consciousness, detachment, contentment, peace, and a feeling of oneness or connectedness to all things. These profound states of being, however, must be integrated into the personality as enduring character traits. Otherwise, shadow issues and lack of maturity in one or more aspects of one's life may undermine awakening.

Notes

1 C. G. Jung, *The Red Book: Liber Novus: A Reader's Edition*, ed. Sonu Shamdasani. New York: W. W. Norton, 2009, 119–23.

2 C. G. Jung, *Psychology and Alchemy*, vol. 12, *The Collected Works of C. G. Jung*, 2nd ed., trans. R. F. C. Hull. Princeton: Princeton University Press, 1968, § 44. The Self, for Jung, is the archetype of wholeness; a superordinate, organizing principle of psychic selfhood. The editors of *The Collected Works of C. G. Jung* do not capitalize the self, whether referring to the archetype or simply one's individual ego, leaving it to the context of the passage to indicate which meaning is intended. I follow the convention of most contemporary Jungian writers and use the upper case (Self) to distinguish the archetype of wholeness from the ego personality except when quoting Jung.

3 C. G. Jung, *Psychological Types*, vol. 6, *The Collected Works of C. G. Jung*, trans. R. F. C. Hull. Princeton: Princeton University Press, 1971, § 188.

4 C. G. Jung, *The Archetype of the Collective Unconscious*, vol. 9i, *The Collected Works of C. G. Jung*, 2nd ed., trans. R. F. C. Hull. Princeton: Princeton University Press, 1969, § 490.

5 C. G. Jung, *Memories, Dreams, Reflections*, rev. ed., ed. Aniela Jaffe, trans. Richard and Clara Winston. New York: Vintage Books, 1963, 44.
6 Ibid., 44–45.
7 Ibid., 45.
8 Ibid., 45.
9 David Rosen, *The Tao of Jung: The Way of Integrity*. New York: Viking/Arkana, 1966, 56–58.
10 Jung, Memories, *Dreams, Reflections*, 179.
11 Ibid., 188.
12 Ibid., 196.
13 Ibid., 197.
14 Curtis D. Smith, *Jung's Quest for Wholeness: A Religious and Historical Perspective*. Albany: State University of New York Press, 1990, 93.
15 Jung, Memories, *Dreams, Reflections*, 199.
16 Harold Coward, *Jung and Eastern Thought*. Albany: State University of New York Press, 1985, 34–35.
17 Jung, Memories, *Dreams, Reflections*, 177.
18 James Hillman, "Psychological Commentary," in *Kundalini: The Evolutionary Energy in Man* by Gopi Krishna. Berkeley, CA: Shambhala, 1971, 40–41.
19 M.-L. von Franz, "Process of Individuation," in *Man and His Symbols*, ed. C. G. Jung and M.-L. von Franz. London: Aldus Books, 1964, 210.
20 Jeffrey Raff, *Jung and the Alchemical Imagination*. Berwick, ME: Nicolas-Hays, 2000, 2–13.
21 Smith, *Jung's Quest for Wholeness*, 118.
22 Murray Stein, foreword to *No Other Gods: An Interpretation of the Biblical Myth for a Transbiblical Age*, by Phyllis Boswell Moore. Wilmette, IL: Chiron Publications, 1992, viii.
23 C. G. Jung, "The Structure of the Psyche" (1931), in *The Collected Works of C. G. Jung*, vol. 8, 2nd ed., trans. R. F. C. Hull. Princeton: Princeton University Press, 1969, § 342.
24 C. G. Jung, Symbols of Transformation, in *The Collected Works of C. G. Jung*, vol. 5, 2nd ed., trans. R. F. C. Hull. Princeton: Princeton University Press, 1956, § 30.
25 C. G. Jung, "Psychology and Religion" (1937), in *The Collected Works of C. G. Jung*, vol. 11, 2nd ed., trans. R. F. C. Hull. Princeton: Princeton University Press, 1969, § 127.
26 C. G. Jung, *Psychology and Alchemy*, in *The Collected Works of C. G. Jung*, vol. 12, 2nd ed., trans. R. F. C. Hull. Princeton: Princeton University Press, 1968, § 20.
27 Ibid., § 22.
28 C. G. Jung, "A Psychological Approach to the Dogma of the Trinity" (1948), in *The Collected Works of C. G. Jung*, vol. 11, 2nd ed., trans. R. F. C. Hull. Princeton University Press, 1969, § 233.
29 Jung, *Psychology and Alchemy*, § 20.
30 C. G. Jung, "The Spiritual Problem of Modern Man," in *The Portable Jung*, ed. Joseph Campbell. New York: Viking Press, 1971, 476.
31 Jung, "Yoga and the West" (1936), in *The Collected Works of C. G. Jung*, vol. 11, 2nd ed., trans. R. F. C. Hull. Princeton: Princeton University Press, 1969, § 876.
32 Murray Stein, *The Principle of Individuation: Toward the Development of Consciousness*. Wilmette, IL: Chiron Publications, 2006, xiii–iv.
33 Ibid., 5–6.
34 Ibid., 15.
35 C. G. Jung, "The Transcendent Function," in *The Collected Works of C. G. Jung*, vol. 8, 2nd ed., vol. trans. R. F. C. Hull. Princeton: Princeton University Press, 1969, § 131.
36 Stein, *The Principle of Individuation*, 25–26.
37 C. G. Jung, *C. G. Jung Letters*, selected and edited by Gerhard Alder in collaboration with Aniela Jaffé, vol. 1. Princeton: Princeton University Press, 1973, 377.
38 Stein, *The Principle of Individuation*, 32.
39 Ibid., 34.

40 Ibid., 35–36.
41 Ibid., 48.
42 Murray Stein, *Minding the Self: Jungian Meditations on Contemporary Spirituality*. New York: Routledge, 2014, 5–6.
43 Ibid., 6–7.
44 C. G. Jung, *Answer to Job*, fiftieth-anniversary ed., trans. R. F. C. Hull. Princeton: Princeton University Press, 1973, 93.
45 Stein, *Minding the Self*, 7–8.
46 Ibid., 8–12.
47 Ibid., 11.
48 Ibid., 19.
49 Andrew Harvey and Anne Baring, *The Divine Feminine: Exploring the Feminine Face of God Around the World*. Berkeley, CA: Conari Press, 1996, 6–7.
50 Marion Woodman, Kate Danson, Mary Hamilton, and Rita Greer Allen, *Leaving My Father's House: A Journey to Conscious Femininity*. Boston: Shambhala, 1993, 1–2.
51 Anne Baring and Jules Cashford, *The Myth of the Goddess: Evolution of an Image*. London: Arkana, 1991, 660–61.
52 Ibid., 663–64.
53 Anne Baring, *The Dream of the Cosmos: A Quest for the Soul*. Dorset, England: Archive Publishing, 2013.
54 Ibid., 27.
55 Coward, 3.
56 Jung, "Yoga and the West," § 873.
57 Sonu Shamdasani, introduction to *The Psychology of Kundalini Yoga: Notes of the Seminar Given in 1932 by C. G. Jung*, by C. G. Jung, ed. Sonu Shamdasani. Princeton: Princeton University Press, 1996, xxiii.
58 C. G. Jung, *The Psychology of Kundalini Yoga: Notes on a Seminar Given in 1932 by C. G. Jung*, ed. Sonu Shamdasani. Princeton: Princeton University Press, 1996, 21–22.
59 Ibid., 61. Jung explains that his own interest in kundalini developed through an encounter with a European woman brought up in the East who presented dreams and fantasies that he could not understand until he came across Sir John Woodroffe's book entitled *The Serpent Power*. Jung claims that the symbolism of kundalini yoga suggests that the bizarre symptoms that patients present may actually result from the awakening of the kundalini. Jung states that knowledge of such symbolism enables one to see the symptoms as a meaningful symbolic process. See Shamdasani, "Introduction," pp. xxv–xxvi.
60 Ibid., 61–62. Shamdasani, like the translators of *The Collected Works of C. G. Jung*, uses lower case for the term *self* leading the reader to discern from the context if the word refers to the ego or the archetypal self. In this the passage, *self* refers to the latter since it distinguished from the ego.
61 Ibid., 27–28.
62 Ibid., 17.
63 Ibid., 33–35.
64 Joseph Campbell, The *Inner Reaches of Outer Space: Metaphor as Myth and as Religion*. New York: Harper and Row, 1986, 66.
65 Jung, *The Psychology of Kundalini Yoga*, 39.
66 Ibid.
67 Ibid., 45–46.
68 Ibid., 66.
69 Ibid., 47.
70 Ibid., 49–50.
71 Ibid., 50.
72 Ibid., 57.
73 Ibid.
74 Ibid., 83.

75 Ibid.
76 Ibid.
77 Jung, *Memories, Dreams, Reflections*, 323.
78 Ibid., 324.
79 Ibid., 325.

7
CONTEMPLATIVE YOGA AND AWAKENING

Yoga is the state in which the mental and emotional fluctuations become still. Then we abide in our true nature.
—*Yoga Sutras*

I regard myself to be a Western Hindu because I have embraced yoga spirituality. Contrary to popular belief in the West, yoga is far more than physical postures for cultivating flexibility and engendering good health. I use the term *contemplative yoga* to emphasize its spiritual dimension and to distinguish it from the modern postural forms of yoga now being widely practiced by over twenty million Americans in yoga studios throughout the country. Yoga is a vast body of spiritual teachings and practices that have been developed in India for five millennia and that may be regarded as the very foundation of the ancient Indian civilization.[1] Yoga's principal teachings and practices emerge from important developmental phases in the Hindu tradition and from their associated texts. Among the most distinctive characteristics of Indian spirituality is the way in which it preserves, synthesizes, and refreshes itself again and again; accordingly, the yoga tradition has great recombinant power. An unbroken tradition of philosophy and spiritual disciplines, yoga is undergoing further development as it takes root in the West.

I have practiced Hindu contemplative yoga for over four decades. As I noted in the Introduction, I have received initiations, empowerments, and guidance from Indian yogis (Sri Raushan Nath and Gurumayi Chidvilasananda) and more recently from Western yogis (Swami Shankarananda, Mark Griffin, Sally Kempton, and Paul Muller-Ortega). My love and reverence for contemplative yoga deepen with each year of practice. I take heartfelt refuge in the teachings and disciplines that are the primary means by which I engage the process of spiritual awakening.

The preceding chapter discussed Jungian practices that foster individuation by working with dreams, symbols, and disavowed or repressed shadow material—a lifelong project that leads to greater integration of the personality and to wholeness.

By contrast, the aim of contemplative yoga is spiritual awakening—recognizing the deepest dimension of being that is unconditioned by thought, emotions, and action. In this chapter, I elucidate the primary forms of yoga spirituality that have been effectively transmitted to the West, giving special emphasis to Kashmir Shaivism, a tantric yoga tradition that most deeply informs my spirituality. While the focus here is on yoga, my conviction is that individuation and awakening, while distinctly different, are complementary processes that can be integrated in fulfilling and efficacious ways to open us to the Spirit within.

Indian philosophy and yoga

Classical systems of Indian philosophy are called *darshanas*, a term that means "viewpoints" or "visions." Derived from the verbal root *drish*, the word *darshana* means "to see." Thus, this philosophy provides a way of seeing the nature of reality that Hindus regard as veiled or obscured by our conditioned existence. As Heinrich Zimmer observes, "the chief aim of Indian thought is to unveil and integrate into consciousness what has been resisted and hidden by the forces of life."[2] As he asserts, the ancient sages' greatest achievement was the discovery of the Self, an independent, imperishable entity underlying the conscious personality and physical body. To know this Self and make this knowledge effective in human life has been the persistent effort of Indian philosophy. Naïve unawareness of the Self's hidden truth is regarded as the primary cause of all the misplaced emphases, misguided attitudes, and self-inflicted existential suffering that characterize the human condition.[3]

The fundamental factor responsible for the problems of ordinary existence is ignorance (*avidya*). Hindu mythology and Vedantic philosophy stress the concept of *maya*, which means both "creative power" and "illusion." Maya is both a cosmic and psychological concept; in the latter sense, it is the net of entanglement that distorts our understanding of the nature of both the world and ourselves. To get beyond this, to know how it works and transcend its cosmic spell, is the primary human task; it is, as Zimmer explains, "to learn the secret of the entanglement, and, if possible, to cut through into a reality outside and beneath the emotional and intellectual convolutions that enwrap our conscious being."[4] Hindu tradition calls this goal *moksha*, or "liberation." The primary means of achieving it is yoga.

Yoga refers both to the traditions of mental and physical discipline and the goal achieved by these disciplines. Yoga scholar Georg Feuerstein provides the best comprehensive definition: Yoga is "the generative name for the various Indian paths of ecstatic self-transcendence—the methodical transmutation of consciousness to the point of liberation from the spell of the ego-personality."[5] In other words, yoga refers to *paths* that lead to freedom from a small, contracted sense of identity. Yoga is also the *goal* of the practice, a state of being. As one is freed from a contracted mode of being, one realizes or recognizes one's true nature. Therefore, this state of being is called Self-realization.

The Upanishads and Vedanta

All yoga traditions can be found in seed form in the Vedas, the most ancient scriptures of India. Vedic yoga primarily takes the form of rituals that connect participants to the divine, that which pervades and energizes all things. The Upanishads are the contemplative portion of the Vedas; in these texts, the external or exoteric Vedic rituals are interiorized in the yoga practitioner's bodymind.[6] The practice of yoga, in fact, can be aptly described as the interiorization of awareness.

The Upanishads describe an all-inclusive and all-pervading principle designated as *Brahman*, which derives from the root *brih*, meaning "to grow" or "to expand." Sages and philosophers maintain that while it is impossible to explain Brahman in words, it is possible to characterize its nature as being (*sat*), consciousness (*chit*), and bliss (*ananda*). These texts also teach that Brahman is the ground and innermost essence of a human being, described as the *atman*, or "the Self." *Atman* is said to be self-luminous, birthless, deathless, and ever-present. The terms *Brahman* and *atman* are discussed extensively in the Upanishads, and the text includes concise statements that summarize the meaning of dialogues between sages and students. These "great sayings" (*mahavakas*) include "That Thou Art" (*tat tvam asi*) and "I am Brahman" (*aham brahmasmi*). Both affirm that Brahman, or ground of being, and Atman are identical. However, this truth needs to be recognized; this is the meaning of the term Self-realization. Knowledge of the Self is occluded by mental and emotional afflictions that must be removed through contemplative spiritual practices for Self-realization to be achieved.

Discovery of the Self entails self-discipline and discriminating awareness. "Subtler than the subtlest is this Self, and beyond all logic," states the *Katha Upanishad*. "The ancient, effulgent being, the indwelling Spirit, hidden in the lotus of the heart, is hard to know."[7] The text continues with another image that epitomizes the Upanishadic teachings on yoga:

> Know that the Self is the rider, and the body the chariot; that the intellect is the charioteer, and the mind the reins ... When a person lacks discrimination and his mind is uncontrolled, his senses are unmanageable, like the restive horses of a charioteer. But when a person has discrimination and his mind is controlled, the senses, like the well-trained horses of a charioteer, lightly obey the rein.[8]

The Sanskrit word for discrimination is *viveka*, a term that refers to the ability to differentiate the temporal from the eternal or what is unimportant from what truly matters; it is the distinguishing characteristic of *jnana yoga*, the yoga of knowledge, or discriminating wisdom.

The *Katha Upanishad* provides additional guidance regarding what is to be known. "There are two selves, the apparent self and the real Self. Of these it is the real Self, and he alone, who must be felt as truly existing."[9] The apparent self is akin to Jung's notion of personality No. 1, while the real Self is the Atman, analogous to Jung's personality No. 2. It is noteworthy that the Self must be felt or *realized*, not merely cognized. The text further explains how this is to be done:

> None beholds him with the eyes, for he is without form. Yet in the heart he is revealed, through self-control and meditation. When all the senses are stilled, when the mind is at rest, when the intellect wavers not—then, say the wise, the highest state is reached. This calm of the senses and the mind has been defined as yoga. He who attains it is free from delusion.[10]

The Upanishads are interpreted by different schools of Vedantic philosophy. The non-dual school, *Advaita Vedanta*, which has been particularly influential, is associated with Shankara, the great ninth-century philosopher-sage. The yoga associated with this philosophy is *jnana-yoga*.[11] Advaitins describe our ordinary existential condition in terms of the epistemological process of *superimposition* or, in Jungian terms, projection. Superimposition is the process whereby, through ignorance, a thing and its properties are perceived as something else. The classic examples given by Advaitins include the mistaken perception of a rope appearing as a snake or the presence of a mirage in the desert. In the same manner, the attributes of the non-Self are falsely superimposed upon the Self.[12] The Self, or pure consciousness, appears as the individualized person. In actuality, the Self is *misidentified* with the five coverings or sheaths in which it is enveloped, described as the physical, vital, mental, consciousness, and bliss bodies. The aim of the Advaita Vedantin is to realize the Self that underlies these coverings; the yogic method for doing so is called Self-inquiry. Through inquiry one negates the identifications that conceal the Self. For example, one acknowledges that one has a body, but is not one's body; one has feelings, but is not one's feelings; one has thoughts, but is not one's thoughts. The Self is that which remains—the witness, aware of all objects that arise in consciousness.

The tradition of Vedantic Self-inquiry remains a vital one. In the past century, Ramana Maharshi and Nisargadatta Maharaj, two great sages who exemplify the *experiential* rather than *doctrinal* aspect of Vedanta, taught this method, each in his own way.[13] For Ramana, inquiry takes the form of the question, "Who am I?" In his view, this method surpasses all other yogic sadhanas or practices. He describes the practice in this way:

> When other thoughts arise, one should not pursue them, but should inquire: "To whom did they arise?" It does not matter how many thoughts arise. As each thought arises, one should inquire with diligence, "To whom has this thought arisen?" The answer that would emerge would be "To me." Thereupon, if one inquires, "Who am I?" the mind will go back to its source, and the thought that arose will become quiescent. With repeated practice in this manner, the mind will develop the skill to stay in its source. When the mind that is subtle goes out through the brain and the sense organs, the gross names and forms appear; when it stays in the heart, the

names and forms disappear. Not letting the mind go out but retaining it in the Heart is what is called "inwardness" (*antar-mukha*). Letting the mind go out of the Heart is known as "externalization" (*bahir-mukha*). Thus, when the mind stays in the Heart, the "I" which is ever the source of all thoughts will go and the Self which ever exists will shine.[14]

Ramana describes this state as quietude. As he says, "Remaining quiet is what is called wisdom-insight. To remain quiet is to resolve the mind in the Self."[15] In Nisargadatta's view, inquiry is essentially a path of negation. He insists that it is crucial to know what you are *not*. His approach also enjoins the seeker to go deep into the felt sense of "I am."[16] The teachings of Ramana and Nisargadatta both carry forward the yoga of the deep Self originally taught in the Upanishads by Vedantic philosophers such as Shankara. Taken together, their methods exemplify *jnana yoga*. The hallmark of this path of contemplative inquiry is a capacity for interiority that generally requires renunciation from the activities of worldly life.

The *Yoga Sutras* of Patanjali

The classical system of yoga philosophy contained in the *Yoga Sutras* is comprised of 196 aphorisms compiled by the sage Patanjali around the second-century of the Common Era. Also referred to as *raja yoga*, or the royal yoga, the text delineates psycho-physical practices that liberate a yogi from the mental and emotional afflictions that bind a person and block the realization of the Self, called *purusha* in the text. *Purusha*, a term analogous to *atman* in the Upanishads, describes the true nature of one's being; both refer to the Self, which is pure consciousness, the witness, or Seer, by which all things are known.

Like depth psychology, the *Yoga Sutras* identifies psychological factors outside conscious awareness that afflict our consciousness and give rise to suffering. In addition, the text provides practitioners with a methodology for neutralizing these psychological forces and accessing and realizing the Self—a realization that bestows a profound freedom from conditioning and gives rise to the positive mental states of bliss, peace, fearlessness, loving-kindness, equanimity, and compassion.

What is the nature of the unconscious psychological factors that cause existential suffering? Every experience leaves an impression in the psyche. Stored in the unconscious, these impressions, called *samskaras*, influence and often distort our perceptions. Strong negative impressions are the root of psychological wounds that cause emotional distress and conflict in our relationships. Conglomerations of samskaras generate repetitive patterns of behavior, called *vasanas*. Vasanas are habit energies, behaviors that often occur automatically or compulsively because they arise from the unconscious.

The *Yoga Sutras* also specifies five primary emotional/mental afflictions, called *kleshas*, which deeply condition our attitudes and behaviors. The first and foremost klesha is ignorance. Ignorance is more than simply not knowing; it is the limited knowledge that we receive from our senses and mind. Closely related to the first is egotism, the second klesha, the egocentric attitude that develops out of ignorance or limited knowledge. From the perspective of yoga, our greatest problem is that *we think that we know*. While we do know something, what we know is partial, one-sided, and superficial; the body, senses, and mind are inadequate for knowing the truth. Yoga, by contrast, entails humility and a journey into the unknown. Yoga teaches that there is an adequate vehicle for knowing—the silent mind, the mind in a state of stillness, equanimity, peace, and balance. Yoga bestows knowledge by identity, or knowledge from direct experience. The yogic term for such knowledge is *samadhi*—the ability to see things clearly and calmly when the mind is unified, focused, and one-pointed; it is to know holistically rather than partially, and whole-heartedly. The third klesha is attachment—we cling to what is pleasurable and seek more of it. The fourth is aversion—we avoid what is unpleasant and push it away. The fifth is fear of death—we cling to life and live in denial of the inevitable fact that we will die. These five afflictions are the primary causes of our inner restlessness and give rise to less subtle sources of distress familiar to most of us—desirous craving, greed, anger, hubris, envy, and jealousy.

While samskaras, vasanas, and the kleshas are the cause of human suffering, yoga is the means by which they may be overcome. Yoga is clearly defined in the opening sutras of the text:

> Complete mastery over the roaming tendencies of the mind is Yoga.
>
> Then the Seer becomes established in its essential nature.
>
> Elsewhere [the Seer] conforms to the roaming tendencies of the mind.[17]

These sutras underscore the fact that the mind is typically distracted, unfocused, and undisciplined. Yogic practice reins in the mind so that one can abide in the Seer or Witness that is the luminous substrate of the mind. When we identify with consciousness itself, rather than its contents and fluctuations, we experience the bliss that is our inherent nature.

The *Yoga Sutras* prescribes eight limbs, or components, of spiritual practice that alleviate and ultimately eliminate the impact of negative samskaras, vasanas, and kleshas in our lives. The first two limbs (*yama* and *niyama*) provide the ethical basis for practicing yoga. *Yama* refers to behaviors we need to restrain—harming others, being dishonest, taking what belongs to others; *niyama* entails activities and attitudes we need to cultivate—study, self-discipline, and devotion.[18] *Asana*, or posture, is the third limb. It may come as a surprise that the *Yoga Sutras* teaches only one posture—a comfortable position that one can maintain for the length of time one meditates (2.46). This might be sitting in a cross-legged position on the floor or a chair. The fourth limb is *pranayama*, or breath control (2.49–51). While yogic traditions teach many subtle, complex forms of pranayama, the form that matters most is breathing that is steady, slow, and mindful. When one breathes in this way, the mind can settle and allow meditation to unfold through the remaining limbs of yoga.

The first four limbs are outer limbs of yoga that focus on the body and its activities, our senses, and the breath. The fifth limb, *pratyahara*, is withdrawal of the senses (2.54). When you sit still in a steady posture and observe the breath, consciousness turns inward—it becomes introverted rather than engaged and distracted by objects of sense perception. Pratyahara is the gateway to the inner limbs of yoga in which consciousness undergoes unification, purification, and awakening. *Dharana*, the sixth limb, is concentration on a single object (3.1). The *Yoga Sutras* describes many options for focus, like the breath, an image, or the mantra *Om*. Whichever one is chosen, the practice is to return to that object again and again whenever attention wavers. When the practitioner's concentration deepens, it becomes one-pointed. One-pointed concentration is the seventh limb, *dhyana*, or meditation (3.2). Gradually, through repeated practice of meditation, a yogi becomes absorbed into or one with the object of meditation, the state called *samadhi*, the final limb of yogic practice (3.3–4).

Samadhi, the culmination of practice, is the state that ultimately confers Self-realization, the freedom from conditioned and existential suffering that is the promise of yoga. The psychological content that afflicts the psyche is neutralized. Practitioners experience freedom from conditioning and abide in their true nature. Strikingly, there are degrees of samadhi and complete spiritual awakening rarely comes from a single experience of this state, however profound it may be. In actuality, one needs to experience samadhi many times before one can integrate the realization of the Self into one's life.

While human beings must contend with the tenacious unconscious factors that cause suffering, the *Yoga Sutras* insists that we also have extraordinary potential within us to overcome these. As Pandit Rajmani Tigunait explains, the mind has two kinds of attributes: *inherent* and *acquired*. The *inherent* attributes of the mind are luminosity, joy, wisdom, and the power of discernment; the *acquired* tendencies of the mind make it dull, sluggish, dissipated, disturbed, and distracted.[19] Yoga sadhana is the means by which we can unveil the inherent potential residing within us.

Tigunait asserts that the secret of the *Yoga Sutras* may be discerned through a careful study of Vyasa's commentary on the text. Referring to the secret as the lotus of the heart, a beautiful metaphor for the Self in the aforementioned discussion of the Upanishads, he describes an approach to meditation that reclaims our inner luminosity and joy. The key verse is sutra 1.36: "By concentrating on the lotus of the heart, there arises a state of sorrowless joy [*vishoka*], which is infused with inner light [*jyotishmati*]; upon its emergence, such a state anchors the mind to a peaceful flow free from all thought constructs."[20] The first, *vishoka*, refers to a state free from doubt, fear, anger, grief, guilt, regret, and shame. The mind is so clear that one is able to see one's deeply rooted samskaras without being disturbed by them. We can differentiate our conscious or witnessing awareness from the consciousness that is entangled with deeply rooted subtle karmic impressions. We discover that we are the creator of our personal world. This realization, affirms Tigunait, frees us from the fear of losing ourselves by becoming engulfed in our personal world;

we are able to live in the world while remaining above it.[21] The second state, *jyotishmati*, is a condition of inner luminosity. The feeling of I-am-ness (the second of the aforementioned kleshas) is fully illuminated by the light of pure consciousness. The little self begins to see *purusha*, or the Self, and as it does, our notion of ourselves as an isolated individual consciousness dissolves.

Both states are strikingly similar to what Jung describes in his comments pertaining to kundalini yoga, regarding the parallels between yoga and the transpersonal phase of individuation:

> What has caused one to be previously seized with panic is not panic anymore; one is capable of seeing the tension of the opposites of the world without agitation. One does not become apathetic but is freed from entanglement. Consciousness is removed to a sphere of objectlessness. This experience has its effects in practical life, and indeed in the most palpable way.[22]

This parallel between the *Yoga Sutras* and Jung allows us to glimpse the promise of integrative spirituality—a way of being in the world that is both enlightened and individuated. In the language of yoga, this is the state of embodied liberation called *jivanmukti*—freedom or liberation in the body while one is still active in the world.

The *Yoga Sutras* stresses two factors that are essential for one to realize the goal of yoga. The first is *abhyasa*, or diligent and persistent practice (1.13–14). Yoga requires the discipline of an accomplished musician or athlete—perhaps more; in this case, it is a question of achieving mastery of the mind. Reining in the roaming tendencies of the mind and neutralizing powerful unconscious tendencies and patterns requires nothing less. The second essential element of yoga is *vairagya*, translated variously as renunciation or detachment (1.15–16). A practitioner must learn how to let go of habitual attitudes, expectations, and behaviors that impede the ability to become established in the Self. Clearly, when you are troubled by someone or something that causes you to suffer, you need somehow to let it go. All the limbs of yoga make this possible—provided that you practice daily. Yogic practices must be integrated into the rhythm of one's daily existence. Ultimately, then, yoga becomes a way of life.

Yoga in the Bhagavad Gita

The *Bhagavad Gita* is a synthesis of important teachings on yoga within the context of the great Indian epic, the *Mahabharata*. Though placed within this context, it is essentially an Upanishad, a spiritual discourse between a spiritual teacher, or guru, and a disciple. The main storyline of the *Mahabharata* traces the rivalry between two groups of cousins for control of the family kingdom. After Yudhishthira, the eldest of the Pandavas, loses a gambling match, he and his brothers and their common wife are forced into exile for thirteen years with the promise that, if they meet certain conditions during that period, they will receive back half of the kingdom. The conditions are met, but Duryodhana, eldest of the rivaling Kauravas, refuses to keep the promise even under the threat of war. All efforts to negotiate fail.

The rival sides each gather together an enormous army of allies for a final showdown. The armies assemble into two mighty opposing lines on the field of Kurushetra, poised and eager for battle. At this critical moment, Arjuna, greatest of the Pandava warriors, rides to the forefront of the battle line with his charioteer Krishna, but loses his will to fight. In response to this moral crisis, Krishna engages Arjuna in a sustained dialogue on yoga. While the battlefield is an effective backdrop, the *Gita's* subject is the war within, the struggle for self-mastery that every person must wage in order to live wisely and skillfully.

The discourse begins with Arjuna's dilemma—to fight or not to fight. His failure of will has been brought on by his concern over those whom he might kill. This anxiety, Krishna says, is misplaced. The body is mortal, he explains, but the Self that dwells within the body is immortal. That Self is unborn, eternal, and immutable. It does not die when the body dies (2.18–20).[23] This is the wisdom of Samkhya philosophy and *jnana yoga*. In the *Gita*, Samkhya refers to the intellectual or analytical discrimination between the eternal non-material soul (*purusha*) and the embodied world of nature and persons (*prakriti*).

Jnana yoga, as it is initially defined in the text, seems to imply the withdrawal from activity in the world. However, the *Gita* then proceeds to conjoin the contemplative yoga of knowledge with *karma yoga*, a path of action or work (3.3). It is not action itself that Krishna wants to eliminate, but the bondage of action that leads to continuing rebirth. The attempt to abstain from action is not the solution to bondage. The solution is a purified intellect (*buddhi*), which eliminates the attachment that brings rebirth. This teaching repudiates inaction and provides one of the most well-known definitions of yoga contained in the *Gita*:

> You have a right to work, but never to the fruit of work. You should never engage in action for the sake of reward, nor should you long for inaction. Perform work in this world, Arjuna, as a man established within himself— without selfish attachments, and alike in success and defeat. For yoga is perfect evenness of mind. (2:47–48)[24]

Krishna makes clear that there is no alternative to action in the world; complete inaction is not a real possibility. "One who shirks action does not attain freedom; no one can gain perfection by abstaining from work. Indeed, there is no one who rests even an instant; every creature is driven to action by his own nature" (3.4–5).[25] The question, then, is not whether to act or not to act, but how to act wisely and skillfully. Yoga, in fact, is also defined in the text as "skill in action" (2.50).[26] The way to unify consciousness is by performing every action mindfully with complete awareness (4.18). The proper stance of the yogi may be described as passionate equanimity. One acts with clear and courageous intention, but is open to how things play out in experience.

Krishna also reinterprets action in relation to the ancient Vedic idea of ritual sacrifice (*yajna*). The rituals involve making an offering to the gods by pouring an oblation into the sacred fire. In this way humanity nourishes the gods, and the gods, in turn, nourish the earth and its creatures. This idea is transformed in the karma yoga taught in the *Gita*. All work may be performed as an offering and a way of contributing to the maintenance of the world. Sacrifice, understood in this manner, means non-egocentric action performed with an attitude of service. One acts not for personal gain, but for the sake of the world—without attachment to outcomes.

Another component of the *Gita's* teachings on yoga is *bhakti yoga*, the path of devotional love, which enables a practitioner to focus on the divine in a personal, intimate manner. Krishna stresses the need to conquer the egocentric personality through instructions for meditation that are similar to Patanjali's classical yoga. The difference here is that Krishna himself becomes the object of meditation. Krishna teaches that yogis must gain control of their senses through self-discipline and one-pointed concentration, a process he describes in a concise manner and amplifies with a famous image:

> Once seated, strive to still your thoughts. Make your mind one-pointed in meditation, and your heart will be purified. Hold your body, head, and neck firmly in a straight line, and keep your eyes from wandering. With all fears dissolved in the peace of the Self and all desires dedicated to Brahman, controlling and fixing it on me, sit in meditation with me as your only goal. With the senses and mind constantly controlled through meditation, united with the Self within, an aspirant attains nirvana, the state of abiding joy and peace in me . . . When meditation is mastered, the mind is unwavering like the flame of a lamp in a windless place. In the still mind, in the depths of meditation, the Self reveals itself. Beholding the Self by means of the Self, an aspirant knows the joy and peace of complete fulfillment. (6.11–15; 19–21)[27]

In subsequent chapters, Krishna reveals that his nature includes both *purusha* and *prakriti*, and he provides a way to overcome the delusions engendered by maya. He tells Arjuna that his higher nature supports the whole universe and is the source of life in all beings—"There is nothing that exists separate from me, Arjuna. The entire universe is suspended from me as my necklace of jewels" (7.7). While Krishna acknowledges that the *gunas*, the modalities of nature (*prakriti*) that make up his divine maya, are difficult to overcome, those who take refuge in him cross over them. They are united with him and liberated by their devotion. For them, he is "the dearest beloved," and his devotees are very dear to him. When devotees enter a state of union (yoga) with him, Krishna conveys that they "may be regarded as my very Self" (7.14). He further teaches that devotion is the means by which those excluded from Vedic knowledge can reach the highest goal. It is an inclusive yoga, available to all, whatever their birth, race, sex, or caste (9.32). His instruction to all is clear—"Fill your mind with me; love me; serve me; worship me always. Seeking me in your heart, you will at last be united with me" (9.34).[28]

The *Gita* may be read as a progressive teaching that moves from partial answers about yoga to a comprehensive text that integrates the paths of knowledge (*jnana*), action (*karma*), and devotional love (*bhakti*). Each path is integrally related to and supports the others.[29] In this way, the *Gita* validates all the strands of yoga that precede it while offering innovative paths involving action and love. Contemplative knowledge is conjoined with action, renunciation is reconceived as service, while love unifies and motivates sadhana, or spiritual practice.

Although in Hindu tradition the *Gita* belongs to the category of "remembered" or recollected wisdom (*smriti*), it has achieved a status comparable to the Veda and has elicited commentaries from great yoga masters and philosophers. Mahatma Gandhi's commentary is among those that align most closely with my views and Jung's depth psychology. In Gandhi's view, the epic battle in the *Mahabharata* is a struggle between *dharma*, or moral duty and right conduct, and its opposite—a battle between forces of good and evil, personified in us as virtues and vices.[30] The author of the epic, Vyasa, has not established the necessity of physical warfare; on the contrary, he has proven its futility. As Gandhi explains, "He has made the victors shed tears of sorrow and repentance and has left them nothing but a legacy of miseries."[31] We are not at peace with ourselves until becoming like unto God, says Gandhi, and the endeavor to reach this state is the only ambition worth having. He calls this state "Self-realization," and the purpose of the *Gita* is to show the most excellent way to attain this. It is attainable, he insists, only through "constant heart-churn."[32] In other words, as in Jung's psychology, we must deal with conflict, both inner and outer, by engaging our shadow material, holding the tension of the opposites, and allowing the transcendent function to show us how to move forward in our lives.

The *Gita* may be interpreted in a Jungian manner. Viewed in this way, the text presents a dialogue between Arjuna (the ego) and Krishna (the Self). As Arjuna prepares to fight, he experiences a struggle with the opposites. As Jung explains: "Nothing so promotes the growth of consciousness as this inner confrontation with the opposites. The ego becomes ambivalent and ambiguous, and is caught between hammer and anvil."[33] This, precisely, is Arjuna's dilemma. His confusion is conditioned by his unconscious, colored by an influence hidden from his conscious awareness, or ego attitude. Underlying this confusion is a lack of self-knowledge (*avidya*); we do not know who or what we really are. Until we realize or connect with the Self, we are divided within ourselves. We behave like separate creatures in a struggle with the rest of life.

The *Gita* presents this dilemma as a conflict between a lower self (*manas*) and a higher one (*buddhi*). The Sanskrit word for what makes us identify with the lower, separate self is *ahamkara*; literally, this is the "I-maker," the component of the personality that presents us to ourselves as separate from the rest of life. In Jungian terms, ahamkara is the ego complex. To call the ego personality the "lower" self simply reflects that it is limited, only a portion of what we are as human beings. Compared to what we really are, this lesser self (the ego personality) is a cage of separateness; identifying ourselves with it is the source of insecurity, conflict, and dissatisfaction. How, then, do we free ourselves from such a limited self-understanding? The *Gita* teaches that our conditioned mind (*manas*) must be brought under control by means of the discriminating intellect (*buddhi*), and this becomes possible when the ego enters into dialogue with the Self. As this occurs, we become more capable of making decisions that are independent, emerging from unconscious and collective forces; one becomes more conscious and creative. In this way, we become free from the cycle of impulse-driven behaviors and overcome the egocentricity that divides us within and alienates us from other persons and our environment.

The battlefield is not only Kurushetra, a geographical location in which the Indian confrontation takes place; the *Gita* also indicates that it is the field of dharma (*dharmashetra*). In psychological terms, the field of action is the human bodymind—the field where all the activities of life occur. As an archetypal figure, Arjuna represents a turning point in consciousness, a place of opposing perceptions. He signifies the moment when one state of mind shifts to another, by first descending into the darkness of doubt and unknowing. As Arjuna surveys his situation, he questions his motives and revolts against his one-sidedness. Instead of rushing into battle, he detaches himself and enters into dialogue with Krishna, or the archetypal Self. Gradually, he deeply engages powerful emotions such as anger and gives up cherished illusions regarding his role as a warrior. In other words, Arjuna's crisis is the call to individuation. Initially he sinks into despair or depression, but it is through this descent that he becomes connected to his depths, to the Self. Through dialogue with this deeper dimension of his being, he is able to relinquish his naïve way of viewing the world.

In chapter 11 of the *Gita*, Arjuna is granted a vision of Krishna's wholeness, whose luster is said to be greater than a thousand suns. The vision overwhelms Arjuna and dissolves what remains of his doubt. For a brief time, he sees the coincidence of opposites; it is a profound experience of the Self. Arjuna, however, does not merge with or dissolve into Krishna, but asks to see him again in the form that is familiar to him. Arjuna's relationship with Krishna is changed now that he has seen how Krishna really is. This may be described as "Self-realization," a mode of being that goes beyond the acquisition of greater ego strength. Marie-Louise von Franz clarifies Jung's use of the term:

> Jung . . . meant something entirely different, consciously entering into relationship with another psychic content, which drawing on the Upanishads, he calls the Self. In this case also, a more continuous and stable ego identity develops, but a rather different sort. It is less egocentric and has more human kindness.[34]

In Jung's psychology, the ego must be in relationship with the Self; it must remain in dialogue with the Self, for the Self can only be known by the conscious ego. The dynamic relationship is somewhat paradoxical. On the one hand, the efforts of the ego create consciousness; on the other, something larger and more encompassing is required. An extended passage from Jung's magnum opus, *Mysterium Coniunctionis*, clarifies this process:

> The self, in its efforts at self-realization, reaches out beyond the ego-personality on all sides; because of its all-encompassing nature it is brighter and darker than the ego, and accordingly confronts it with problems which it would like to avoid. Either one's moral courage fails, or one's insight, or both, until in the end fate decides. The ego never lacks moral and rational counter-arguments, which one cannot and should not set aside so long as it is possible to hold on to them. For you only feel yourself on the right road when the conflicts of duty seem to have resolved themselves, and you have become victim of a decision made over your head or in defiance of your heart. From this we can see the numinous power of the self, which can hardly be experienced in any other way. For this reason *the experience of the self is always a defeat for the ego.*[35]

For Jung, the biblical Book of Job represents an individual ego's decisive encounter with the Self in Western spiritual literature. Jung continues: "The ego enters into the picture only so far as it can offer resistance, defend itself, and in the event of defeat still affirm its existence. The prototype of this situation is Job's encounter with Yahweh."[36] Arjuna's encounter with Krishna's cosmic form is, I contend, the Eastern analogue of Job's encounter with Yahweh.

This Jungian interpretation of the *Gita* is, I believe, compatible with theistic/bhakti-oriented Hindu perspectives. As long as the divine, or God-image, appears in a personal form, as it does in the *Gita*, a relationship persists between the soul and the divinity; in Jungian terms, the ego-Self axis, or relationship, is preserved. This reading can be summarized as follows:

- Krishna, or the Self, lovingly guides Arjuna through his despair or depression toward Self-realization.

- In this process, the ego attitude is wounded and descends into despair. The descent compels the ego to seek guidance and enter into a dialogue with the Self.

- The dialogue is informed by detachment from outer and material concerns; by introverted attention, or self-inquiry; and by deep listening to the guidance that unfolds from within.

- As the process intensifies, the ego experiences a numinous encounter with the transpersonal Self.

- Arjuna's egocentric doubts and one-sided perspective are overcome. He finds the courage to be himself and act as the situation requires. Action informed in this way may be described as non-attached, non-egocentric action—action that is aligned with the restoration of harmony in the world, or *dharma*.

In developmental terms, such action is worldcentric rather than egocentric or ethnocentric.

Tantra and the yoga of Kashmir Shaivism

While the *Gita* effectively integrates ancient teachings on yoga from sources such as the Upanishads and Patanjali's *Yoga Sutras*, an even greater synthesizing perspective emerges from the tantric traditions during the eighth to twelve centuries of the Common Era. *Tantra* derives from the verbal root *tan* meaning "to expand" and, according to esoteric explanations, is that which expands knowledge or wisdom. Tantra also stands for "continuum," the seamless whole that comprises transcendence and immanence, being and becoming, universal consciousness and mental consciousness, spirit and matter.[37] The teachings and practices from tantric traditions are known collectively as Kashmir Shaivism. I have embraced this form of yoga spirituality because it articulates a vision of spirit inherent in matter and the body, valorizes the divine feminine, and provides an array of practices that cultivate intellectual, affective, and somatic capacities in an integrated manner.

The Shaiva teachings I have received and practice integrate several tantric traditions associated with great contemplative yogis who lived during the eighth to twelfth centuries in Kashmir. Focusing on the divine feminine energy known as Shakti, the Spanda tradition teaches that the universe consists of vibrating awareness; its spiritual practices aim at discerning and aligning with this creative, pulsating energy in one's thoughts, feelings, and action.[38] Pratyabhijna is a wisdom tradition whose teachings are reminiscent of those of the Upanishads; it teaches that the goal of yoga is to recognize that one's true nature *is* Shiva, which, in this context, means the Self, or universal consciousness.[39] A synthesis of these traditions with other tantric schools, known as the Trika, was created by the tenth-century, philosopher-sage Abhinavagupta.[40]

Most importantly, the ultimate aim of tantric yoga, as with the individuation process delineated by Jung, is the integration of the masculine and feminine principles symbolized by the *hieros gamos*, or sacred marriage. In Tantra, the masculine principle is personified as Shiva and symbolizes universal consciousness, or Spirit, whereas Shakti, personified by goddesses such as Parvati and Kali, symbolizes energy and the embodiment of consciousness in matter. Tantra places great emphasis on Shakti, the divine feminine, as the means by which humanity can realize its inherent divinity in a world-embracing vision of life. Since I am among those who believe that recovering the feminine principle, or Goddess, is the spiritual imperative of our time, I regard aspects of tantric yoga traditions to be among the most important forms of integrative spirituality available to us in the twenty-first century.

The most concise articulation of the philosophy and yoga spirituality of Kashmir Shaivism is found in the *Pratyabhijna-hridayam* ("The Heart of Recognition"), a text ascribed to one of Abhinavagupta's disciples, Kshemaraja. In twenty short sutras, or aphorisms, the text describes the process by which an individual recognizes the Self through this form of world-affirming yoga.[41] The *Pratyabhijna-hridayam* depicts the cosmos as a play of consciousness enacted by Shakti, the creative energy of Shiva. She becomes the universe of diverse forms through the power of maya, the principle of differentiation and limitation. In the process, Shiva (universal consciousness) becomes the *jiva*, an individual soul, who enacts the powers of Shiva, or the Self, albeit without conscious awareness. We become deluded by our own mental and sensory powers, failing to realize that we are the *subjects* who enact these abilities. Through spiritual awakening, we recognize that we are the author of these powers; this recognition is accomplished by "inward movement" and "unfoldment of the center," yogic practices that enable us to realize the Self and embody this awakening in the myriad activities of life.

According to the text, the individual "has the universe as his body in a contracted form" (sutra 4), conveying the idea that the macrocosm is fully present within a human being. The feminine creative principle resides in the subtle body of the individual as *kundalini shakti*, coiled at the base of the spine in the root chakra. However, it is dormant until awakened and, consequently, one's personal power or energy is limited, a condition called the "poverty of Shakti." Spirituality, then, involves expanding our latent spiritual energy until we recognize our true nature.

Kundalini awakening occurs through *shaktipat*, a descent or influx of cosmic Shakti into a spiritual aspirant. Power flows from the cosmos into the subtle body and effects a new birth, an initiation that impels the spiritual journey of an individual seeker. Traditionally *shaktipat* is transmitted to a seeker by a spiritual master or guru through a touch or look, though it can occur in other ways—while gazing at a picture of a spiritual master; when one is asleep and dreaming; or even, in rare instances, spontaneously. No matter how it comes, even if an individual teacher is the vehicle, *shaktipat* comes through the Goddess. While *kundalini* awakening can be activated through hatha yoga techniques such as forceful breathing exercises (*pranayama*) and muscular contractions (*bandhas*), the Kashmir Shaiva traditions utilize gentler methods, approaching *kundalini* as a goddess, an intelligent energy that guides spiritual awakening. The intention is to allow *kundalini* to awaken herself and move through us in her own spontaneous way, by her own will. Instead of trying to dominate the energy, seekers gently invoke her. This approach may include mindful breathing, prayer, a devotional attitude, visualizing her in the form of a goddess, or recitation of mantra.[42] Approaching *kundalini* in this manner, I feel, aligns with the attitude toward the unconscious that Jung recommends—a respectful, dialogical stance in which one does not force or manipulate the dynamics of the psyche.

Returning to the *Pratyabhijna-hridayam*, the phrase "inward movement" refers to the yogic process of dis-identifying with all thoughts, feelings, and physical objects in which the yogi realizes that one is the subject, or Self. The mind, or *chitta*, is released from contraction and expands or rises to the status of universal consciousness, or *Chiti* (sutra 13). This movement generates the fire of yoga (*tapas*), the psychic heat that transforms the constraining tendencies stored in the unconscious. The expansion of consciousness consumes the emotional reactivity and constraining thoughts that obscure the Self (sutra 14). The Self-inquiry practices of Shaiva yoga de-potentiate such content by "burning [the seeds] to sameness with the fire of Consciousness." In contemporary language, one inquires into what one is feeling. Instead of allowing that feeling to affect one's mood or behavior, one purifies the feeling by working with it until that which is painful or negative is processed. The feeling is dissolved back into consciousness and the person is again at peace.[43]

Likewise, through Self-inquiry, experiences of pleasure and aesthetic delight can be the means to experiencing the Self. When one savors the joy or pleasure that arises from eating, drinking, sexuality, or music, the mind expands. For this reason, yogis are instructed to identify with the joy they feel, rather than with the object itself.[44] As a contemplative exercise from the *Vijnana Bhairava Tantra* explains, "Wherever the mind of the individual finds satisfaction (without agitation), let it be concentrated on that. In every such case, the true nature of the highest bliss will shine forth."[45] Thus, ordinary experiences of life can be vehicles of spirituality if they are engaged in the right way. This approach allows the mind to focus on whatever it loves, then to shift from that object to *the feeling the object awakens*, and to meditate on that.[46]

There are a variety of ways of "unfolding the center" and knowing the Self (sutra 18). Different forms of yoga sadhana, which Kashmir Shaivism categorizes as *upayas*, are utilized to mitigate the *malas*, or the forms of contraction that constrain and bind human existence. These limiting conditions that block the recognition of our nature are threefold—contractions pertaining to action; to knowledge; and to will, or emotion. The *malas* correspond to the physical, subtle, and causal bodies.

Karma mala pertains to the physical body; it is the result of selfish and fearful actions. Actions we perform that are harmful to ourselves or others produce negative karma. The limitation or bondage of karma is that we have to live with the results of our actions. Physical karmas can be overcome by good actions, actions that benefit others or that are dedicated to the divine. Spiritual practices called *anavopaya*, or "the way of the body," that transform negative karma include karma yoga, the yoga of service, ritual worship, hatha yoga postures, and breathing exercises.[47]

Mayiya mala, associated with the subtle body, is the limitation that causes us to feel separate from all other beings; it is a contraction of knowledge that generates the perception of duality. *Shaktopaya*, or "the way of the mind," is comprised of practices such as repeating a mantra, self-inquiry, and contemplating ideas that uplift consciousness. These practices work by means of the effect that language (spoken aloud and inward self-talk) has on consciousness. In *shaktopaya*, the focus is on Shakti, the feminine principle that is the power of the Self. A Shaiva aphorism says that Shakti is the doorway, or portal, to Shiva, a principle that underscores the great importance given to the divine feminine in Kashmir Shaivism.[48]

Anava mala, the contraction of will, reduces universal consciousness to the feeling of being a small, limited entity. As a deep feeling within us, centered in the heart, this limitation affects our causal body, the place in us where our Shiva nature (the Self) becomes our individuality (the ego complex). All other limitations emerge from this contraction of will. Since will is associated with affect, or feeling, anava mala ushers in our first negative emotions. Shiva becomes limited. "The archetypal statement of *anava mala*," Swami Shankarananda explains, "is 'I am a person!' This is, unfortunately, not the triumphant shout of a humanist, but the sad cry of one who has been something great."[49] *Shambhavopaya*, or "the way of pure consciousness," provides the remedy. No physical or mental means can ameliorate this condition. Instead, a yogi focuses on pure consciousness or pure awareness, free of mental movements. This consciousness, vast and silent, is Shiva. The object of meditation is the thought-free consciousness out of which thoughts arise, the witnessing awareness underlying thought. This form of meditation is very subtle and is often misunderstood. A practitioner does not need to eliminate all thoughts, but pays no attention to the *content* of thought. Thoughts continue to play in the mind, but the meditator stays focused on the space beyond thought, the space that contains thought.[50]

The *upayas* of Shaiva yoga provide an integral approach to yoga spirituality, that is, the methods that can be combined as needed to help a practitioner holistically engage the physical, emotional, cognitive, and intuitive capacities that can be most effectively utilized by that individual. The Shaiva approach has been my primary form of yogic practice.

There is also a fourth *upaya* beyond those I have described, called *anupaya*, or the non-means. This is actually a way of being—the state of enlightenment—and the goal of Shaiva yoga. No effort is made, since one's vision of life has been fully transformed. The whole world is seen as the sport of the divine, a play of consciousness. *Anupaya* is also called "recognition" since it is based on a penetrating insight into reality or on how things really are. Here one experiences *sahaja samadhi*, the natural state; it is not a "high" state in the sense of intoxication, but an open-eyed state of awareness that is profoundly balanced and integrated.[51]

Although most of us need to engage in the practices that belong to the prior three *upayas*, Kashmir Shaivism emphasizes that awakening can arise at any time and place when we perceive the radiance that permeates the world and our own bodies. The *Vijnana Bhairava Tantra*, a compilation of 112 *dharanas*, or meditation techniques, enjoins practitioners to recognize the divine in a vast array of experiences that include breathing, music, sexuality, intense emotion, the beauty of nature, and other portals into the wonder and bliss that expand our awareness. These practices point to what is perhaps the most distinctive teaching of Shaiva yoga—it is not enough to go inside and experience bliss in the meditative state of introverted concentration, known as *atma-vyapti*, or merging in the Self; the ultimate aim of spiritual practice is *Shiva-vyapti*, or merging with the world. *Atma-vyapti*, the conventional yoga of inwardness, turns the seeker away from the world in order to realize the Self. The Shaiva view is that *atma-vyapti* becomes complete and reaches fruition in *Shiva-vyapti*, a state synonymous with *sahaja samadhi*, the natural state of liberation.[52] One who lives in this condition is liberated while living in the body (*jivanmukti*), free to creatively express the physical, emotional, and mental powers of one's being in the world for the good of all.

Like the other yogic traditions discussed in this chapter, Shaiva yoga enables one to overcome the entanglements with sense objects that constrain and contract. But once this is achieved, one becomes the subject of their desires—subjectivity is no longer projected—and the senses become powers for enjoying the world. Shaivism reveals that the self/world distinction is part of *maya*, or the spell of the ego personality, an illusion created by the contractions of the bodymind; it is a distorted and limited vision of life. The Shaiva yogas are the means for overcoming this spell and releasing the ego-contraction that binds the individual. They expand one's vision of life and engender the experience of wonder that emerges from seeing the grandeur and splendor of the Self in its myriad expressions in the world. First one sees the divinity within; then one beholds it everywhere.

Insights for integrative spirituality

Forms of contemplative yoga that have been effectively transmitted to the West provide many teachings and practices that support integrative spirituality:

* Contemplative yoga traditions offer contemporary spiritual seekers paths that lead to Self-realization, or spiritual awakening, suitable for individuals with different temperaments. Through self-inquiry, intellectual persons can discover the luminous Self, or witness that which lies beneath all forms of self-identification (*jnana yoga*). Through meditation, persons endowed with a capacity for introversion can enter the silence deep within the cave of the heart and behold the divine dwelling within their being (*raja yoga*). Deeply-feeling individuals can cultivate devotional love as a means of relating to the divine (*bhakti yoga*). Those with vital personalities may connect to the divine by viewing their work and actions as a form of worship, or service (*karma yoga*). While each of these can be a sufficient path to spiritual awakening, individual practitioners can combine them in any way that proves to be desirable and effective. The *Bhagavad Gita* and the tantric traditions of Kashmir Shaivism, for example, promote integral approaches to spiritual life that engage the body, emotions, intellect, and intuition as synergistic instruments for embodying Self-realization in the world.

* Contemplative yoga involves the interiorization of awareness. To realize one's true nature, one needs to turn within and dis-identify with the myriad objects of experience. Authentic practice, however, is not dissociative. To dis-identify is to stop projecting and entangling the Self with limited and conditioned aspects of our being (body, feelings, thoughts), and with persons, relationships, or objects toward which we feel strong attraction or aversion. By differentiating the Seer (subject) from the seen (object), we recover who we truly are

(the Self). This process of discernment, of course, is more easily said than done. Consequently, some monastic yoga traditions encourage practitioners to renounce the world. Alternatively, the *Bhagavad Gita* reinterprets renunciation as non-attachment to the results of our actions; yogis are encouraged to act in the world, but to dedicate their work to the divine as service or a form of worship. Tantric traditions go a step further through practices that divinize our sensory capacities; thereby, food, sexuality, music, the beauty of nature, and other activities become portals to the divine. These differing approaches—detachment and engagement—allow us to partake in yoga practices that are appropriate for our psychological tendencies. People struggling with addictive behaviors, for example, may need to learn how to detach or decathect from objects in order to learn that fulfillment comes from within one's self rather than from substances or other persons. Conversely, a person who has overemphasized detachment may need to discover the presence of the divine within the myriad forms of life. Otherwise, there is a danger that one will lose zest for life or the capacity to perceive the radiance and beauty that inheres in the world.

- Contemplation functions as inner-work in depth psychology insofar as it provides us with a way to recognize and ameliorate subjective impressions, behavior patterns, and deep-seated emotional afflictions residing in the unconscious. Practices such as Self-inquiry and meditation can enable a practitioner to gradually let go of these conditionings and, as a result, experience a freedom that may have seemed unimaginable. These practices generate *tapas*, the yogic fire of transformation, which depotentiates the unconscious content that otherwise afflicts consciousness. While the aim is similar to psychotherapeutic or analytic work, the process of yoga differs as it focuses on the concentration of awareness itself rather than engaging or interpreting the contents uncovered in the unconscious.

- The teachings on yoga in the *Bhagavad Gita* present an important parallel to Jungian psychology. As we have seen, the text can be read as a dialogue between the ego and the Self. Human existence often entails conflicts of duty, a struggle with opposites. Our perspective in these situations is typically one-sided and naïve, and is further distorted by emotional complexes that are activated by the struggles that confront us. To resolve these dilemmas, the ego needs to descend into the depths of the psyche in order to connect with a deeper psychic intelligence. Gradually, as doubts and illusions dissolve, wisdom dawns and Self-realization unfolds. In yogic terms, a person experiences the transpersonal Self in the form of the Beloved, a God-image such as Krishna, or the inner guide or guru who dispels ignorance; in Jungian language, the Self manifests through the transcendent function, producing a symbol that integrates the opposites. In either case, constant "heart-churn," as Gandhi puts it, is required. A person must deal with conflict (inner and outer), engage unconscious shadow material, and allow the Transcendent (yoga) or transcendent function (Jungian psychology) to show one how to move forward in one's life. Whether through yoga, depth psychology, or both modes of inner work, we become more conscious and creative persons, capable of making decisions that are less egocentric and more human-hearted. Through these means, we, as living examples, help promote peace and greater harmony in a world besieged by violence and conflict.

• By extolling the integration, or sacred marriage, of the masculine and feminine principles, tantric yoga aligns closely with Jungian psychology. Tantra's emphasis on Shakti, which is both the creative energy that manifests as the cosmos and the power of awakening residing in the bodymind, offers us a form of spirituality that fully recovers the divine feminine. Shakti-based spirituality values the body and the earth. She is not a transcendent or wholly Other, as is the case with the masculine God-images that predominate in the most prevalent forms of Abrahamic religions. She is fully immanent as the world. Consequently, ordinary experiences of life can be portals to the divine if they are engaged in a conscious manner. By practicing the contemplations, or *dharanas*, prescribed in the *Vijnana Bhairava Tantra*, for example, we can become the subject of our desires and identified with the Self, rather than entangled with or addicted to sense objects. Genuine happiness and bliss, we come to understand, arise from within and are not dependent on something or someone other than us. Moreover, through meditation and other contemplative practices, we merge not only with the Self, but with the world as well. We realize the self/world distinction as the spell of the ego personality, an illusion generated by the contractions of the bodymind. Ultimately, tantric yoga offers its practitioners a world-embracing spirituality that aims at nothing less than liberation in the body. Free from conditioning and self-imposed limitations, we become free to express the physical, emotional, and mental powers of our being in the world, for the good of all.

Notes

1 Georg Feuerstein, *The Yoga Tradition: Its History, Literature, Philosophy and Practice*, 3rd ed., Chino Valley, AZ: Holm Press, 2008, p. 6.
2 Heinrich Zimmer, *Philosophies of India*, ed. Joseph Campbell. Princeton: Princeton University Press, 1951, 3.
3 Ibid., 12.
4 Heinrich Zimmer, *Myths and Symbols in Indian Art and Civilization*, ed. Joseph Campbell. Princeton: Princeton University Press, 1946, 26.
5 Feuerstein, *The Yoga Tradition*, 6.
6 In Hindu tradition, body and mind are inextricably connected; both are prakriti (matter) rather than purusha (consciousness or spirit). I use the term bodymind, as do many scholars, to refer to the psycho-physical organism.
7 Swami Prabhavananda and Frederick Manchester, *The Upanishads: Breath of the Eternal*. New York: Signet Classic, 1957, 17.
8 Ibid., 19.
9 Ibid., 24.
10 Ibid. In this passage the Self (*atman*) is referred to as "he" for literary purposes though the Atman, like Brahman, is beyond gender.

11 Feuerstein, *The Yoga Tradition*, 207.
12 Swami Nikhilananda, *Self-Knowledge (Ātmabodha): An English Translation of Sankarāchārya's Ātmabodha with Notes, Comments, and Introduction*. New York: Ramakrishna-Vivekananda Center, 1974, 42.
13 Arvind Sharma, *The Experiential Dimension of Advaita Vedanta*. Delhi: Motilal Banarsidass, 1980, xiv.
14 Ramana Maharshi, *The Spiritual Teaching of Ramana Maharshi*. Boston: Shambhala, 1988, 5–6.
15 Ibid., 11.
16 Sri Nisargadatta Maharaj, *I Am That: Talks with Sri Nisargadatta Maharaj*, ed. Sudhakar Dikshit, trans. Maurice Frydman. Durham, NC: Acorn Press, 1973. The text is replete with this teaching. For illustrative passages, see pp. 2, 18–19, 48, 224, 230–31, 537. Appendix I also summarizes the teaching: "To delve into the sense of 'I'—so real and vital—in order to reach its source is the core of Nisarga Yoga. Not being continuous, the sense of 'I' must have a source from which it flows and to which it returns . . . The gateway to reality, by whatever road one arrives to it, is the sense of 'I am.' It is through grasping the full import of the 'I am,' and going beyond its source, that one reaches the supreme state, which is also the primordial and the ultimate."
17 Sutras 1:2, 1:3, and 1:4. Translation from Pandit Rajmani Tigunait, *The Secret of the Yoga Sutra: Samadhi Pada*. Honesdale, PA: Himalayan Institute, 2014, 265–66.
18 Sutras 2:29–2:32 describe the yamas and niyamas. See Edward F. Bryant, *The Yoga Sūtras of Patañjali: A New Edition, Translation, and Commentary*. New York: North Point Press, 2009, pp. 242–54, for an excellent commentary.
19 Tigunait, xvi–xix.
20 Ibid., 188.
21 Ibid., 188–89.
22 Jung, *The Psychology of Kundalini Yoga*, 83.
23 All passages from the Bhagavad Gita are from Eknath Easwaran's *The Bhagavad Gita*. Tomales, CA: Nilgiri Press, 2007.
24 Ibid., 94.
25 Ibid., 104.
26 Ibid., 95.
27 Ibid., 141–42.
28 Ibid., 177.
29 Many commentators on the Gita take this view. See, for example, Swami Rama, *Perennial Psychology of the Bhagavad Gita*, Honesdale, PA: The Himalayan International Institute of Yoga Science and Philosophy of the U.S.A, 1985; Eknath Easwaran, *Essence of the Bhagavad Gita: A Contemporary Guide to Yoga*, Meditation, and Indian Philosophy. Tomales, CA: Nilgiri Press, 2011; and Sri Aurobindo, *Essays on the Gita*. Pondicherry: Sri Aurobindo Ashram, 1972. Aurobindo's view, in particular, is a strong articulation of the view that the Gita is a comprehensive teaching that synthesizes knowledge, action, and devotion.
30 Mohandas K. Gandhi, *The Bhagavad Gita According to Gandhi*, ed. John Strohmeier. Berkeley, CA: Berkeley Hills Press, 2000, 22.
31 Ibid., 16.
32 Ibid., 18.
33 Jung, *Memories, Dreams, Reflections*, 345.
34 Marie-Louise von Franz, *Psychotherapy*. Boston: Shambhala, 1993, 1.
35 C. G. Jung, *Mysterium Coniunctionis, The Collected Works of C. G. Jung*, vol. 14, 2nd ed., trans. R. F. C. Hull. Princeton University Press, 1969, § 778.
36 Ibid., 546.
37 Georg Feuerstein, *Tantra: The Path of Ecstasy*. Boston: Shambhala, 1998, 1–2.
38 Shakti is Shiva's creative energy. In Kashmir Shaivism, spanda is a term that describes Shakti as the divine pulse, or vibration, that creates and pervades all life. The aim of the yogi is to discern and align with this principle.

39 See B. N. Pandit, *Iśvara Pratyabhijña Kārikā of Utpaladeva: Verses on the Recognition of the Lord*. New Delhi: Muktabodha Indological Research Institute, 2003, for a key text of this tradition.

40 See Swami Shankarananda, *Consciousness is Everything: The Yoga of Kashmir Shaivism*. Mt. Eliza: Victoria: Shaktipat Press, 2003, for a description of the influential traditions, texts, and practices of Kashmir Shaivism.

41 See Jaideva Singh, *Pratyabhijñahṛdayam: The Secret of Self-Recognition*. Delhi: Motilal Banarsidass, 1980, for a translation and commentary of the text. See also Appendix B in Shankarananda, *Consciousness is Everything*, for a translation of the verses I utilize in this chapter.

42 I am indebted to Sally Kempton, one of my spiritual teachers, for my understanding regarding the Goddess being the source of *shaktipat* and her views on how to approach *kundalini*. See her *Awakening Shakti: The Transformative Power of the Goddesses of Yoga*. Boulder, CO: Sounds True, 2013.

43 Shankarananda, 146–47.

44 Ibid., 186.

45 Jaideva Singh, *Vijñānabhairava or Divine Consciousness: A Treasury of 112 Types of Yoga*. Delhi: Motilal Banarsidass, 1979, 70.

46 Shankarananda, 186–87.

47 Ibid., 120.

48 Ibid., 121–22.

49 Ibid., 123.

50 Ibid., 124.

51 Ibid., 125.

52 Ibid., 150; 285.

8

INTEGRATING SPIRITUAL AWAKENING AND PSYCHOLOGICAL DEVELOPMENT

> True self-cultivation involves the holistic integration of mind, body, and spirit. Balancing yin and yang through the various practices of the Integral Way, one achieves complete unity without and within.
> —*Lao Tzu*

Thus far we have journeyed with religious thinkers, Jungian analysts, and contemplative yogis whose modes of thinking and practice have informed my own path of spirituality. This way of exploring, I contend, may serve as a valuable map or model for your own seeking, given that our quest is occurring in the context of a postmodern world characterized by cross-pressured cultural dynamics—the death of traditional God-images, secularization, religious pluralism, Jungian depth psychology, and the emerging presence of contemplative yoga in the West.

I have been persistently drawn, following Jung's lead, to go beyond the spirit of the times to encounter the depths, that is, our interiority and the dimensions of being that are conveyed by the terms spirit and soul. As we have seen, *Spirit* concerns awakening, discovering the unconditional ground of our being; *soul* pertains to individuation, our embodied growth and development throughout the life cycle toward greater wholeness. While we may devote ourselves to cultivating spirit *or* soul, my conviction is that each endeavor without the other is one-sided and incomplete. Integrating both endeavors—awakening and individuation—is the passion that impels my intellectual studies, teaching, and inner work.

This integration process, like all the aforementioned aspects of the spiritual journey, is a personal matter; we must find our own way of mining and integrating the spiritual and psychological depths of our lives. I have found it useful and profoundly illuminating to explore the works of two contemporary individuals who have dedicated their lives to this purpose. In this penultimate chapter, I highlight selected teachings of Ken Wilber and A. H. Almaas, whom I regard to be the most pioneering and encompassing exemplars of integrative spirituality. They are sophisticated writers and the scope of their respective writings is vast, so I offer a concise overview of their foundational concepts regarding psychological and spiritual development, a distillation, as it were, as an introduction to those unfamiliar with their work. I focus on their ideas regarding the relationship between spiritual awakening and psychological development, on integrative practices, and how different views of the ultimate are valid apprehensions of reality, truly fascinating concepts that inform and enrich my spiritual practice.

The integral approach of Ken Wilber

Wilber, like Jung, discovered his real calling after he abandoned a conventional intellectual path that he had been successfully pursuing, but which left his life bereft of existential meaning. Describing his life as "built upon logic, structured by physics, and moved by chemistry," he became disillusioned with science's limited and narrow scope. Reading a passage from the *Tao Te Ching*, a contemplative text attributed to the Chinese sage Lao Tzu, initiated a passionate quest for the kind of knowledge that nourishes his soul and awakens his spirit:

> The Way (or Tao) that can be told is not the Eternal Way.
> The name that can be named is not the Eternal Name.
> The Nameless is the origin of Heaven and Earth.
> The Named is but the mother of ten thousand things.
> Truly, only he that rids himself of desire can see the Secret Essences;
> He that has never rid himself of desire can only see the Outcomes.
> These two things issue from the same Source, but nevertheless are different
>   in form.
> This Source we can but call the Mystery,
> The Doorway whence issues all Secret Essences.[1]

"The old sage," he says, "had touched a chord so deep in me that I suddenly awoke to the silent but certain realization that my life, my old self, my old beliefs could no longer be energized. It was time for a separation."[2] The separation demanded an entirely new mode of inquiry. "Intellectually," he explains, "I began an obsessive venture in reading, devouring books on Eastern philosophy at a terrifying rate. I cut chemistry classes to read the *Bhagavad Gita*; I skipped calculus to study Kabbalah. I was introduced to Huxley and the psychedelics, Watts and Beat Zen."[3]

The next two years were spent in solitary reading and research, eight to ten hours a day. He pursued degrees in chemistry and biology; these came so easily to him that he didn't have to waste much time studying.[4] During this period, he felt unhappy and dissatisfied with life. As he recollects:

This simple unhappiness is really the way Gautama Buddha used the word *dukkha*; although it is usually translated as "suffering," it more accurately means "sour." The Buddha's first truth: life as normally lived is sour, and awakening to this sourness is the first step on the path to liberation.

Life for me *was* sour; it was unhappy. And in part I was obsessed with reading all the great psychologists and sages because I was searching for a way out of the sour life; reading was motivated by personal existential therapy, to put it in dry terms. The point is that I had to "read everything" because I was trying mentally and emotionally to put together in a comprehensive framework that which I felt was necessary for my own salvation.[5]

Wilber was drawn to a diverse array of writers who exemplify how reading can animate one's spiritual quest and lead to integrative insights. While he was particularly drawn to the work of Fritz Perls, C. G. Jung, and the existentialists, his thinking was also captivated by mystics (Krishnamurti, Zen masters, Vedantic sages, Meister Eckhart), traditionalists who espouse the perennial philosophy (Ananda Coomarswamy, Rene Guénon, Frithjof Schuon), and psychoanalysts (Sigmund Freud, Sándor Fernenczi, Otto Rank, Melanie Klein). Now he was confused as well as unhappy; these authorities all disagreed with one another. Wilber's cognitive dissonance triggered an insight—each theory is true, but partial:

For my part, I simply could not imagine any mind of genius (whether Freud's or Buddha's) could manufacture *only* falsehoods and errors. This was inconceivable to me. Rather, if we must form a conclusion, the only possible one would be: Freud was correct but partial; Buddha was correct but partial; and so with Perls, Kierkegaard, the existentialists, the behaviorists. And it was on that tentative basis that I proceeded. We are faced not with several errors and one truth, but with several partial truths, and how to fit them together is then the supreme puzzle.[6]

Well on his way to a Ph.D. in 1972, he abandoned his doctoral studies in biochemistry to write his first book, at age 23, on the spectrum of personal and transpersonal forms of human consciousness, a leitmotif that informed his work for the next four decades. Wilber's studies also included the vast scope of Western philosophy, from the ancient pre-Socratics to the postmodernists, as well as the writings of pioneering twentieth-century physicists. By reading everyone from East to West, from Shankara to Sartre, Buddha to Freud, Jesus to Jung, and Aristotle to Bohr, he endeavored to be as inclusive, comprehensive, and integrative as possible in his presentation of theoretical ideas and psycho-spiritual practices.

Wilber's wide-ranging studies of diverse fields of knowledge impelled him to formulate his Integral Theory, Integral Approach, or, more technically, the Integral AQAL Approach, an acronym for "all quadrants, all levels, all lines, all states, all types."[7] Briefly explained, *quadrants* refer to four different domains of knowledge (subjective interiority, inter-subjective culture, objective nature, inter-objective systems); *levels* designate stages of psycho-social development; *lines* denote types of intelligence; *states* pertain to consciousness; and *types* pertain to typological or temperamental characteristics. These categories, elucidated later in this chapter, are the theoretical basis of Wilber's holistic theory of reality, a meta-perspective or super-map of the territories germane to understanding the multidimensional aspects of human existence.

Returning to Wilber's personal odyssey, his quest was as profoundly experiential as it was intellectual. From the outset, he committed to a rigorous practice of Zen Buddhist meditation. He investigated many esoteric traditions, from Western mysticism to the modern twentieth-century mystics of India, particularly the Vedantic sage Ramana Maharshi (see Chapter 7) and the Shabd Yoga master Kirpal Singh. Most influential was the evolutionary integral yoga of Sri Aurobindo (see Chapter 4). Wilber's initial practice was integrative, a combination of Gestalt psychology and Zen meditation. He studied with many prominent Zen masters, but also engaged in the somatic practices of Rolfing, sensory awareness, the Alexander technique, hatha yoga, and tai chi chuan. In so doing, his aim was to balance body-mind-spirit, an approach that developed into "integral transformative practice," or "integral life practice," an integrative repertoire of practices discussed later in this chapter.[8]

Over the decades, Wilber was initiated into and practiced all three vehicles of Buddhism—Theravada or Hinayana (the "Lesser Vehicle"), Mahayana (the "Great Vehicle"), and Vajrayana ("the Diamond Vehicle"), with particular emphasis on the latter. Although a practicing Buddhist, he is quick to explain: "I do not think that Buddhism is the best way or the only way. And I would not call myself a Buddhist; I have too many affinities with Vedanta Hinduism and Christian mysticism, among many others. But one has to choose a particular path if one is to actually *practice*, and my path has been Buddhist."[9] Here and elsewhere throughout his writings, Wilber insists on the primacy of practice and the importance of developing the full range of our human capacities.

Through his meditation practice he was able to move beyond the fluctuations of mental contractions and to experience profound states, including the subtle realm of the archetypes and of archetypal deities, which he describes as his first direct experience of the sacredness of the world. Gradually it dawned on him that there are limits to superconscious experience; such experiential displays can go on forever. This cured him of a subtle-level fixation that was an obstacle to moving from the subtle realm of soul to that of causal spirit. His Zen training and his studies of mystics informed him that the ultimate state is not a particular experience, however blissful or profound, but the ground of *all* experiences, high or low.[10]

A profound realization came to him during a retreat led by Katagiri Roshi, Wilber's primary Zen master, as his separate egoic self dissolved into radiant, all-pervading, unobstructed awareness. Wilber describes this *kensho*, the Zen term for a small satori or initial awakening, the first of several in his life, in language that evokes the reality that lies beyond the ego or separate sense of self:

There was no subject anywhere in the universe; there was no object anywhere in the universe; there was only the universe. Everything was arising moment to moment, and it was arising in me and as me; yet there was no me. It is very important to realize that this state was not a loss of faculties but a peak enhancement of them; it was no blank trance but perfect clarity; not depersonalized but transpersonalized. No personal faculties—language, logic, concepts, motor skills—were lost or impaired. Rather, they all functioned, for the first time it seemed to me, in radical openness, free of defenses thrown up by a separate self sense. This radically open, undefended, and perfectly nondual state was both incredible and profoundly ordinary, so extraordinarily ordinary that it did not even register. There was nobody there to comprehend it, until I fell *out* of it. (I guess about three hours later.)[11]

Although Wilber says there was nobody (no ego) to comprehend his experience while he was awash in it, there was a need for processing afterwards. In other words, spiritual awakening needs to be interpreted in order for it to be integrated into one's life, and one's understanding or perspective reflects one's level of psychological development. His insight regarding the limitations of exalted states of consciousness also points to the need for some form of inquiry. Self-reflexive questions such as "Who am I?" or "Who desires release?" disengage attention from objective displays in consciousness and turn it on consciousness itself.[12] In this way, one penetrates through and beyond all identifications to realize one's true, unconditioned nature. Expressed in the language of a Zen koan, a person discovers her Original Face, the face she had before her parents were born. In other words, she discovers the timeless ground of her being. Such is the nature of spiritual awakening. But how does it relate to psychological development?

In Wilber's view, human beings engage in two different types of growth and development, which he refers to as *growing up*, a process of psychological maturation, and *waking up*, the process of spiritual awakening. Historically we have focused on one or the other type of growth. Consequently, we have produced individuals who might be quite "grown up," or psychologically mature, but not awakened or enlightened. Humanity has produced, Wilber explains, awakened or enlightened individuals—persons who have followed a contemplative path of waking up—but who remain relatively immature in many of their human capacities. For instance, they might be poorly developed psychosexually and take advantage of their students; they might be morally undeveloped despite their spiritual interests; or they might be xenophobic, racist, sexist, homophobic, or authoritarian.[13] The two different modes of human development, he believes, are relatively independent. Wilber correlates waking up with states of consciousness whereas growing up pertains to levels and lines of development. I will consider each of the five components of the AQAL framework—states, levels, lines, types, and quadrants—to better understand how they may be effectively integrated in spiritual practice.

States of consciousness

Waking up is a growth process that leads to what is variously known as awakening, enlightenment, realization, and freedom. A spiritually awakened person becomes identified with reality in a state the Sufis call "the Supreme Identity," the realization that the individual and the ultimate reality are one. This realization releases one from the original sin, separation, or dualism of identifying with the small, finite, temporal sense of self. Waking up, Wilber maintains, is present within the esoteric core of the world's great religions: in Judaism as Kabbalah and Hasidism; in contemplative branches of Christianity exemplified by St. John of the Cross, St. Teresa of Avila, and Meister Eckhart; in the Sufi orders of Islam; in the Hindu traditions of Yoga, Vedanta, and Kashmir Shaivism; in the meditative traditions of Buddhism such as Zen; and in China as contemplative Taoism and Neo-Confucianism.[14]

These great wisdom traditions, says Wilber, distinguish four or five major states of consciousness—the waking state; the dream state; the deep dreamless state; the empty witness state; and the nondual or unity state. While most of us are familiar with the first three states, the other two—witnessing and unity consciousness—may be unknown territory. To gain access to these states, one must engage in contemplative practices. Witness consciousness is known in Sanskrit as *turiya* in the Upanishads, which literally means "the fourth" state, that beyond waking, dreaming, and dreamless sleep. The highest state, *turiyatita*, which means "beyond the fourth," is a state of pure unity or radical oneness with everything that is.[15]

In many of his books Wilber describes how the highest states of consciousness may be cultivated through contemplative practices. For instance, in the instructions below, he describes a process of dis-identification, a *via negativa*, as a means of recognizing the witness. After adopting a comfortable posture, one is directed to silently recite the following statements, while trying to realize as vividly as possible the importance of each statement:

> I *have* a body, but I am *not* my body. I can see and feel my body, and what can be seen and felt is not the true Seer. My body may be tired or excited, sick or healthy, heavy or light, but that has nothing to do with my inward I. I *have* a body, but I am *not* my body.
>
> I *have* desires, but I am not my desires. I can know my desires, and what can be known is not the true Knower. Desires come and go, floating through my awareness, but they do not affect my inward I. I *have* desires but I am *not* my desires.
>
> I *have* emotions, but I am *not* my emotions. I can feel and sense my emotions, and what can be felt and sensed is not the true Feeler. Emotions pass through me, but they do not affect my inward I. I *have* emotions but I am *not* my emotions.
>
> I *have* thoughts, but I am *not* my thoughts. I can know and intuit my thoughts, and what can be known is not the true Knower. Thoughts come

to me and thoughts leave me, but they do not affect my inward I. I *have* thoughts but I am *not* my thoughts.

This done—perhaps several times—affirm as concretely as possible: I am what remains, a pure center of awareness, an unmoved witness of all these thoughts, emotions, feelings, and desires.[16]

If one persists with this practice, one may begin to intuit a deep inward sense of freedom, lightness, and stillness, as well as a feeling of release from anxiety or other distressing emotions. Discovering the witness, says Wilber, is much like diving below the waves on the surface of a stormy ocean to the quiet and secure depths below. At first one may only be a few feet beneath the agitated waves of emotion but, with persistence, one can gain the ability to fathom the quiet depths of the soul.[17]

The process of discovering the witness involves two selves. One is the *self* that one is aware of as an object, with characteristics one identifies with. For instance, "I am a woman," "I am a father," "I am an American," "I am a musician," "I am middle-aged," and so on. These descriptions are all attributes one can see—all things that are seen about oneself—but there is also the *Self* that is doing the seeing. This Self does the seeing but cannot itself be seen; it is a pure subject or pure Seer, not an object or something seen. Ramana Maharshi, the Vedantic sage, calls this the "I-I," the big "I" who is aware of the small "I." The first self, the one comprised of descriptions, is what you are *not*. This is why, says Wilber, the meditative traditions maintain that we are the victims of a case of mistaken identity. As Patanjali says in the *Yoga Sutras* (2.6), the ignorant or unenlightened ego is due to "the identification of the Seer with the instruments of seeing" (sutra 2.6).[18]

Spiritual awakening involves discovering the deeper Self, one's true nature that is revealed through witness consciousness. The deeper Self is characterized as a vast, open, empty clearing or spaciousness in which everything is arising, moment to moment.[19] Wilber also describes this vast opening as pure "I AMness," which is present, whether one has realized it yet or not, even in deep dreamless sleep. I AMness is timeless; it lives in the pure now-moment, never entering the stream of time. Citing the philosopher Ludwig Wittgenstein, he clarifies the real meaning of eternity—"If we take eternity to mean not everlasting temporal duration but a moment without time, then eternal life belongs to those who live in the present."[20] All of us, Wilber points out, have access to eternity. The timeless now, he says, is not something you have to work to achieve; rather it is something that you cannot avoid. It is all we are ever aware of and it includes and embraces thoughts of the past, present, and future. Spiritual awakening is thus a matter of *recognizing* the ground of our being—a matter of *realization*, of making it real, a waking up to what is always already the case.

Discovering the witness through dis-identification is a major landmark in the process of spiritual awakening, and it has been the goal of many mystics and contemplative practitioners. For others, including Wilber, the goal is unity consciousness, the state that is "beyond the fourth" (*turiyatita*). In this state, says

Wilber, the witness collapses into everything witnessed; a person feels identified with everything that is arising. Before that can occur, he explains, one must first discover the transpersonal witness, which provides a "jumping off point" for unity consciousness.[21] There are different views regarding the highest state of consciousness. Hindus, for instance, often regard the witness state as the highest, whereas Buddhists hold that there is a state beyond it. In my view, both states confer spiritual awakening.

Wilber clarifies the distinction between the witness and the nondual unity state in a passage that also distinguishes soul and spirit:

> So "soul" is both the highest level of individual growth we can achieve, but also the final barrier, the final knot, to complete enlightenment or supreme identity, simply because as transcendental witness it stands back from everything it witnesses. Once we push through the witness position, then the soul or witness dissolves and there is only the play of nondual awareness, awareness that does not look at objects but is completely one with all objects. (Zen says, "It is like tasting the sky.") The gap between subject and object collapses, the soul is transcended or dissolved, and pure spiritual or nondual awareness—which is very simple, very obvious, very clear—arises. You realize that your intrinsic being is vast and open, empty and clear, and everything arising anywhere is arising within you, as intrinsic spirit, spontaneously.[22]

While the nondual state of unity consciousness may be the highest state, cultivating witness consciousness is an indispensable aspect of spiritual awakening and, as we shall see, can be utilized in the growing up process described below.

Levels or stages of psychological development

Levels or stages of psychological development are a second component of the AQAL framework.[23] States of consciousness come and go; peak experiences and mystical states, no matter how profound, will come, stay a bit, then pass. Where *states* of consciousness are temporary, *stages* of consciousness endure. Stages represent actual milestones of growth and development. For instance, once a child develops through the linguistic phase of development, the child has permanent access to language. The same thing, says Wilber, happens for other types of growth. Once a person becomes stabilized in a stage of growth and development, one has access to the qualities of that stage—such as greater consciousness, more encompassing love, or higher ethical values. Passing states become permanent traits.[24]

There are many ways to study development and, therefore, there are all sorts of stage conceptions. In Wilber's view, all of them can be useful. We have considered several in this book—Jean Gebser's five stages of cultural history (Chapter 1); James Fowler's stages of faith (Chapter 2); and the chakra system of kundalini yoga (Chapter 6). Each stage represents a level of organization or a level of complexity. This dynamic is an essential principle in Wilber's Integral Approach. Each stage of development, says Wilber, involves a *transcend-and-include* of its predecessor, which means that each new stage of development enfolds or includes its previous stage, but then adds something new, novel, and emergent. For instance, biological evolution entails a developmental sequence that progresses from atoms to molecules to cells to organisms. The same transcend-and-include dynamic operates within the stages of human growth and development. However, if something goes wrong with the "transcend" part, the higher or emerging stage fails to move beyond the previous stage in a healthy manner, and parts of the new stage remain stuck or fixated at the previous stage. The new stage will develop an addiction to those parts to which it is fixated. If something goes wrong with the "include" part—one does not integrate the previous stage, but instead dissociates and denies and splits off parts of it—it will develop an allergy to those disowned and unwanted aspects of itself.[25]

The Integral Approach uses mindfulness to work through developmental fixations and allergies. The practice of mindfulness generally entails bringing attention to bear in the present moment on whatever is arising. Integral mindfulness brings neutral, non-judgmental attention to an issue that is a source of distress or difficulty in a person's life. For example, one might have an eating disorder pertaining to the oral stage of development. When the drive to eat arises, it may temporarily take over the person. Some part of the person is still identified with this stage. When the drive arises, a person won't simply have or possess that drive, the person will *be* that drive. All other concerns will be shoved to the side.[26] Using integral mindfulness, the person can begin to let go of the drive's tendency to overwhelm. One is able to dis-identify with it—to look *at* the drive instead of looking *through* it.[27] Similarly, mindfulness may be used to work through psychological problems associated with all stages of development, such as instinctual fixations, emotional attachment/dissociation issues, ideological views, and attachment to blissful or visionary meditative states.

Integral mindfulness, Wilber explains, is like videotaping something. This he expresses in the form of instructions for practice:

> Observe the issue of concern like a camera, seeing everything *just as it is* without any judgment. Don't criticize it, condemn it, or identify. Simply be aware of it neutrally, and pervasively, from all angles. Where is it located? What shape is it? What does it smell like? Feel its urgency directly. Make the subjective drive the object of mindfulness, an object of awareness. Look at it long and steady.[28]

This process, says Wilber, exemplies the essential dynamic of human development. As Robert Kegan, a pioneering developmental researcher from Harvard University, puts it: "I know no better way to describe development than that *the subject of one stage becomes the object of the subject of the next stage.*"[29] Wilber's Integral Approach applies this principle to his stage conception theory. At the *archaic stage*, the self is identified with the simple sensorimotor or physiological dimension. This is its subject or self. It cannot see this stage as an object; it sees the world through this stage as a subject. It cannot look at it, it is looking through it. As the next stage emerges, the *magical-impulsive stage*, the self lets go of its exclusive identity with the previous archaic stage, and switches its self, its subject, its identity, to this new stage. Now the self can see its previous stage as an object. The subject of the previous stage has become the object of the new subject of this stage.[30] And so the process continues through the subsequently emergent and more inclusive stages of development, all the way to Supreme Identity or spiritual awakening.

Lines of development

A third component of the Integral AQAL framework, lines of development, acknowledges the fact that individuals evolve unevenly.[31] Human beings possess a variety of intelligences—cognitive, moral, emotional, psychosexual, interpersonal, and intrapersonal—as well as other capacities that can be further developed if they are effectively cultivated through appropriate practices. Some people have highly advanced cognitive development but lack mature emotional intelligence. Most of us excel in one or two aspects, but do poorly in others. The Integral Approach involves becoming aware of strengths (the intelligences with which we can shine) as well as our weaknesses (where we do poorly or even pathologically), so we can develop more balanced and integrated lives. Developmental lines can be viewed as existential questions that life poses:

- What am I aware of? (cognition)
- What do I need? (needs)
- Who am I? (self-identity)
- What is important to me? (values)
- How do I feel about this? (emotional intelligence)
- What is beautiful or attractive to me? (aesthetics)
- What is the right thing to do? (moral development)
- How should I interact? (interpersonal development)
- How should I physically do this? (kinesthetic ability)
- What is of ultimate concern? (spirituality)

The Integral Approach does not require that a person become hyper-developed in each of these intelligences. The point is to be aware of them since awareness itself has a balancing effect on one's life.[32] The questions associated with lines of development can be utilized to powerful effect in the practice of self-inquiry to remove blocks in awareness and to activate latent potentials. For instance, I have characterized myself as a scholar-practitioner and thus have invested much of my time and energy in the cognitive, self-identity, and spiritual developmental lines. To balance these, I need to cultivate somatic awareness and physical well-being through regular exercise and hatha yoga. And, as a householder yogi, it is imperative for me to nurture intimacy in my marriage and cultivate warm, collaborative relationships with colleagues. These intentional efforts have brought fulfillment and a sense of wholeness that would have eluded me had I limited my devotion, one-sidedly, to the life of the mind and spiritual practice.

Types

Types, a fourth component of the AQAL framework, pertain to different human temperaments. Hinduism, as we have seen (see Chapters 4 and 7), offers different spiritual paths for people who are by nature intellectual (*jnana yoga*), devotional (*bhakti yoga*), active (*karma yoga*), and contemplative (*dhyana yoga*). Psychological types are also an important aspect of Jungian psychology. Jung distinguishes several contrasting tendencies and functions—introversion/extroversion, intuition/sensation, thinking/feeling—that have been incorporated in the Myers-Briggs Type Indicator, an instrument widely used in therapy, education, and business. The Integral Approach encourages practitioners to increase their self-knowledge by using one or more of the typological systems available in our culture. The Enneagram, for instance, which distinguishes nine interconnected personality types, is particularly attractive to people practicing contemplative Christianity and several of the Western esoteric traditions.[33]

Wilber utilizes a masculine/feminine typology derived from Carol Gilligan's research on women's development.[34] Her research reveals that males tend to be focused on autonomy, justice, and rights; by comparison, females tend to center on relationship, care, and responsibility. For Wilber, men seek freedom, and women seek fullness. As he puts it, "Men tend toward agency; women toward communion. Men follow rules; women follow connections."[35] There are exceptions, of course, since all typologies reveal general tendencies. Wilber draws from two important implications of Gilligan's research in his Integral Approach. One is that female development moves through stages that she designates as *selfish*, *care*, and *universal care*. Wilber incorporates these stages of moral development into his AQAL framework. Stage 1 is centered entirely on "me," a preconventional level that is *egocentric*. Stage 2 is centered on "us." Identity expands beyond "me" to "us," including others who belong to one's group, a conventional level that is *ethnocentric*, traditional, and conformist. With stage 3, identity expands again from "us" to "all of us," a *worldcentric* identity in which one cares and has compassion for all of humanity, regardless of race, color, or creed. Beyond this is postconventional stage 4, which Wilber calls *kosmocentric*, where one identifies not only with all of humanity but, as Buddhists say, with "all sentient beings." The second implication of Gilligan's research is that in stage 4, a person integrates and balances capacities for autonomy and agency with those pertaining to relationship and communion. Thus, in moral development, as with other developmental sequences such as Fowler's stages of faith, we see one of the many ways in which the human journey moves toward integration and wholeness.

Quadrants

A fifth component of the AQAL framework involves the quadrants, four domains of knowledge that Wilber distinguishes within his Integral Approach for understanding reality. Quadrants are the basis of his integral methodological pluralism, an attempt to comprehend the complexity of the kosmos without succumbing to reductionism.[36] *Kosmos* is the word the ancient Greeks used to denote a universe that includes not just the physical reality of stars and planets (what *cosmos* usually means), but also the realms of mind, soul, society, art, and Spirit.[37] In Wilber's model, the quadrants represent four fundamental perspectives or ways of looking at any occasion, that is, from the inside and outside of the individual and of the collective. The upper left quadrant is the domain "I," or subjective interiority (the inside of an individual), whereas the lower right belongs to "we," the intersubjective realm of culture (the inside of the collective). The upper and lower quadrants depict the exteriority of the objective world—"it" and "its"—the individual and collective aspects of nature. One can look at any phenomenon from the point of view of the "I" (how I personally see and feel about the event); from the point of view of the "we" (how others, as well as I, see the event); and as an "it" (the objective facts of the event). An integrally informed approach takes all of these dimensions into account. As Wilber explains, if you leave out one or more of these dimensions, something will be missing and our understanding will be fragmented and incomplete.[38]

Figure 8.1 provides a differentiated depiction of the quadrants, delineating developmental levels contained within each. In each case, development transcends and includes the preceding level or stage. For instance, the lower left quadrant, pertaining to culture, shows a sequence that moves from archaic (traditional), scientific-rational (modern), and pluralistic (postmodern) worldviews to the most encompassing ones designated as holistic and integral. Likewise, the levels depicted in the three other quadrants exemplify the granularity of the AQAL framework.

There are several ways an understanding of the quadrant model supports integrative spirituality. First and most importantly, it embraces the interiority or subjectivity that is ignored or given little significance within the dominant paradigm of secular, scientific materialism discussed in Chapter 1. This model recovers the realms of soul and spirit, the subtle dimensions of the Great Nest of Being, that are the territories cultivated by Jungian depth psychology and contemplative yoga (upper level quadrant).

Second, an understanding of the quadrants helps individuals develop the capacity to adopt and integrate different perspectives into their worldviews (lower left quadrant). In other words, the model helps a person move from the egocentric and ethnocentric stages to a more inclusive form of worldcentric and kosmocentric identity that engenders a greater degree of care and compassion for others.

Third, the quadrants reflect different perspectives by which we envisage the divine, which Wilber calls the "three faces of spirit" or the "1-2-3 of God." One may have a first-person experience of spirit in which divinity is experienced as the true I, the deepest dimension of one's being—this is the experience of unitive

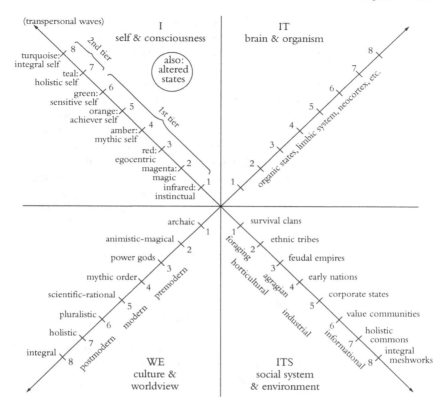

FIGURE 8.1 Some aspects of the four quadrants as they appear in humans

Figure from *Integral Spirituality*, by Ken Wilber. Copyright © 2006. Reprinted by arrangement with The Permissions Company, Inc. on behalf of Shambhala Publications.

mysticism. More common to theistic traditions is the second-person, I-thou experience of communion with the divine, cultivated through prayer and devotion. In addition, there are those who experience spirit through a third-person relationship to nature or the great web of life. While factors such as temperament, religious tradition or cultural conditioning often incline individuals to experience spirit in a singular manner, the Integral Approach validates each of the modes of experience and encourages individuals to cultivate all of them within the context of their spiritual practice.

Integral Life Practice

Integral Life Practice (ILP) is the pragmatic aspect of Wilber's Integral AQAL framework. ILP combines practices from the wisdom traditions of the world's religions with those developed by modern psychology, consciousness studies, and other fields, as well as those devised by Wilber and his associates. An individual practitioner engages practices that promote physical health, emotional balance, mental clarity, and spiritual awakening. Practice is viewed as an adventure that is creative, fluid, and that evolves over time.

ILP is a modular to integrated spirituality. The four core modules are body, mind, spirit, and shadow. Traditional spiritual paths, says Wilber and his associates, have usually emphasized only two or three of these and have rarely included the shadow module. Modern psychological approaches to self-development may include shadow work, but some neglect the mind, and most lack the depth and rigor of the meditation traditions that focus on spirit. Additional ILP modules include ethics, sexual yoga, work, emotions, relationships, and communication.[39] Engagement with these is based on one's priorities, available time for practice, and how imperative they are for one's individuation process. Illustrative practices for the four core modules include:

- Body—aerobics, sports, swimming, weightlifting, hatha yoga, qigong, diet, nutrition
- Mind—reading, intellectual study
- Spirit—prayer, meditation, chanting, devotional worship
- Shadow—psychotherapy, self-inquiry, taking back projections

Through these means, ILP offers a cross-training approach to spirituality and psychological development that is integrated, synergistic, and adaptable to an individual's unique journey toward spiritual awakening and psychological wholeness.

The Diamond Approach of A. H. Almaas

Born in Kuwait in 1944, A. H. Almaas, the pen name for A. Hameed Ali, moved to the United States at the age of eighteen to study physics at the University of California, Berkeley. He studied physical science because he wanted to discover objective truth, truth independent from personal bias. As he pursued his studies, he realized that the truth he was interested in had more to do with the nature of being human. This realization initiated his search for inner spiritual understanding. He engaged in experiential workshops focused on inner growth and openness, underwent several years of bioenergetics analysis, and began to study Sufi and Zen thought. His inner journey was fully launched when he joined a group led by the Chilean psychiatrist Claudio Naranjo, who taught him how psychological approaches and spiritual practices can work together. The psychological elements included Gestalt therapy, Karen Horney's self-analysis, the Enneagram, as well as group and interpersonal work. The spiritual aspect emphasized the spiritual teachings of G. I. Gurdjieff, who distinguishes Essence from personality.[40]

Almaas reports that his real transformation began with the discovery that *Essence*, the true nature of Being, is experienced as *presence*, and with his desire to learn how to stay anchored in this presence. "This recognition and realization of my essential nature as an ontological presence," he says, "had a volcanic effect on my life and my process."[41] It became the central focus and meaning of his life from then on. This living presence gradually expanded and deepened, revealing various dimensions of Being. In his words, "This process was a spontaneous unfoldment, what felt like a magical unveiling, a self-revelation of Being's mysteries."[42] He viewed this unfolding process as the result of a particular manifestation of Essence, which he came to recognize as *essential guidance*. "This precise, diamond-like guidance," he explains, "became the inner guide that has functioned more truly than any external guide I have ever known."[43] The realizations that followed became the basis for the Diamond Approach, teachings that he continues to transmit to students and teachers of the Ridhwan School. The core premise of his approach is that psychological work and spiritual practice are two inseparable elements of the same method.

Inquiry into personal experience is the main method of the Diamond Approach, in which psychological understanding opens the soul to deeper experiences that are typically regarded as spiritual. "Inquiry," for Almaas, "is mainly a matter of being aware of one's experience, both inner and outer, recognizing what is and what is not understood, with a curiosity about it that expresses a heart-felt love for the truth."[44] He says that he continues to be in awe of the knowledge that arises from his own inquiry, leading him to appreciate that the knowledge is not his own personal creation, rather it arises from the guidance of Being. For this reason, he asserts that the Diamond Approach is not the result of an intellectual synthesis of what he has read, heard and experienced; it is an articulation of an actual process of transformation.[45] "Being," he further explains, "has been continually revealing to me its many facets and dimensions, always in spontaneous and unexpected revelations."[46] Even so, Almaas has engaged in extensive studies of depth psychology and spiritual traditions. Psychological sources include Sigmund Freud, ego psychology, self psychology, object relations theory, and Reichian somatic therapy; and the spiritual literature and practices that comprise Buddhism, Vedanta, Sufism, and mystical Christianity.[47] These fields and teachings contribute to the Diamond Approach, particularly its conceptual elaboration in Almaas's many books, but the emphasis, in the practice, is always on personal and direct experience of the perspectives expressed in these sources.

Practice

Almaas, like Wilber, emphasizes the primacy of practice. In the Diamond Approach practice is not limited to meditation. For Almaas, practice is continual—it means that one practices being present through all moments of life, during all one's daily activities. As one's commitment to align with reality deepens, he explains, devotion to realness intensifies, and a quality of consciousness manifests that is more concentrated and clear. This concentrated consciousness is presence, being in touch with the immediacy of our being. When presence is experienced and understood, a person sees that practice is already realization—that the process and goal are inseparable.[48] This stage of living realization, says Almaas, is epitomized by a classic expression from Dogen Zenji, one of the most celebrated Zen masters— "Practice is realization and realization is practice."[49]

Why practice, we might ask? Because we want to live fully, says Almaas. We want to be free, fulfill our purpose, and discover the mysteries of our existence. All of this requires that we fully engage reality, a process he describes as a ceaseless journey without destination. In the Diamond Approach, the central practice of inquiry embodies this open-ended view of reality. From the very beginning of doing this work, Almaas explains, practitioners engage in the wholehearted exploration of direct, lived experience. Fully realized practice, he adds, is mature enough to accept the ordinary simplicity of whatever is happening as the realization of that moment. Engaging practice so completely and so totally requires a particular maturation of the soul.[50]

The enlightenment drive

Our lives are driven by powerful inner forces that support our survival and express our sexual and social energies. Drives permeate our feelings, attitudes, and actions. The motivation of the soul that leads to psycho-spiritual practice, says Almaas, involves the awakening of what he calls *the enlightenment drive*. The enlightenment drive is not completely biological or instinctual; it is about the quality of our inner experience. We may recognize it as the religious drive, the longing for God or divine union, the desire for enlightenment or truth, or the love of discovering the secrets of the universe. True nature, our inherent beingness, is a dynamic force. As the soul matures, this dynamic impels us to go toward greater actualization of that nature, to bring it forward and display it in full consciousness.[51]

The enlightenment drive, Almaas explains, is something we all have that can wake up at any point. For most people, this drive awakens first through the head center as "the thought of enlightenment"—the idea that there is such a thing as enlightenment, that one can pursue a spiritual life or practice. When the drive wakes up in the heart center, it appears as love, compassion, and as an irresistible passion for the truth of the inner life. Practice fully matures when the drive wakes up in the belly, called the Hara or Kath center. This is the center of action, which shifts one's functioning from the realms of ideas and feelings to that of action and direct down-to-earth engagement.[52]

Essence, soul, and personality

According to the Diamond Approach, the true nature of existence is *Being* and the true nature of a person is called *Essence*. The soul is the individualized consciousness of a person. The content of awareness is the content of the soul. Sensations, perceptions, emotions, thoughts, and concepts are all forms flowing within the soul. Soul can be structured by personality or Being or Essence. When structured by personality, the soul can feel stuck, dead, reactive, fearful, and frustrated. Experience filtered through a rigid and defensive structuring of the soul is inauthentic. When the soul is patterned by Essence, the soul is authentic; it is present, open, intelligent, and fluid. One function of the Diamond Approach is to soften, develop, and then integrate personality structures into the soul. When the soul is more open and refined, there is less need to control the flow of reality. One is more fully present to whatever is.[53] It is the soul that makes the journey of awakening from conditioned and constricted patterns to the realization of its true nature. The work of the soul is to open, clarify, and purify itself to experience Essence more directly, more completely, and with fewer obscurations or blocks.[54]

Developments in Western psychology and psychotherapy, in Almaas's view, allow us to see how people are stuck in and controlled by conditioning from infancy and childhood. Historically speaking, this understanding of emotional suffering offers something that traditional spiritual traditions lack. Conversely, the notion of Essence is not generally recognized in psychology and psychotherapy. Alienation from one's true nature is not seen and thus not taken into consideration in psychological theory. Recent attempts to combine these two approaches, he says, tend to be sequential rather than integrated. The pattern is that psychological work is expected to take persons from point A to point B; then spiritual practice takes them to point C. Psychological work is undertaken to dissolve the false self or personality; only then is Essential development possible. The Diamond Approach engages these two processes simultaneously. Without working on Essence, Almaas explains, there is no resolution to our suffering and no opportunity to realize our true nature.[55]

Emptiness and space

Almaas's way of integrating psychological and spiritual work is exemplified in his teachings on self-images, emptiness, and space. When a person engages in psychotherapy or spiritual practice, she often experiences a sense of emptiness, deficiency, disorientation or weakness. These experiences, he explains, pertain to her self-image. A self-image arises through interactions with the world, significant others, and the body; it is a collection of structures and boundaries that form in the course of ego development. Psychoanalytic psychologists see emptiness as an indicator of an unhealthy and unintegrated ego. The typical psychological view is that we should avoid emptiness by strengthening and integrating our boundaries and intrapsychic structures. On the other hand, many spiritual systems, especially Buddhism, see emptiness as the objective nature of reality and the truth behind any sense of self or identity. The Diamond Approach brings these two views together by distinguishing two kinds of emptiness: the first—*space*—is the open and clear nature of Being; the latter is *deficient emptiness*, also described by Almaas as a hole.[56]

Deficient emptiness, for Almaas, arises from the loss of Essence during ego development. As Essence is abandoned in the psychological development of a young child, contact with Being is lost. This lack of Being is felt as a hole in the psyche, as if a part of oneself is missing. A person feels empty in a deficient way. Ego structures and self-image develop, in part, to avoid this sense of deficiency, yet they can never fill the emptiness. What is missing is not a self-image, but rather, Essence. Dissolving a self-image through Diamond Approach inquiry brings to consciousness the hole that is covered by the self-image. The hole functions as a filter for mental structures, mistaken beliefs, feelings, memories, and misunderstandings. Without these structures, deficient emptiness is revealed as space. As unpleasant as it may be to experience, on the other side of deficient emptiness lies space, clarity, and freedom.[57]

The pearl beyond price

Psychological approaches promote the development of an integrated, stable, coherent, and enduring ego. Spiritual systems generally emphasize the need to transcend this sense of self. Some transpersonal psychologists take a sequential view. The ego must first be developed and then transcended as one moves from personal to transpersonal levels of personality development. This view, summarized as "You must be somebody to become nobody," can be mistaken to mean that spiritual awakening requires the loss of one's personhood. There appears to be a contradiction between impersonal Beingness ("the nobody") and our personal autonomy ("the somebody"). Almaas resolves this contradiction by recognizing an aspect of Essence called the *Personal Essence*, the *Pearl Beyond Price*, or simply the *Pearl*. The qualities of the Pearl are autonomy, personhood, authenticity, and contact. One's ability to live in fulfilling ways and to have genuine personal contact with others is rooted in the Pearl, but its origin is Essential, spiritual, and unconditioned, rather than historical and conditioned.[58]

From the perspective of the Diamond Approach, the ego, or personality, develops in response to situations in the world to support functioning and to provide a sense of personal dignity and worth. A healthy ego, however, is not the end of development. Ego characteristics are not abandoned in self-transcendence, but emerge in a fuller and integrated way in the Pearl. As a refinement of ego development, the Pearl embodies the functional qualities of the ego in a way that is authentic, open, and flowing; it is the true personality. The ego and the Pearl are seen as parallel developments, one inauthentic and the other authentic. Rather than sequential steps, the ego is gradually metabolized into the Pearl.[59]

The spiritual teachings of the mystical traditions, says Almaas, regard personal life to be less important than the spiritual realm. The ego is taken to be a falsehood that must die in order for realization to occur. Almaas holds a different view. For him, ego is a reflection, albeit an imperfect one, of true reality. Understanding ego, rather than transcending it, resolves the contradiction between personal and spiritual life.[60] As he explains:

> The Personal Essence can be seen as the integration or absorption of personality into Being, as the synthesis of the man of the world and the man

of spirit. However, it is more accurate to see it as the natural product of ego development. In other words, ego development and spiritual enlightenment are not two disjointed processes but parts of the same process. The understanding of the Personal Essence shows how they are linked. This point is a radical departure from the understanding of both traditional spiritual teachings and modern psychology.[61]

This view exemplifies a truly integrative spirituality, one that values psychological development, including the Jungian notion of individuation, and the transpersonal or spiritual domain cultivated by mystical traditions such as contemplative yoga.

Essential identity: self-realization or the point

As the psycho-spiritual process unfolds, a shift occurs from *having* Essence to *being* Essence. The center of experience shifts from the ego, which has experiences of Essence, to Essence itself. Almaas calls this *Essential Identity* or the *Point*. The realization of Being is a movement from the surface to the depth of one's true nature. The Personal Essence or *Pearl* brings Being into one's life so that it can be expressed in one's feelings, thoughts, actions, and relationships. The Point is the realization of one's identity as Being.[62]

Self-realization arises from penetrating the shell of the personality, a process that entails working through the narcissistic wound—the gap between Essence and what we take ourselves to be. Through sustained inquiry, the false self or shell of the personality gradually dissolves and, eventually, the Point appears. The Point is described as a brilliant star, a radiant point of light. Everywhere, all at once, moving in every direction, it feels like the source of all perception.[63] Diamond Approach teacher John Davis provides a rich description of its impact on a practitioner's life:

> It is experienced as a sense of balance, completeness, simplicity, and purity. There is no longer any gap between our immediate experience, our identity, and our true nature. The Point also brings a simplicity into awareness and our lives . . . Our souls gain a greater focus on Being and feel uncontaminated. We are able to drop our guard, and we can simply "be" without concern about anything, including Essence or self-realization.
>
> The Point also brings about a realization of our uniqueness. Such uniqueness is not about our doing our own thing or holding our own unique perspective, although these follow naturally and spontaneously. It is also not about rejecting any teaching, teacher, or influence. Rather, we abide in our own nature, we cannot help but manifest our own path and opportunities.
>
> Each time the Point arises, we are self-realized, and the more expansive the Point, the more deeply we realize our true nature. We are no longer an ego that has an Essence. We are that Essence itself. We recognize ourselves as whatever Essential states or dimensions arise. If fullness arises, we know

ourselves as fullness, not as a self that is experiencing the state of fullness. If compassion arises, we are not compassionate; we are compassion. We know ourselves as Being. We become the Point sensing and knowing itself. And this self-realization becomes the flow of Being, never static and never finished.[64]

This account of spiritual awakening is noteworthy in several respects. It closely aligns with Wilber's characterization of the nondual state of unity consciousness (*turiyatita*); there is no separation between the experiencer and what is experienced. Almaas's notion of the Point also affirms that spiritual awakening includes the experience of one's uniqueness. Furthermore, awakening or realization is pluralistic; other teachings and teachers are included within the path that unfolds for each individual. Finally, the Diamond Approach regards spiritual realization, like the Jungian journey of individuation, to be an ongoing process with no finality.

True nature and the boundless dimensions

While the realization of Essence is profound and liberating, Almaas delineates five boundless dimensions that arise as the psycho–spiritual process continues to deeply unfold. These nondual and formless dimensions, experienced without the bounds of a separate self, are undistorted by personal history. The boundless dimensions are said to be the deepest foundation of the Diamond Approach. The true nature of Being is not constructed; it is recognized when one penetrates the subjective biases that obscure it. True nature is not a state of consciousness; it is the ground of all consciousness. The boundless dimensions of Being are always present, though we are usually asleep to them.[65]

Divine Love

Davis elucidates how each of the boundless dimensions is experienced by practitioners. Being reveals its nature as beauty and love. We discover that we are always held in the arms of a limitless loving light. Experienced through the mental function, this dimension is a consciousness that is alive and radiant, revealing the beauty of existence. Experienced through the heart center, it is more like a boundless love. Experienced through the belly center, Divine Love is felt as a conscious loving presence holding and enfolding us and the world.[66]

Pure Being and the Supreme

When beauty and love are experienced deeply enough without attachment, their nature is revealed as a fullness and presence. Beauty is now seen as a surface quality, and its substance or depth is pure existence. The world has a quality of presence, significance, profundity, and realness. The world is experienced as pure presence that is differentiated into universal noetic forms. This is the realm sometimes referred to as Gnosis or the *nous*. The world and our experience are revealed as an exquisitely differentiated and luminous existence, palpable and precious.[67]

Nonconceptual reality and the Nameless

When we penetrate the pure presence and unity of the world, we discover its ground as awareness with no content or concepts. We encounter the realm of nonconceptual awareness and emptiness, the ground of the Supreme. The quality of emptiness is more fundamental than form; giving a name to this dimension would fix it and make it into a concept. Thus, Ali [Almaas] also calls it the Nameless. This dimension has a sense of freshness to it. Perception has the quality of bare awareness without concepts and labels. It is as if each perception is brand-new, undistorted by memories or expectations. Perception is mirror-like without commentary or reaction. Being is experienced as completely clear, crystalline, and spacious; it is a luminous emptiness.[68]

The Logos

The Logos is Being as dynamic flow, revealing the world's aliveness and its continual unfoldment and flowering. Coexistent with the other boundless dimensions, the Logos is a constant movement of creation and renewal. Logos is the "original Word" or harmonious and organized unfoldment of Being, and it is the basis for our knowing and communicating about Being.[69]

The Absolute

The Absolute is a deeper reality fundamental to each of the boundless dimensions. The fifth one is beyond beauty, fullness, emptiness, and becoming; it is the unknowable origin and ultimate nature of Being. Initially, it is experienced only as a cessation and an absence. It may be compared to the state of consciousness in deep sleep or the state of the universe before the Big Bang. Later on it is experienced as an ultimate, unconditional, imperturbable peace. Yet this peace is not an end or goal. The Absolute begins to unfold with a preciousness and luminosity that are beyond words. This brings the understanding that everything we experience is only the surface, with the Absolute as the back or inside of the surface. Everything we see exists as a thin bubble over this complete mystery. All of creation arises from this mysterious ground and is therefore never separate from it. This is the source of the experience of complete liberation and complete duality.[70]

These descriptions of the boundless dimensions express the further reaches of psycho-spiritual development. These are profound experiences of the spirit of the depths that, in Wilber's words, *transcend-and-include* Jung's notion of individuation while embracing states of consciousness that may be cultivated through contemplative forms of spirituality. Here we glimpse the mode of existence that may arise when the psychological and spiritual modes of inner work are deeply conjoined.

The view of totality

Almaas characterizes The Diamond Approach as a path that includes ascent and descent, a journey toward enlightenment and a journey toward becoming a complete human being. The journey of ascent, he explains, entails realizing one dimension after another all the way to the absolute dimension. Experiencing that dimension, we realize the vastness and mystery of reality as the ground of everything. The journey of descent is a matter of integrating our lives into our realization.[71] In actuality, ascent and descent are two aspects of a singular and unending process. As he explains, "Learning about reality—realizing it and understanding it in a particular, awakened way—always means going beyond that reality."[72] We get established in a particular dimension, he continues, and then reality moves us elsewhere; we focus a great deal on how to integrate and stabilize that particular condition but then, as that happens, without our expecting it, the realization moves to a different dimension, to a different mode of experience. In this way, he says, we learn about all kinds of realizations.[73]

The notion that spiritual awakening or realization takes multiple forms is one of the most distinctive aspects of the Diamond Approach, one that embraces religious pluralism as well as other views of reality. Almaas refers to his teaching as "the view of totality." The search for meaning, he says, is at the heart of most human activity; it is expressed in our sciences, philosophies, and our spiritual traditions. Each of us mirrors that impulse for finality in our daily calibrations of who we are and what we care most deeply about. In this context, conflicts—whether personal, cultural, intellectual, political, or religious—can be seen as a clash of competing ultimates. But what if reality is not limited to a single ultimate? The view of totality recognizes that no single view or combination of views can exhaust the richness of reality. All possible views—the dual, nondual, theistic, scientific, philosophic, and others—are valid. Each is a complete understanding of its own particular truth, but none is a complete understanding of reality because reality is inherently free and cannot be captured in any single view. Reality, for Almaas, is limitless in the ways in which it reveals itself; it can accommodate all manner of different views and yet remain indeterminate. This indeterminacy is radical openness, not ambiguity. Reality is not static and unchanging; it is a dynamic and unfolding process, and spiritual realization is not about arriving at some ultimate truth, but an ongoing adventure.[74]

Insights for integrative spirituality

Ken Wilber and A. H. Almaas elucidate leading edge approaches to integrative spirituality grounded in their own practices and personal discoveries. While Wilber's developmental model regards spiritual awakening and psychological maturation to be two relatively independent forms of development, Almaas regards these two modes of inner work to be inseparable. This difference notwithstanding, both writers insist that both spiritual awakening and psychological growth are essential if we want to be balanced and integrated individuals. The Integral

Approach and the Diamond Approach are complementary models with values that distinguish integrative forms of spirituality. Both promote visions of spirituality that integrate body, mind, soul, and spirit; both affirm the personal and transpersonal dimensions of human existence; and both embrace teachings from the great wisdom traditions and modern schools of psychology. In my view, Wilber and Almaas offer critically important insights for individuals who are committed to pursuing an integrative path to individuation and awakening:

• Our lives are driven not only by instincts but also by an enlightenment drive, a quality of our deeper nature that impels us toward greater actualization of that nature. Integrative spirituality involves two modes of growth and development—the psychosocial maturation process of growing up and the spiritual process of waking up. One without the other is one-sided and incomplete.

• Contemplative practices engender states of consciousness that are more expansive than the perspective of ego awareness. Practitioners cultivate the state of the witness or pure subject and dis-identify with objects (sensations, feelings, thoughts) arising in consciousness. Gradually they recognize the ground of their being, described by different terms such as the Self, the Supreme Identity, or true nature. For some individuals, the witness collapses into everything witnessed, a nondual state of unity consciousness in which they feel one with everything that is arising. People experiencing this nondual state may experience the world as a living embodiment of divinity. States of consciousness, however profound, come and go. Authentic spirituality must transform the embodied lives of practitioners. Passing states must become enduring traits.

• An understanding of levels or stages of consciousness may help people engaging in spiritual practices integrate their realization into their lives. A stage represents a level of complexity. Each stage transcends and includes its predecessor. Just as biological development progresses from atoms to cells to organisms, psycho-spiritual development leads to greater capacities for consciousness, care, and compassion. Integrative spirituality impels movement from egocentric and ethnocentric to worldcentric and kosmocentric forms of identity.

• Psychological development is arrested when people are unable to move from one developmental stage to the next emergent stage in a healthy manner. Individuals become fixated at a certain stage and addicted to certain needs, or they dissociate and split off unwanted aspects of their selves. The Integral Approach demonstrates how mindfulness can be utilized to work through fixations and aversions. Practitioners learn how to dis-identify with a problematic drive or impulse, to look *at* it instead of *through* it. Similarly, the Diamond Approach exemplifies how open, nonjudgmental inquiry can dissolve self-images and adaptive personality structures and reveal one's Essence or true nature. Both approaches provide practitioners with methods of working with the content of consciousness.

- Wilber's notion of the three faces of spirit and Almaas's description of the boundless dimensions of Being avow that the divine or ultimate reality can be experienced in multiple ways. As Wilber elucidates, we may cultivate a first-person experience of spirit in which divinity is experienced as the true I; a second-person, I-thou experience of communion with the divine; and a third-person relationship to nature, the great web of life. Almaas reveals that Being manifests itself variously as Divine Love; Pure Being or the Supreme; nonconceptual, nameless emptiness; as the dynamic and creative Logos; and as the peace and luminosity of the Absolute.

Integrative spirituality is thus an ever-unfolding adventure of ascent and descent—a journey toward awakening and a journey toward becoming a complete human being. A truly integrative spirituality must include practices that cultivate the multidimensionality of our humanity. The autobiographical disclosures of Wilber and Almaas exemplify this imperative. Just as they each engage in an array of somatic, psychotherapeutic, and contemplative practices, those of us who are called to be whole as well as to be awake must do the same. Integral Life Practice offers useful ways to configure our spirituality. While each person's path will differ and change as it unfolds over time, we are well advised to engage in practices that address body, mind, soul, and spirit, as well as shadow issues that may arise at any stage of our journey toward wholeness and awakening. Ultimately, however, spirituality is not a matter of techniques or doing; it is a mode of being that fully embraces the divinity inherent in us and in the world.

Notes

1 Quoted in Ken Wilber, "Odyssey: A Personal Inquiry into Humanistic and Transpersonal Psychology," in *The Collected Works of Ken Wilber*, vol. 2. Boston: Shambhala, 1999, 15.
2 Ibid., 16.
3 Ibid., 16–17.
4 Ibid., 17.
5 Ibid., 18.
6 Ibid., 19.
7 Ken Wilber, *Integral Spirituality*, ix–x; 1–32.
8 Brad Reynolds, *Embracing Reality: The Integral Vision of Ken Wilber*. New York: Jeremy P. Tarcher/Penguin, 2004, 9–11.
9 Ken Wilber, *Grace and Grit: Spirituality and Healing in the Life and Death of Treya Killam Wilber*. Boston: Shambhala, 1993, 246.
10 Wilber, "Odyssey: A Personal Inquiry into Humanistic and Transpersonal Psychology," 44.
11 Ibid., 46.
12 Ibid., 45.
13 Ken Wilber, *Integral Meditation: Mindfulness as a Path to Grow Up, Wake Up, and Show Up in Your Life*. Boulder, CO: Shambhala, 2016, 2.
14 Ibid., 86.
15 Ibid., 88.
16 Ken Wilber, *No Boundary: Eastern and Western Approaches to Personal Growth*. Boulder, CO: Shambhala, 1981, 128–29.
17 Ibid., 129.

18 Wilber, *Integral Meditation*, 99–100.
19 Ibid., 101.
20 Quoted in Wilber, *Integral Meditation*, 101.
21 Wilber, *No Boundary*, 129–30.
22 Ken Wilber, *The Eye of Spirit: An Integral Vision for a World Gone Slightly Mad*. Boston: Shambhala, 1997, 47.
23 Wilber stresses that the term *level* is not meant in a judgmental or exclusionary fashion, but to indicate that there are important emergent qualities that tend to come into being in a discrete or quantum-like fashion.
24 Wilber, *Integral Spirituality*, 5.
25 Wilber, *Integral Meditation*, 21.
26 Ibid., 22.
27 Ibid., 24.
28 Ibid.
29 Quoted in Wilber, *Integral Meditation*, 45.
30 Ibid., 46.
31 Wilber notes that lines of development represent probabilities of behavior and more like probability clouds than ruler-straight lines. For this reason, some researchers refer to developmental lines as developmental *streams* and call levels *waves*. See Wilber, *Integral Spirituality*, 61.
32 Ken Wilber et al., *Integral Life Practice: A 21st Century Blueprint for Physical Health, Emotional Balance, Mental Clarity, and Spiritual Awakening*. Boston: Integral Books, 2008, 86.
33 There are many excellent books on the Enneagram. See, for example, Helen Palmer, *The Enneagram*. San Francisco: Harper & Row Publishers, 1988; Don Riso and Russ Hudson, *Personality Types*, rev. ed. Boston: Houghton Mifflin Co., 1996; and A. H. Almaas, *Facets of Unity: The Enneagram of Holy Ideas*. Boston: Shambhala, 2002. I especially recommend the latter work since Almaas's writings on psychological development and spiritual awakening are featured in this chapter.
34 Carol Gilligan, *In a Different Voice: Psychological Theory and Women's Development*. Cambridge, MA: Harvard University Press, 1993.
35 Wilber, *Integral Spirituality*, 12.
36 Ibid., 33–49.
37 Wilber et al., *Integral Life Practice*, 9.
38 Wilber, *Integrative Spirituality*, 19–20.
39 Wilber et al., *Integral Life Practice*, 11–16.
40 A. H. Almaas, *Luminous Night's Journey: An Autobiographical Fragment*. Boston: Shambhala, 2000, x–xi.
41 Ibid., xii.
42 Ibid., xiii.
43 Ibid.
44 Ibid., xiii–xi.
45 Ibid., xiv.
46 Ibid., xv.
47 Ibid.
48 A. H. Almaas, *Runaway Realization: Living a Life of Ceaseless Discovery*. Boston: Shambhala, 2014, pp. 16–18.
49 Ibid., 19.
50 Ibid., 22–23; 27.
51 Ibid., 27–28.
52 Ibid., 28–30.
53 John Davis, *The Diamond Approach: An Introduction to the Teachings of A. H. Almaas*. Boston: Shambhala, 1999, 48–49. I am indebted to Davis for his elucidation of the core teachigns of Almaas. I highly recommend this book to readers who are interested in learning more about the Diamond Approach.

54 Ibid., 10–11.
55 A. H. Almaas, *Diamond Heart, Book 1: Elements of the Real in Man*. Berkeley, CA: Diamond Books, 1987, 35–36.
56 Davis, 65.
57 Ibid., 66.
58 Ibid., 111–12.
59 Ibid., 113–14.
60 A. H. Almaas, *The Pearl Beyond Price: Integration of Personality into Being: An Object Relations Approach*. Boston: Shambhala, 2001, 16–17.
61 Ibid., 153–54.
62 Davis, 128–29.
63 Ibid., 131–34.
64 Ibid., 134–35.
65 Ibid., 145–47.
66 Ibid., 148–49.
67 Ibid., 149–50.
68 Ibid., 150–51.
69 Ibid., 151–52.
70 Ibid., 152–53.
71 Almaas, *Runaway Realization*, 125.
72 Ibid., 81.
73 Ibid.
74 Zarina Maiwandi, editor's preface to A. H. Almaas, *Runaway Realization: Living a Life of Ceaseless Discovery*. Boston: Shambhala, 2014, x–xiii.

9

CREDO

I offer salutations to the God and the Goddess:
the infinite parents of the world.
The lover, out of boundless love, has become the beloved.
Because of Her, He exists
And without Him, She would not be.
—*Jnaneshwar Maharaj*

I have presented an array of perspectives—from the religious thought of three traditions, and from Jungian depth psychology, contemplative yoga, Integral Theory, and the Diamond Approach—to glean insights that I believe are useful for those who wish to craft their individual paths to wholeness and awakening. Yet, spirituality is a matter of direct experience, and is, therefore, inherently personal. Each of us, I have maintained, must find our own way. While our ideas, insights, and practices are most alive when they remain open to change, it is important to know where one stands as the process of individuation and awakening unfolds. In the Introduction, I recounted some of the experiences that impelled my own spiritual quest. Here in this final chapter, I share my credo and the contours of my integrative practice with the hope that it may inspire you to clarify your own faith convictions and to engage in forms of inner work that align with what the spirit of the depths calls you to do and to be.

The word *credo* may lead us to think of creedal statements or articles of belief we must affirm to be a member of a religion. My discussion of faith and belief in Chapter 2, however, clarified that *belief* originally meant "to love" and "to hold dear." Recalling this meaning, credo, or "I believe," means I *commit* myself or I *engage* myself. And faith, we have seen, pertains to how we orient ourselves and interpret reality and, at a practical level, is about doing things that engender love and compassion toward others. William James expresses this pragmatic stance in his classic work *The Varieties of Religious Experience*, where he notes the intimate connection between how we see the world and how we act in it. He argues, as I have in this book, that the visible world is but a part of a more spiritual universe from which it draws its significance, and that union or harmonious relationship to that vaster, nonmaterial domain is the true aim of our existence. Through prayer or other forms of inner communion with that world, spiritual energy flows in and produces psychological and material effects within the phenomenal world. How we understand that which is beyond, yet continuous with, our higher nature is a matter of what he calls *over-beliefs*. Over-beliefs elude empirical proof but are the ideas that one finds most persuasive for understanding life's ultimate questions and for deciding how to act in the world. James expresses his own over-belief in God or the divine, asserting the hypothesis that by opening ourselves to it we not only fulfill our deepest destiny, but the universe takes a turn, for the worse or for the better, to the extent that we fulfill that destiny.[1]

View

In the Indian traditions, the first and most important step on the spiritual path is getting oriented to the View (*darshana*) of the path you will walk. Recall that *darshana* means worldview, vision of reality, and way of seeing. View, then, serves as an understanding of reality that inspires and supports the efficacy of spiritual practice; the term is analogous to the Western notion of credo and James's over-beliefs. While I accept all forms of contemplative yoga presented in Chapter 7, I align most closely with the nondual, tantric Shaiva theology of Kashmir Shaivism, referred to here as Shaiva Tantra.

I regard God as the creative energy that underlies, animates, and sustains all existence. God is the ground of all being, the source of all that is, and the power that sustains and regenerates the universe. I am a panentheist. Panentheism is formed by inserting *en*, which means "in," to pantheism. While pantheism affirms that all is God, panentheism means that God is *in* the world but not that the world *is* God. In other words, God is transcendent and formless and fully immanent in the myriad manifestations of divinity that comprise the world. As Judith Plaskow explains, God is more than the totality of creation while including and unifying creation. Panentheists affirm that, "Despite the fractured, scattered, and conflicted nature of our experience of both the world and ourselves, there is a unity that embraces and contains our diversity and that connects all things to each other."[2] Though Plaskow is Jewish, this statement expresses the essence of the Hindu conception of divinity. The world, for Hindus, is a unity-in-diversity, and is exemplified in the nondual Shaiva Tantra vision of reality rendered by scholar-practitioner Christopher Wallis, which I paraphrase below:

- All that exists is one infinite divine Consciousness, free and blissful, which projects within the field of its awareness a vast multiplicity of apparently differentiated subjects and objects. Each object is an actualization of a timeless potentiality inherent in the Light of Consciousness, and each subject is that plus a reflexive movement of self-awareness.

- Creation is a divine play, the result of a natural impulse within the divine to express the totality of its self-knowledge in action. This is a purely voluntary movement of the universal into the particular. Infinite Consciousness contracts into multiple finite embodied loci of awareness out of its own free will.

- When finite subjects identify with the limited and circumscribed cognitions that make up this phase of their existence, instead of identifying with the trans-individual overarching pulsation of pure Awareness that is their true essence-nature, they experience existential suffering.

- To rectify the suffering, we may feel an inner urge to take up the path of spiritual gnosis and yogic practice to undermine our misidentification and to trigger a recognition that one's real identity is that of the highest divinity, the All-in-all.

- This experiential gnosis is repeated and reinforced through various means until it becomes the non-conceptual ground of every moment of experience. Through such contemplative practice, our contracted sense of self and separation from the whole are finally annihilated in the incandescent radiance of the complete expansion into integrated wholeness.[3]

This View, for me, is a joyous cosmology to which I give my heart's full consent. To be sure, suffering is an integral part of the picture. But the good news is that suffering can be ameliorated through diligent practice, and the salutary results reveal the grandeur and splendor of our true nature and the divinity that inheres in the world. The French philosopher Blaise Pascal, a Christian, formulated a famous wager. He proposed that humans all bet with their lives whether God exists or not. Expressed in its most succinct form: If one bets that God *does* exist, and he does, you win everything, to lose, you lose nothing. Should one bet that God *does not* exist, and win, you win nothing, but to lose? You lose everything.[4] While I don't accept the Christian premise, the point is well taken. I wager that by engaging in inner work, especially contemplative yoga, I gain the opportunity to transform the suffering that arises from the unconscious and my habitual behavior into a more conscious—potentially enlightened—mode of being that is personally fulfilling and beneficial to others. If the cosmology and over-beliefs I hold are not accurate, I may flourish nevertheless. Conversely, if I do not engage in inner work, I may forfeit opportunities to reduce my suffering and to benefit others irrespective of whether or not the divine exists in the way I envision it. Therefore, I engage in sadhana with enthusiasm and joy!

I also embrace nondual Shaiva Tantra because it enables me to view God as both formless and with form and to personify the divine as both masculine and feminine. The God-image of Shaiva Tantra is Shiva-Shakti, a singularity that of Consciousness (Shiva) and Creative Energy (Shakti). Hinduism, ...ay, is polymorphously perverse; I revel in its diverse ways of imaging ... relating to the divine! As the description of my practice below reveals, I engage the divine in multiple ways that enliven and actualize different aspects of my being.

Integrative practice

Whether a practice is daily or occasional, the aim is to cultivate balance, integration, peace within, and harmonious relationships with others. Here I share the array of practices that address the somatic, psychological, interpersonal, and spiritual aspects of my life.

Somatic practices

My daily sadhana begins in the morning with an Integral Life Practice (ILP) called the 3-Body Workout that attunes me to the causal, subtle, and physical bodies. Standing and breathing naturally, I notice the suchness, the is-ness of the present moment. Silently I affirm to myself, "I am this suchness in which all things arise." The palms of my hands are together at the heart and then crossed over the chest. With the last exhale, I release into the spacious, formless source of my being. Next, I move my arms in a sweeping, circular motion for several rounds and nourish the subtle, energetic body by breathing into the fullness of life; breathing out, I return to the source of vital energy that animates life. Finally, I touch my belly and silently affirm, "Infinite freedom and fullness appear in my precious human body"; I touch the earth declaring that "I am connected to all beings." I complete the practice, bowing in the four directions, with a silent dedication—"May my consciousness and all my behavior be of service to all beings, liberating all into the suchness of this and every moment."[5] I follow with twenty minutes of hatha yoga asanas. In the late afternoon, I alternate aerobic exercise with yin yoga classes to alleviate the stress of the day and to stay physically fit. Yin Yoga consists of holding select poses for five to seven minutes and surrendering to gravity in a gentle fashion that increases somatic awareness and flexibility in the joints.

Contemplative reading

After morning exercise, I engage in contemplative reading for a half-hour while drinking tea. Over the years, I have slowly read and re-read books from different traditions that inspire my spiritual practice. Some of the works include classic contemplative texts like the Upanishads, *Dhammapada*, *Tao Te Ching*, *Bhagavad Gita*, and St. Teresa of Avila's *The Interior Castle*. Other reading, by psychological writers, include works such as *The Red Book: Liber Novus* by Jung, Wilber's *The Religion of Tomorrow: A Vision for the Future of the Great Traditions*, and Almaas's *The Inner Journey Home: Soul's Realization of the Unity of Reality*.

I also engage in more formal study of scriptural and yogic texts with spiritual teachers who are steeped in the traditions that inform my practice. I have studied the *Yoga Sutras* and *Pratyabhijna-hrydayam* (*Heart of Recognition*) with Christopher Wallis, the *Bhagavad Gita* and *Spanda Karikas* with Sally Kempton, and the *Shiva Sutras* and Abhinavagupta's *Tantraloka* with Paul Muller-Ortega. I agree with these scholar-practitioners who maintain that yoga sadhana is most efficacious when knowledge obtained through intellectual study is conjoined with the wisdom that arises from experiential practice.

Puja

The Hindu word for worship is *puja*. When I first started meditating in my early twenties, I had little interest in ritual or prayer. I proceeded directly to meditation, first chanting *Om* in the manner of my teacher, until the chant dissolved into silence. Later in my early forties, after joining the faculty at Pacifica Graduate Institute, I felt a desire to pray, but was unsure how to begin or whether it was even a possibility for me. Engaging in a willful suspension of disbelief, I tried an experiment—I put aside the question of whether there was a being or beings who could hear me; instead, I assumed a creative attitude, believing that prayer could be viewed as an imaginal activity that evoked the energies and qualities in my unconscious. Within a few weeks I not only felt comfortable doing this, but also began with relative ease to create a personal liturgy that has evolved and changed over time. My liturgy, which includes invocations to great beings and spiritual teachers, has kindled my devotion and is a core element of my practice. In this way, I cultivate a second person, I-Thou relationship to the divine. In recent years, I have focused on the divine feminine, personified by the Hindu goddesses of yoga, as expressed in my daily puja described below:

I cut a fresh flower from the garden each morning and place it on my puja table or altar. I chant *Om* three times and quietly chant in Sanskrit a prayer to Shiva (rendered in English):

> You are my Self. Parvati [Shiva's consort] is my reason.
>
> My five pranas are Your attendants, my body is Your house, and all the pleasures of my senses are objects for Your worship.
>
> My sleep is Your state of samadhi. Wherever I walk, I am walking around You.
>
> Everything I say is in praise of You.
>
> Everything I do is in devotion to You, O benevolent Lord.[6]

I light a candle, place it on a tray, and wave it before the objects and images on my puja. This practice, called *arati* in Hindu tradition, is performed in India by priests in the temples and by householders in their homes.

My liturgy continues with invocations, including the *bija* (seed) mantras, which invite the divine into my life while activating archetypal energies in my psyche. Bija mantras are concise syllables that evoke the energetics of deities represented below in bold font with diacritical marks for the long vowel sound. Because they are most potent when pronounced as precisely as possible, they are best learned from a practiced teacher. I learned these mantras from Sally Kempton, one of my primary teachers, in her Wisdom Goddess Empowerment courses. She has written a splendid book, *Awakening Shakti*, on the transformative power of the goddesses of yoga.[7]

> O Ganesha, salutations you. I seek your blessings. Remove the obstacles that impede my sadhana and that block the flow of divine creativity and spontaneity in my life.
>
> *Om gum ganapatayai namaha*

> O Shiva, salutations to you. I seek your blessings and take refuge in you. By the closing and opening of your eyes the world is absorbed and comes into being. Empower my sadhana, deepen my meditation, and establish my awareness in the Heart.
>
> *Om namah shivaya*

> O Ma, salutations to you. I seek your blessing and take refuge in you. Descend into my body-mind and awaken in my body-mind.
>
> I invoke you as Kali to experience liberation from kleshas, malas, samskaras, vasanas, complexes, and karmas that bind my existence so that I may realize the freedom and bliss inherent in my true nature.
>
> *Om aim hrīm klīm chamundaye viche svaha*

> O Ma, I invoke you as Saraswati to expand wisdom and to receive inspiration for my teaching, writing, and all forms of communication.
>
> *Om aim saraswatyai namaha*

> O Ma, I invoke you as Bhuvaneshwari to experience and express the spacious, loving awareness in which all things arise, are supported and held, and into which they dissolve.
>
> *Om hrīm bhuvaneshwarayai namaha*

> O Ma, I invoke you as Lalita Tripur Sundari to perceive life and the world as a play of Consciousness and to experience and express divine Eros.
>
> *O aim hrīm shrīm lalita ambikayai namaha*

O Ma, I invoke you as Sri Lakshmi to experience and express beauty and abundance.

Om shrīm maha lakshmyai namaha

O Ma, I invoke you as Kundalini Shakti to experience and express the power of awakening in, as, and through this body-mind.

Om aim hrīm shrīm krīm namaha

O Sri Guru, salutations to you. Lead me from the unreal to the real, from darkness to light, from samsara to freedom. Salutations to all enlightened beings, gurus, and teachers who support my journey to wholeness and awakening.

Chanting and svadhyaya

I have also cultivated the affective aspect of sadhana through *kirtan*, the devotional group chanting of the names of divinities in a call and response manner, a practice common among Hindus, especially in bhakti traditions. Siddha Yoga, for instance, includes kirtan as a core practice, one that I thoroughly enjoy. Cultivating devotion in this way engages my emotions, kindles longing for the divine, and deepens my capacity to feel love for others; it also makes it easy to glide into meditation. *Svadhyaya*, the chanting of texts, focuses more on internalizing the meaning of scriptures, though it can also be done as a prelude to meditation. Hindu traditions regard the chanting of texts as study of the Self. While kirtan engages affect, svadhyaya focuses more on the cultivation of self-knowledge (*jnana*). I have found both practices to be edifying and regard them as essential, complementary elements of my sadhana.

Mantra and japa

Hindu traditions place great emphasis on mantra, or sacred sounds that attune one to the divine. My personal liturgy includes bija or seed mantras to invoke different aspects of the divine feminine, and I also use *Om namah shivaya* and the heart-seed mantra I received from my meditation teachers to invoke the divinity that dwells within me. In the nondual tradition of Shaiva Tantra, Shiva is not an anthropomorphic deity but pure Consciousness, the formless Self from which all forms take shape; thus, *Om namah shivaya* means "I bow to the Self," an understanding expressed in Swami Muktananda's signature teaching:

> Honor your own Self.
> Meditate on your own Self.
> Worship your own Self.

> Kneel to your own Self.
> Understand your own Self.
> Your God dwells within you as you.[8]

During the day, I often practice *japa*, repetition of a mantra, to turn my mind toward the divine and to ease stress or break free from troubling thoughts that feel unproductive or are likely to lead to unskillful action. Typically I do japa while walking or while easing into sleep.

Meditation

While devotional practices are intrinsically valuable, I engage them as preparation for meditation, which I regard as the royal path to spiritual awakening. The attitudes and feelings engendered by devotional practices ease the entry into silent meditation. For each hourly session, I set a timer so I can forget about tracking time and use a mantra until it dissolves into a state that is relatively free of thoughts and emotions. When thoughts and feelings do arise, I merely witness them; if necessary, I return to silent repetition of the mantra until I am able once again to settle into the simple feeling of being. When the timer chimes to signal the end of the sitting, I pray that I may integrate the meditation for the benefit of all.

Self-Inquiry and Bhavana

Self-inquiry is essential to my practice in two respects. At the most practical level, it is a way to become aware of unconscious feelings that block awareness and that impede conscious functioning. While journaling about troubling matters serves this purpose, I also use a form of Self-inquiry called Shiva Process that I learned from Swami Shankarananda. Inquiry, he explains, asks us to be present and to investigate present experience. The basic practice is to make *A-statements*, accurate statements of present feeling.[9]

- I feel afraid.
- I feel angry.
- I'm bored.
- I want . . .
- I feel depressed.
- I feel hopeless.
- I feel peaceful.
- I feel happy.
- I feel energized.

Though this process is simple to perform, it has powerful effects. It has enabled me to be much more conscious of my inner world, to dissolve confusion that impedes decisions, and has allowed me to respond rather than react to troubling interpersonal situations. It has also greatly enhanced my creativity energy.

At a deeper level, Self-inquiry is integral to jnana yoga, the path of knowledge. Ramana Maharshi taught inquiry in the form of the question "Who am I?" This question is to be brooded over, like a Zen koan, rather than repeated like a mantra. Shankarananda's Shiva Process entails another form of such inquiry in the form of G-*statements* (great or God statements), such as, "I am the Self."[10] G-statements include great sayings of the Upanishads such as "That Thou Art" (*tat tvam asi*) and the 112 *bhavanas* or contemplations contained in the *Vijnana Bhairava Tantra*, a core text of Shaiva Tantra.[11] I find these particularly beautiful, ecstatic, and inspiring since they focus on both somatic and aesthetic experience as well as introverted meditative states. Moreover, they arise from a dialogue between Shiva and his beloved Goddess, two aspects of the singular divinity that personify the Shaiva Tantra vision of reality. These contemplations provide glimpses of awakening that can expand awareness gradually, evoke wonder, and synergistically inspire the practices we engage to cultivate an integrative spirituality.

Journaling

Keeping a journal functions as a form of self-inquiry and a way of metabolizing daily experience. I track important aspects of my life—dreams, physical health, emotions, marital dynamics, work, and spiritual practice. While narrative writing is mostly a form of witnessing life experiences, I also use it for active imagination dialogues that help me see issues from a less egocentric perspective. Writing about interpersonal conflicts enables me to attend to shadow material by identifying and investigating complexes that have been triggered and feelings I may be projecting onto others.

Council

Nath-ji, my root guru, was a householder yogi who extolled not only the Hindu ideals of Self-realization but also what he referred to as *marriage realization*. Like many of the great Shaiva Tantra masters, he regarded the sadhana of householder yogis to be as noble as the paths traversed by renunciates and monastics. Inspired by this ideal, I view marriage as *relational yoga*, an intimate relationship in which partners engage in a mutual process of individuation and awakening. Naturally there are challenges and crises along the way. While my partner and I have on occasion engaged in marriage therapy to deal with particularly complex difficulties, we have consistently been able to deepen our connection and work through issues on our own by utilizing the practice of council. Derived from Native American tradition, council involves one person speaking for as long as they wish without interruption of any kind from the other. The partner who listens intentionally suspends grievances, reactions, defenses, questions, comments, and judgments and attempts to open to what needs to be understood; the partner who speaks can then be fully seen and completely heard. The experience of being keenly attended to is profound—relationship tensions soften and issues often resolve themselves when both partners learn to hold space for one another and lovingly work to understand the other's perspective.

Service

Central to the Hindu worldview is the idea of *yagna*, often translated as "sacrifice." The meaning in contemporary terms, however, is best rendered by the notions of exchange and service—"Gotta serve somebody," as Bob Dylan puts it. For Hindus the entire universe is a process of mutual sacrifice or exchange,[12] wherein the elements sacrifice to each other, plants and animals sacrifice for humans, and parents for their children. In Hindu spirituality, *yagna* takes the form of *seva*, selfless service or karma yoga. "Selfless" action, in my view, means non-egocentric action that takes others into account and that is beneficial to them. We, in turn, benefit from the non-egocentric actions of others. I view my work as a professor—my relationships with students and colleagues—as karma yoga. Serving in the role of program chair for eighteen years provided me with ample opportunity to perform my work, as best I could, for the sake of others. I believe that a great deal of my psycho-spiritual development has resulted from navigating the needs of students and working through issues, including interpersonal conflicts, that arise in collegial relationships.

Retreat and pilgrimage

Daily practice is, I believe, the most essential element of spirituality. In addition, the efficacy of daily practice is greatly enhanced by periodic experiences of deep spiritual retreat. For the past twenty-five years, I have engaged in full-day meditation intensives about six times a year as well as longer retreats. I have also made six pilgrimages to India to visit the home and sanctuary of Nath-ji; the ashrams of Ramana Maharshi, Sri Aurobindo and the Mother, Swami Muktananda, Mark Griffin, and Meher Baba; and other sacred sites including Varanasi, Vaishno Devi in north India, and Kanyakumari at the southernmost location of the Indian subcontinent. As I pen the final pages of this book, I am anticipating my seventh sojourn to India. Once more, with a grateful heart, I will pay homage to the sages and places that have inspired my journey to wholeness and awakening.

In closing, I dedicate this book to my kindred travelers on the path to an integrative spirituality. I offer the heartfelt prayer I repeat each morning as I emerge from daily meditation.

May all beings be safe.

May all beings be free from suffering.

May all beings discover the freedom and bliss of their true nature.

May all beings enjoy material well-being: clean water, nourishing food, adequate shelter, and quality healthcare.

May all beings dwell in peace.

Om shantih, shantih, shantih

Notes

1 William James, *The Varieties of Religious Experience*, ed. Martin E. Marty. New York: Penguin Books, 1982, 504–19.
2 Carol P. Christ and Judith Plaskow, *Goddess and God: Conversations in Embodied Theology*. Minneapolis: Fortress Press, 2016, 184.
3 Christopher D. Wallis, *Tantra Illuminated: The Philosophy, History, and Practice of a Timeless Tradition*. Petaluma, CA: Mattamayūra Press, 2012, 55.
4 James A. Connor, *Pascal's Wager: The Man Who Played Dice with God*. San Francisco: HarperSanFransico, 2006, 179–87.
5 Wilber et al., *Integral Life Practice*, 136–49.
6 "Śiva Mānasa Pūjā: Mental Worship of Shiva." In *The Nectar of Chanting*. South Fallsburg, NY: SYDA Foundation, 1983, 166–67.
7 See Sally Kempton, *Awakening Shakti: The Transformative Power of the Goddesses of Yoga*. Boulder, CO: Sounds True, 2013. For information on her e-courses, other publications, and teaching schedule visit her website at www.sallykempton.com.
8 Swami Muktananda and Gurumayi Chidvilasananda, *Resonate with Stillness: Daily Contemplations*. South Fallsburg, NY: SYDA Foundation, 1995, January 5.
9 Swami Shankarananda, *Self-Inquiry: Using Your Awareness to Unblock Your Life*. Mt. Eliza, Australia: Shaktipat Press, 2007, 85–95.
10 Ibid., 101–04.
11 See Lorin Roche, *The Radiance Sutras: 112 Gateways to the Yoga of Wonder and Delight*. Boulder, CO: Sounds True, 2014, for contemporary, poetic translations of the contemplative exercises contained in the *Vijnana Bhairava Tantra*, a core text of nondual Shaiva tradition. For a more traditional, scholarly translation see Jaideva Singh, *Vijñābhairava or Divine Consciousness: A Treasury of 112 Types of Yoga*. Delhi: Motilal Banarsidass Publishers, 2003.
12 Devdutt Pattanaik, *My Gita*. New Delhi: Rupa, 2015, 99–108.

BIBLIOGRAPHY

Almaas, A. H. *Diamond Heart, Book 1: Elements of the Real in Man*. Berkeley, CA: Diamond Books, 1987.

Almaas, A. H. *Facets of Unity: The Enneagram of Holy Ideas*. Boston: Shambhala, 2002.

Almaas, A. H. *Luminous Night's Journey: An Autobiographical Fragment*. Boston: Shambhala, 2000.

Almaas, A. H. *The Pearl Beyond Price: Integration of Personality into Being: An Object Relations Approach*. Boston: Shambhala, 2001.

Almaas, A. H. *The Inner Journey Home: Soul's Realization of the Unity of Reality*. Boston: Shambhala, 2004.

Almaas, A. H. *Runaway Realization: Living a Life of Ceaseless Discovery*. Boston: Shambhala, 2014.

Anderson, Gerald. *Christianity and World Religions: The Challenge of Pluralism*. Downer's Grove, IL: Inter-Varsity Press, 1984.

Armstrong, Karen. *The Spiral Staircase: My Climb Out of Darkness*. New York: Anchor Books, 2004.

Armstrong, Karen. *Twelve Steps to a Compassionate Life*. Toronto: Alfred A. Knopf, 2011.

Aurobindo, Sri. *Essays on the Gita*. Pondicherry: Sri Aurobindo Ashram, 1972.

Aurobindo, Sri. *The Life Divine*. In *Sri Aurobindo Birth Centenary Library*. Vol. 18. Pondicherry: Sri Aurobindo Ashram Trust, 1970.

Aurobindo, Sri. *Social and Political Thought*. In *Sri Aurobindo Birth Centenary Library*. Vol. 15. Pondicherry: Sri Aurobindo Ashram Trust, 1971.

Baird, Robert D. "The Response of Swami Bhaktivedanta." In *Modern Responses to Religious Pluralism*, edited by Harold G. Coward, 105–27. Albany: State University of New York Press, 1987.

Baring, Anne. *The Dream of the Cosmos: A Quest for the Soul*. Dorset, England: Archive Publishing, 2013.

Baring, Anne, and Jules Cashford, *The Myth of the Goddess: Evolution of an Image*. London: Arkana, 1991.

Barth, Karl. "The Revelation of God as the Abolition of Religion." In *Christianity and Other Religions*, edited by John Hick and Brian Hebblethwaite, 32–51. Philadelphia: Fortress Press, 1980.

Brunner, Emil. *Revelation and Religion.* Translated by Olive Wyon. Philadelphia: Westminster, 1947.

Bruteau, Beatrice. *Worthy is the World: The Hindu Philosophy of Sri Aurobindo.* Rutherford, NJ: Fairleigh Dickinson University Press, 1971.

Bryant, Edwin F. *The Yoga Sūtras of Patañjali: A New Edition, Translation and Commentary.* New York: North Point Press, 2009.

Campbell, Joseph. *The Hero's Journey: Joseph Campbell on His Life and Work.* Edited by Phil Cousineau. Novato, CA: 1990.

Campbell, Joseph. The *Inner Reaches of Outer Space: Metaphor as Myth and as Religion.* New York: Harper and Row, 1986.

Campbell, Joseph. *The Masks of God: Occidental Mythology.* New York: The Viking Press, 1964.

Chopra, Deepak, and Leonard Mlodinow. *War of the Worldviews: Science vs. Spirituality.* New York: Harmony Books, 2011.

Christ, Carol P., and Judith Plaskow. *Goddess and God: Conversations in Embodied Theology.* *Minneapolis*: Fortress Press, 2016.

Combs, Alan. *Consciousness Explained Better: Towards an Integral Understanding of the Multifaceted Nature of Consciousness.* St. Paul, MN: Paragon House, 2009.

Connor, James A. *Pascal's Wager: The Man Who Played Dice with God.* San Francisco: Harper & Rowe, 2006, 180–81.

Coward, Harold. *Jung and Eastern Thought.* Albany: State University of New York Press, 1985.

Coward, Harold. *Pluralism: Challenge to World Religions.* Maryknoll, NY: Orbis Books, 1985.

Coward, Harold. "The Response of the Arya Samaj. In *Modern Indian Responses to Religious Pluralism*, edited by Harold G. Coward, 39–64. Albany: State University of New York Press, 1987.

Dalai Lama XIV. *Beyond Religion: Ethics for a Whole World.* Boston: Houghton Mifflin Harcourt, 2011.

Dalai Lama XIV. *Ethics for a New Millennium.* New York: Riverhead Books, 1999.

Dalai Lama XIV. *Toward a True Kinship of Faiths: How the World's Religions Can Come Together.* New York: Three Rivers Press, 2010.

Dalai Lama XIV. *The Universe in a Single Atom: The Convergence of Science and* Spirituality. New York: Morgan Road Books, 2005.

Davis, John. *The Diamond Approach: An Introduction to the Teachings of A. H. Almaas.* Boston: Shambhala, 1999.

De Bary, William T. ed., *Sources of the Indian Tradition.* Vol 2. New York: Columbia University Press, 1958.

Deutsch, Eliot. *On Truth: An Ontological Theory.* Honolulu: University Press of Hawaii, 1979.

Doniger, Wendy. *The Implied Spider: Politics and Theology in Myth.* New York: Columbia University Press, 1998.

Easwaran, Eknath. *The Bhagavad Gita.* Tomales, CA: Nilgiri Press, 2007.

Easwaran, Eknath. *Essence of the Bhagavad Gita: A Contemporary Guide to Yoga, Meditation, and Indian Philosophy.* Tomales, CA: Nilgiri Press, 2011.

Feuerstein, Georg. *The Deeper Dimension of Yoga: Theory and Practice.* Boston: Shambhala, 2003.

Feuerstein, Georg. *Tantra: The Path of Ecstasy.* Boston: Shambhala, 1998.

Feuerstein, Georg. *The Yoga Tradition: Its History, Literature, Philosophy and Practice.* 3rd ed. Chino Valley, AZ: Holm Press, 2008.

"The Frankfurt Declaration," *Christianity Today* 14 (1970): 844–46.

Franz, Marie-Louise von. *Psychotherapy*. Boston: Shambhala, 1993.

Fowler, James W. *Stages of Faith: The Psychology of Human Development and the Quest for Meaning*. San Francisco: Harper & Row, 1981.

Gandhi, Mohandas K. *All Men Are Brothers: Life and Thoughts of Mahatma Gandhi as Told in His Own Words*. Edited by Krishna Kripalani. Ahmedabad: Navajivan Publishing House, 1960.

Gandhi, Mohandas K. *The Bhagavad Gita According to Gandhi*. Edited by John Strohmeier. Berkeley, CA: Berkeley Hills Press, 2000.

Gandhi, Mohandas K. *An Autobiography: The Story of My Experiments with Truth*. Translated by Mahadev Desai. Boston: Beacon Press, 1993.

Gandhi, Mohandas K. *The Collected Works of Mahatma Gandhi*. 89 vols. Ahmedabad: Navajivan Trust, 1958–1983.

Gebser, Jean. *The Ever-Present Origin, Part One: Foundations of the Aperspectival World*. Athens, OH: Ohio University Press, 1986.

Gilligan, Carol. *In a Different Voice: Psychological Theory and Women's Development*. Cambridge, MA: Harvard University Press, 1993.

Goleman, Daniel. *Destructive Emotions: How Shall We Overcome Them? A Scientific Dialogue with the Dalai Lama*. New York: Bantam Books, 2003.

Gross, Rita M. *Religious Diversity: What's the Problem?* Eugene, OR: Cascade Books, 2014.

Hammond, Phillip E. Introduction to *The Sacred in a Secular Age: Towards Revision in the Scientific Study of Religion*, edited by Phillip E. Hammond, 1–6. Berkeley: University of California Press, 1985.

Harvey, Andrew, and Anne Baring. *The Divine Feminine: Exploring the Feminine Face of God Around the World*. Berkeley, CA: Conari Press, 1996.

Hick, John. *An Autobiography*. Oxford: Oneworld, 2002.

Hick, John. *The Fifth Dimension: An Exploration of the Spiritual Realm*. New York: Oneworld, 1999.

Hick, John. *God and the Universe of Faiths*. Glasgow: Collins, 1977.

Hick, John. *God Has Many Names*. Philadelphia: Westminster, 1982.

Hick, John. *An Interpretation of Religion: Human Responses to the Transcendent*, 2nd ed. New Haven, CT: 2004.

Hick, John. "Jesus in the World Religions." In *The Myth of God Incarnate*, edited by John Hick, 167–85. Philadelphia: Westminster, 1977.

Hick, John. "On Grading Religions." *Religious Studies* 17 (1981): 451–67.

Hick, John. *Philosophy of Religion*, 3rd ed. Englewood Cliffs, NJ: Prentice-Hall, 1983, 107–08.

Hillman, James. "Psychological Commentary." In *Kundalini: The Evolutionary Energy in Man*, by Gopi Krishna. Berkeley, CA: Shambhala, 1971.

Jordens, J. T. F. "Gandhi and Religious Pluralism." In *Modern Indian Responses to Religious Pluralism*, edited by Harold G. Coward, 3–17. Albany: State University of New York Press, 1987.

Judith, Anodea. *The Global Heart Awakens: Humanity's Rite of Passage from the Love of Power to the Power of Love*. San Rafael, CA: Shift Books, 2013.

Jung, C. G. *Answer to Job*. Fiftieth-anniversary ed. Translated by R. F. C. Hull. Princeton: Princeton University Press, 1973.

Jung, C. G. *The Archetypes of the Collective Unconscious*. In *The Collected Works of C. G. Jung*. 2nd ed. Vol. 9i. Translated by. R. F. C. Hull. Princeton: Princeton University Press, 1969.

Jung, C. G. *Jung Letters*. Vol. 1. Edited by Gerhard Alder in collaboration with Aniela Jaffé. Princeton: Princeton University Press, 1973.

Jung, C. G. *Memories, Dreams, Reflections*. Rev. ed. Edited by Aniela Jaffé. Translated by Richard and Clara Winston. New York: Vintage Books, 1963.

Jung, C. G. *Mysterium Coniunctionis*. In *The Collected Works of C. G. Jung*. 2nd ed. Vol. 14. Translated by R. F. C. Hull. Princeton: Princeton University Press, 1970.

Jung, C. G. *Psychology and Alchemy*. In *The Collected Works of C. G. Jung*. 2nd ed. Vol. 12. Translated by R. F. C. Hull. Princeton: Princeton University Press, 1968.

Jung, C. G. *Psychology and Religion: West and East*. In *The Collected Works of C. G. Jung*. 2nd ed. Vol. 11. Translated by R. F. C. Hull. Princeton: Princeton University Press, 1969.

Jung, C. G. *Psychological Types*. In *The Collected Works of C. G. Jung*. Vol. 6. A revision by R. F. C. Hull of the translation by H. G. Baynes. Princeton: Princeton University Press, 1971.

Jung, C. G. *The Psychology of Kundalini Yoga: Notes on a Seminar Given in 1932 by C. G. Jung*. Edited by Sonu Shamdasani. Princeton: Princeton University Press, 1996.

Jung, C. G. *The Red Book: Liber Novus: A Reader's Edition*. Edited by Sonu Shamdasani. Translated by Mark Kyburz, John Peck, and Sonu Shamdasani. New York: W.W. Norton. 2009.

Jung, C. G. "The Spiritual Problem of Modern Man." In *The Portable Jung*, edited by Joseph Campbell, 456–79. New York: Viking, 1971.

Jung, C. G. *The Structure and Dynamics of the Psyche*. In *The Collected Works of C. G. Jung*. 2nd ed., Vol. 8. Translated by. R. F. C. Princeton: Princeton University Press, 1969.

Jung, C. G. *Symbols of Transformation*. In *The Collected Works of C. G. Jung*. 2nd ed. Translated by R. F. C. Hull. Vol. 5. Princeton: Princeton University Press, 1956.

Kempton, Sally. *Awakening Shakti: The Transformative Power of the Goddesses of Yoga*. Boulder, CO: Sounds True, 2013.

Knitter, Paul F. *No Other Name? A Critical Survey of Christian Attitudes Toward the World Religions*. Maryknoll, NY: Orbis Books, 1985.

Knitter, Paul F. *Without Buddha I Could Not Be a Christian*. Oxford: Oneworld, 2009.

Kraemer, Hendrik. *The Christian Message in a Non-Christian World*, 3rd ed. Grand Rapids, MI: Kregel Publications, 1956.

Küng, Hans. "The Freedom of Religions," in *Attitudes Toward Other Religions*. Edited by Owen C. Thomas. New York: Harper & Row, 1969.

Küng, Hans. "No World Peace Without Religious Peace." In *Christianity and the World Religions: Paths of Dialogue with Islam, Hinduism, and Buddhism*, by Hans Küng, Josef van Ess, Heinrich von Stietencron, and Heinz Behert, 440–43. Translated by Peter Heinegg. Garden City, NY: Doubleday & Co, 1986.

Lovejoy, Arthur O. *The Grain Chain of Being*. Cambridge, MA: Harvard University Press, 1964.

Lyotard, Jean François. *The Postmodern Condition: A Report on Knowledge*. Translated by Geoff Bennington and Brian Massumi. Minneapolis: University of Minnesota Press, 1984.

Maiwandi, Zarina. Editor's Preface to *Runaway Realization: Living a Life of Ceaseless Discovery*, by A. H. Almaas. Boston: Shambhala, 2014.

Minor, Robert N. "The Response of Sri Aurobindo and the Mother." In *Modern Indian Responses to Religious Pluralism*, edited by Harold G. Coward, 85–104. Albany: State University of New York Press, 1987.

Minor, Robert N. "Sarvepalli Radhakrishnan on the Nature of 'Hindu' Tolerance." *Journal of the American Academy of Religion* 50 (1982): 276–90.

Muktananda, Swami, and Gurumayi Chidvilasananda. *Resonate with Stillness: Daily Contemplations*. South Fallsburg, NY: SYDA Foundation, 1995.

Nhat Hanh, Thich. *Coming Home: Jesus and Buddha as Brothers*. New York: Riverhead Books, 1999.

Nhat Hanh, Thich. *Old Path White Clouds: Walking in the Footsteps of the Buddha*. Berkeley, CA: Parallax Press, 1991.

Nhat Hanh, Thich. *Peace is Every Step: Meditation in Life: The Life and Work of Thich Nhat Hanh*, directed by Gaetano Kazuo Maida (1997; Oakland, CA: Media Festival, 2005), DVD.

Nietzsche, Friedrich. *The Gay Science, with a Prelude of Rhymes and an Appendix of Songs*. Translated by Walter Kaufman. New York: Random House, 1974.

Nikhilananda, Swami. *Self-Knowledge (Ātmabodha): An English Translation of Sankarāchārya's Ātmabodha with Notes, Comments, and Introduction*. New York: Ramakrishna-Vivekananda Center, 1974.

Nikhilananda, Swami, trans. *The Gospel of Sri Ramakrishna*. New York: Ramakrisna-Vivekananda Center, 1942.

Nisargadatta Maharaj, Sri. *I Am That: Talks with Sri Nisargadatta Maharaj*. Edited by Sudhakar Dikshit. Translated by Maurice Frydman. Durham, NC: Acorn Press, 1973.

Otto, Rudolf. *The Idea of the Holy: An Inquiry into the Non-Rational Factor in the Idea of the Divine and its Relation to the Rational*. Translated by John W. Harvey. 2nd ed. London: Oxford University Press, 1950.

Palmer, Helen. *The Enneagram*. San Francisco: Harper & Row Publishers, 1988.

Pandit, B. N. *Iśvara Pratyabhijña Kārikā of Utpaladeva: Verses on the Recognition of the Lord*. New Delhi: Muktabodha Indological Research Institute, 2003.

Panikkar, Raimundo. *The Intrareligious Dialogue*. New York: Paulist Press, 1978.

Panikkar, Raimundo. *The Unknown Christ of Hinduism: Towards an Ecumenical Christophany*. Rev. ed. London: Darton, Longman & Todd, 1981.

Pattanaik, Devdutt. *My Gita*. New Delhi: Rupa, 2015.

Prabhavananda, Swami, and Frederick Manchester. *The Upanishads: Breath of the Eternal*. New York: Signet Classic, 1957.

Radhakrishnan, Sarvepalli. *Eastern Religions and Western Thought*. London: Oxford University Press, 1969.

Radhakrishnan, Sarvepalli. *The Hindu View of Life*. New York: Macmillan, 1973.

Raff, Jeffrey. *Jung and the Alchemical Imagination*. Berwick, ME: Nicolas-Hays, 2000.

Rahner, Karl. *Theological Investigations*. Vol. 5. Translated by Karl-H Kruger. Baltimore: Helicon, 1966.

Rama, Swami. *Perennial Psychology of the Bhagavad Gita*. Honesdale, PA: The Himalayan International Institute of Yoga Science and Philosophy of the U.S.A, 1985.

Ramana, Maharishi. *The Spiritual Teaching of Ramana Maharshi*. Boston: Shambhala, 1988.

Reynolds, Brad. *Embracing Reality: The Integral Vision of Ken Wilber*. New York: Jeremy P. Tarcher/Penguin, 2004.

Riso, Don, and Russ Hudson. *Personality Types*. Rev. ed. Boston: Houghton Mifflin Co., 1996.

Robinson, John A. T. *Truth is Two-Eyed*. Philadelphia: Westminster, 1979.

Roche, Lorin. *The Radiance Sutras: 112 Gateways to the Yoga of Wonder and Delight*. Boulder, CO: Sounds True, 2014.

Rolland, Romain. *The Life of Vivekananda and the Universal Gospel*. Translated by E. F. Malcolm-Smith. Kolkata: Advaita Ashram, 2009.

Rosen, David. *The Tao of Jung: The Way of Integrity*. New York: Viking/Arkana, 1966.

Scott, Waldron. "No Other Name—An Evangelical Conviction" in *Christ's Lordship and Religious Pluralism*. Edited by Gerald H. Anderson and Thomas F. Stransky. Maryknoll, NY: Orbis, 1981.

Shamdasani, Sonu. Introduction to *The Psychology of Kundalini Yoga: Notes of the Seminar Given in 1932 by C. G. Jung*, edited by Sonu Shamdasani, xvii–xlvi. Princeton: Princeton University Press, 1996.

Shankarananda, Swami. *Consciousness is Everything: The Yoga of Kashmir Shaivism*. Mt. Eliza: Victoria: Shaktipat Press, 2003.

Shankarananda, Swami. *Self-Inquiry: Using Awareness to Unblock Your Life*. Mt. Eliza: Victoria: Shaktipat Press, 2007.

Sharma, Arvind. *The Experiential Dimension of Advaita Vedanta*. Delhi: Motilal Banarsidass, 1980.

Sharpe, Eric. *Faith Meets Faith: Some Christian Attitudes to Hinduism in the Nineteenth and Twentieth Centuries*. London: SCM Press, 1977.

Sharpe, Eric. *Not to Destroy but to Fulfill: The Contribution of J. N. Farquhar to Protestant Missionary Thought in India Before 1914*. Uppsala: Gleerup, 1965.

Singh, Jaideva. *Pratyabhijñāhṛdayam: The Secret of Self-Recognition*. Delhi: Motilal Banarsidass, 1980.

Singh, Jaideva. *Vijñānabhairava or Divine Consciousness: A Treasury of 112 Types of Yoga*. Delhi: Motilal Banarsidass, 1979.

Smith, Curtis, D. *Jung's Quest for Wholeness: A Religious and Historical Perspective*. Albany: State University of New York Press, 1990.

Smith, Huston. *Why Religion Matters: The Fate of the Human Spirit in an Age of Disbelief*. San Francisco: HarperSanFrancisco, 2001.

Smith, James K. A. *How (Not) To Be Secular: Reading Charles Taylor*. Grand Rapids, MI: William E. Eerdmans Publishing Co, 2014.

Smith, Wilfred Cantwell. *Faith and Belief*. Princeton, NJ: Princeton University Press, 1979.

Stein, Murray. *Minding the Self: Jungian Meditations on Contemporary Spirituality*. London: Routledge, 2014.

Stein, Murray. Foreword to *No Other Gods: An Interpretation of the Biblical Myth for a Transbiblical Age*, by Phyllis Boswell Moore, vii–ix. Wilmette, I: Chiron Publications, 1992.

Stein, Murray. *The Principle of Individuation: Toward the Development of Consciousness*. Wilmette, IL: Chiron Publications, 2006.

Tapasyananda, Swami. *The Philosophical and Religious Lectures of Swami Vivekananda*. Madras: Sri Ramakrishna Math, 1984.

Taylor, Charles. *A Secular Age*. Cambridge, MA: The Belknap Press of Harvard University Press, 2007.

Taylor, Mark C. *After God*. Chicago: University of Chicago Press, 2007.

Teresa of Avila, St. *The Interior Castle*. Translated by Mirabai Starr. New York: Riverhead Books, 2003.

Tigunait, Pandit Rajmani. *The Secret of the Yoga Sutra: Samadhi Pada*. Honesdale, PA: Himalayan Institute, 2014.

Tillich, Paul. *Christianity and the Encounter of the World Religions*. New York: Columbia University Press, 1963.

Tillich, Paul. *The Courage to Be*. New Haven, CT: Yale University Press, 1952.

Vivekananda, Swami. *The Complete Works of Swami Vivekananda*. 17th ed. Volume 1. Kolkata: Advaita Ashrama, 1986.

Wallis, Christopher. *Tantra Illuminated: The Philosophy, History, and Practice of a Timeless Tradition*. 2nd ed. Petaluma, CA: Mattamyūra Press, 2013.

Wilber, Ken. *The Eye of Spirit: An Integral Vision for a World Gone Slightly Mad.* Boston: Shambhala, 1997.

Wilber, Ken. *Grace and Grit: Spirituality and Healing in the Life and Death of Treya Killam Wilber.* Boston: Shambhala, 1993.

Wilber, Ken. *Integral Meditation: Mindfulness as a Path to Grow Up, Wake Up, and Show Up in Your Life.* Boulder, CO: Shambhala, 2016.

Wilber, Ken. *Integral Spirituality: A Startling New Role for Religion in the Modern and Postmodern World.* Boston: Integral Books, 2006.

Wilber, Ken. *The Marriage of Sense and Soul: Integrating Science and Religion.* New York: Random House, 1998.

Wilber, Ken. *No Boundary: Eastern and Western Approaches to Personal Growth.* Boulder, CO: Shambhala, 1981.

Wilber, Ken. "Odyssey: A Personal Inquiry into Humanistic and Transpersonal Psychology." In *The Collected Works of Ken Wilber.* Vol. 2. Boston: Shambhala, 1999.

Wilber, Ken. *The Religion of Tomorrow: A Vision for the Future of the Great Traditions—More Inclusive, More Comprehensive, More Complete.* Boulder, CO: Shambhala, 2017.

Wilber, Ken, Terry Patten, Adam Leonard, and Marco Morell. *Integral Life Practice: A 21st century Blueprint for Physical Health, Emotional Balance, Mental Clarity, and Spiritual Awakening.* Boston: Integral Books, 2008.

Wiles, Maurice. "Christianity Without Incarnation." In *The Myth of God Incarnate*, edited by John Hick, xvii–xlvi. Philadelphia: Westminster, 1977.

Woodman, Marion, Kate Danson, Mary Hamilton, and Rita Greer Allen. *Leaving My Father's House: A Journey to Conscious Femininity.* Boston: Shambhala, 1993.

Zimmer, Heinrich. *Myths and Symbols in Indian Art and Civilization.* Edited by Joseph Campbell. Princeton: Princeton University Press, 1946.

Zimmer, Heinrich. *Philosophies of India.* Edited by Joseph Campbell. Princeton: Princeton University Press, 1951.

INDEX

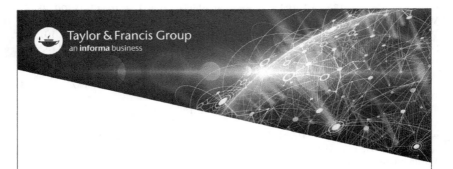